The Entropy Exhibition

When first published in 1983 *The Entropy Exhibition* was the first critical assessment of the literary movement known as 'New Wave' science fiction. It examines the history of the *New Worlds* magazine and its background in the popular imagination of the 1960s, traces the strange history of sex in science fiction and analyses developments in stylistic theory and practice.

Michael Moorcock edited and produced the magazine *New Worlds* from 1964 to 1973. Within its pages he encouraged the development of new kinds of popular writing out of the genre of science fiction, energetically reworking traditional themes, images and styles as a radical response to the crisis of modern fiction. The essential paradox of the writing lay in its fascination with the concept of 'entropy' – the universal and irreversible decline of energy into disorder. Entropy provides the key to both the anarchic vitality of the magazine and to its neglect by critics and academics, as well as its connection with other cultural experiments of the 1960s.

Detailed attention is given to each of the three main contributors to the *New Worlds* magazine – Michael Moorcock, Brian Aldiss and J.G. Ballard. Moorcock himself is more commonly judged by his commercial fantasy novels than by the magazine he supported with them, but here at last the balance is redressed: *New Worlds* emerges as nothing less than a focus and a metaphor for many of the transformations of English and American literature in the past two decades.

'I cannot believe that there is any better criticism of SF in print at the moment.' – *John Sutherland*

The Entropy Exhibition

Michael Moorcock and the British 'New Wave' in Science Fiction

Colin Greenland

Routledge
Taylor & Francis Group

First published in 1983
by Routledge & Kegan Paul Plc

This edition first published in 2012 by Routledge
2 Park Square, Milton Park, Abingdon, Oxon, OX14 4RN

Simultaneously published in the USA and Canada
by Routledge
711 Third Avenue, New York, NY 10017

Routledge is an imprint of the Taylor & Francis Group, an informa business

© 1983 Colin Greenland

Publisher's Note
The publisher has gone to great lengths to ensure the quality of this reprint but points out that some imperfections in the original copies may be apparent.

Disclaimer
The publisher has made every effort to trace copyright holders and welcomes correspondence from those they have been unable to contact.

A Library of Congress record exists under ISBN: 0710093101

ISBN 13: 978-0-415-50062-3 (hbk)

Colin Greenland

The Entropy Exhibition

Michael Moorcock and the British
'New Wave' in science fiction

Routledge & Kegan Paul
London, Boston, Melbourne and Henley

First published in 1983
by Routledge & Kegan Paul Plc
39 Store Street, London WC1E 7DD,
9 Park Street, Boston, Mass. 02108, USA,
296 Beaconsfield Parade, Middle Park,
Melbourne, 3206, Australia, and
Broadway House, Newtown Road,
Henley-on-Thames, Oxon RG9 1EN
Typeset in 10 on 12 pt Times Roman by
Inforum Ltd, Portsmouth
and printed in Great Britain by
Hartnoll Print
Bodmin, Cornwall

Library of Congress Cataloging in Publication Data
Greenland, Colin, 1954–
  The entropy exhibition.

Based on the author's thesis (doctoral)—Oxford, 1980.
Bibliography: p. Includes index.
1. Science fiction, English—History and criticism.
2. English fiction—20th century—History and criticism.
3. Moorcock, Michael, 1939–   —Criticism and interpretation.
4. New worlds (London, England)
5. Aldiss, Brian Wilson, 1925–   —Critisicm and interpretation.
6. Ballard, J. G., 1930–   —Criticism and interpretation.
I. Title.
PR830.S35G73 1982   823'.0876'09   82-15153

ISBN 0-7100-9310-1

To David and Malcolm

The one hazard facing science fiction, the Trojan Horse being trundled toward its expanding ghetto . . . is that faceless creature, literary criticism.

J. G. Ballard

Contents

Preface

New Worlds was always the foremost British science fiction magazine, from its first issue in 1946. When Michael Moorcock took over the editorship in 1964, it became something more: the locus of a vigorous literary movement, organised almost single-handedly by Moorcock himself. His purpose was firstly to publish a more ambitious and flexible kind of science fiction which would no longer subscribe to the narrative conventions established in American 'pulp' magazines. When this policy met with hostility from science fiction fans and professionals who preferred to stick with what they knew, Moorcock opened the magazine to new kinds of imaginative writing beyond the categories of genre fiction. Most prominent in *New Worlds* were the works of Brian W. Aldiss, J.G. Ballard, and Moorcock himself; other major contributors included M. John Harrison, D.M. Thomas, and Langdon Jones, and the Americans, Thomas M. Disch, John Sladek, Norman Spinrad, and James Sallis. The inspirational effect of the magazine can be seen in the large proportion of new young writers whose work it stimulated and published.

Despite the commercial crises which continually threatened *New Worlds*, including censorship by its own printers and distributors, Moorcock and his colleagues never lost sight of their principles and ideals. *New Worlds* was very much a magazine of the 1960s in its commitment to the popular arts, to freedom of imagination, to the original and unconventional, but it remained sceptical about other 'revolutionary' novelties of the period – prophetically, as it turned out. The anarchic movement it generated, called 'New Wave science fiction' by friends and enemies alike, spreads much further than that label indicates. It has helped to make the elements of science fiction more important to contemporary fiction in general and to the popular imagination at large. *The Entropy Exhibition* is a critical examination of *New Worlds* as a singular literary phenomenon, and an insight into how science fiction can articulate some of the elusive, often ambiguous ideas and problems of modernity.

Acknowledgments

This book is the product of several years of research, aided in part by finance from the Arts Council of Great Britain for a Writing Fellowship at NE London Polytechnic. NELP houses the library of the Science Fiction Foundation, the largest and best specialist collection on this side of the Atlantic, invaluable to any scholar of sf. The basis for *The Entropy Exhibition*, however, was a thesis of the same title accepted in 1980 for a doctorate in English Literature at the University of Oxford. Those who are surprised to see work of such brash modernity proceeding from that citadel of tradition and antiquity should know that the papers of both Brian Aldiss and Michael Moorcock are held on deposit by the Bodleian Library. All unpublished sources cited here may be found in those collections, which are unfortunately not yet catalogued: I am extremely grateful to Margaret Aldiss and Brian Hinton for their labours in arranging the collections.

The greatest advantage of studying living writers is that they are often available for consultation. When the idea of this research was little more than a pipe-dream, Brian Aldiss encouraged me, and introduced me to Tom Shippey, then Fellow of St John's College, Oxford, who agreed to supervise my work and was particularly influential on its organisation, and in modulating the rhetoric of enthusiasm to the more sober tones of critical analysis. Michael Moorcock gave me considerable help in the form of discussion, and access to his own bookshelves. Aldiss, Ballard and Moorcock all read some of my earliest drafts and offered useful comments, and many other improvements were suggested by my eagle-eyed examiners, Professor I.F. Clarke, formerly of the University of

Strathclyde, and Dr Peter Hoy of Merton College, Oxford. For
support and assistance of a less official kind I am indebted to Keith
Bowden, Nick Pratt, and other friends too numerous to mention,
and especially to Joyce Day, good spirit of the SFF.

Text of all material quoted from *New Worlds*, © *New Worlds*,
reproduced by kind permission.

Text of David Bowie, 'Oh You Pretty Things' (1971) and 'Starman'
(1972), © Chrysalis Music/Mainman/Bewlay Bros, reproduced by
kind permission.

Text of David Bowie, 'Space Oddity' (1969) used by kind permission of Westminster Music Limited.

Unpublished material by Brian W. Aldiss and Michael Moorcock
used by kind permission of the authors.

Chapter One
The cybernetic cuckoos
science fiction and the popular imagination in the 1960s

In John Wyndham's *The Midwich Cuckoos* extra-terrestrial aliens visit a dull little English village and leave behind an embassy of their own seed implanted in human host-mothers. Though human enough in appearance, the offspring grow at an accelerated pace and soon began to exercise extraordinary mental powers, with violent effect. Gordon Zellaby, who has observed their upbringing, remarks,[1]

> We are presented with a moral dilemma of some niceness. On the one hand, it is our duty to our race and culture to liquidate the Children, for it is clear that if we do not we shall, at best, be completely dominated by them, and their culture, whatever it may turn out to be, will extinguish ours.
>
> On the other hand, it is our culture that gives us scruples about the ruthless liquidation of unarmed minorities, not to mention the practical obstacles to such a solution. . . .
>
> It makes one long for H.G.'s straightforward Martians.

Alien visitors to Earth in Arthur C. Clarke's *Childhood's End*, though less straightforward than Wells's, are more benevolent than Wyndham's. They have been sent to prepare for the emergence of a new species out of the human race. Again it is the children that threaten humanity with extinction, but these are not of alien stock; their superhuman mental capacities are the result of an evolutionary jump. George Greggson, father of the first mutant, consults one of the alien supervisors.[2]

> 'I've only one question,' he said, 'What shall we do about our children?'
>
> 'Enjoy them while you may,' answered Rashaverak gently.

'They will not be yours for long.'

It was advice that might have been given to any parent in any age: but now it contained a threat and a terror it had never held before.

In an essay first presented at a 1965 conference on 'The Idea of the Future', Leslie Fiedler referred to Clarke's novel,[3]

at the conclusion of which the mutated offspring of parents much like us are about to take off under their own power into outer space. Mr. Clarke believes that he is talking about a time still to come because he takes metaphor for fact; though simply translating 'outer space' into 'inner space' reveals that what he is up to is less prediction than description; since the post-human future is now, and if not we, at least our children, are what it would be comfortable to pretend we still only foresee.

Fiedler's justification of science fiction is not by any count of correct predictions, but by its subtext, its inner meaning, what he calls the 'myth' of science fiction:[4]

quite simply the myth of the end of man, of the transcendence or . . . transformation (under the impact of advanced technology and the transfer of traditional human functions to machines) of *homo sapiens* into something else: the emergence – to use the language of Science Fiction itself – of 'mutants' among us.

The 'mutants' Fiedler identifies are his own children, his students, and their contemporaries: 'Beatniks or hipsters, layabouts and drop-outs we are likely to call them with corresponding hostility.' One adolescent is a misfit; a village-full is an invasion; an international host of them is a new species.

Fiedler's proposition, that 'the post-human future is now' and that the Western younger generation in the mid-1960s intentionally made a cultural disconnection equivalent to an evolutionary mutation, however biologically unsound, is a prominent image of its time. He was by no means alone in his claims, nor in his rhetoric; and least of all in assigning a new importance to science fiction.[5]

Surely, there has never been a moment in which the most naïve as well as the most sophisticated have been so acutely aware of how the past threatens momentarily to disappear from the present, which itself seems on the verge of disappearing into the future.

And this awareness functions, therefore, on the level of art as well as entertainment, persuading quite serious writers to emulate the modes of Science Fiction. The novel is most amenable to this sort of adaptation, whose traces we can find in writers as various as William Golding and Anthony Burgess, William Burroughs and Kurt Vonnegut, Jr., Harry Matthews [sic] and John Barth – to all of whom young readers tend to respond with a sympathy they do not feel even toward such forerunners of the mode . . . as Aldous Huxley, H.G. Wells and George Orwell.

Fiedler observes that the evolutionary 'moment' is expressed in fiction that anticipated it, like Vonnegut's, and fiction that followed it, like Barth's. He recognises semi-conscious premonitions in earlier science fiction like Clarke's, and deliberate adjustments in later 'quite serious' fiction, that bracket the moment. This book will look between those brackets to examine the fiction of the moment itself, the work of a group of writers dedicated to the 'awareness' and 'seriousness' of science fiction, and to doing away with naïveté forever.

In *The Midwich Cuckoos* the Children represent a race with a very strong survival imperative which is a certain threat to mankind. In the end, however, they are destroyed by Zellaby in an exercise of a human (and characteristically British) impulse which they could not have foreseen: heroic self-sacrifice. In the terms of his own society Zellaby plays a moral trump, reasserting the endangered culture and so preserving it. In *Childhood's End* the Children are not hostile to Terran life and culture but effectively outgrow it. Their parents accept obsolescence and watch their evolution open-mouthed. As the Children's departure for outer space burns up the old planet behind them the last adult human survivor gives a commentary of approval.

The notion of a 'generation gap', of historical, social and cultural discontinuity between parents and children since the Second World War, is now extensively familiar. The rise of a 'counter-culture' that threatened not just to supplant but to destroy previous forms can be traced back to the 1950s, when England and America attained levels of national prosperity secure and high enough to permit internal diffraction. In *Watch Out Kids*, his history of the youth revolution, Mick Farren describes the split with characteristic cynicism.[6]

During the early fifties a new life style began to evolve;

previous to this, humanity had passed from childhood to maturity with little comment, a kid put on long pants, he went to the factory with his old man and Pow! he was hooked for life. The system had produced another one.

This was fine until the post war boom, when Madison Avenue realised that the fourteen to twenty-one age group had a vast consumption potential, particularly for luxury goods. The problem was to give those kids a collective identity and so the phrase teenager appeared in about nineteen forty-nine. Giving an identity to this group was one thing, controlling them was an entirely different matter. This group identity began to lead to something of a group consciousness and this led to a critical appraisal of the world that had been shaped by the previous generation.

Though stimulated and supplied by the commercial establishment, the teenagers rejected its ideology. Seizing what they had been offered and finding it altogether preferable to the prospects adult society held for their future, they began to develop a counter-culture, deliberately geared to the present and in defiance of the conventions of their parents. They were energetic, sexual and loud; giving full vent to the normal erratic impulses of adolescence, they inverted them into virtues, to be defined and streamlined by a progression of new heroes – from the sullen menace of Marlon Brando, the Wild One, through the frustrated urgency of James Dean, to the sneering aggression of Elvis Presley. Their access to those rebel heroes was, however, controlled by businessmen, the managers, promoters, and producers; their accessories, an integral part of their new culture, were similarly produced and marketed. The young rebels had not rejected consumerism, but their materialism did not show the spirit of compliant placidity which characterised their parents' consumption. The teenagers' taste was for a whole new range of goods, outside the valuation of parental society: leather jackets, jeans, motorbikes, guitars. They conferred their own meanings on them, put them to their own uses, often in opposition to the ideology of their manufacturers. Jerry Rubin, instigator of the anarchist Yippie Party, records this ironic alchemy of wealth, leisure, and technology.[7]

On the surface the world of the 1950's was all Eisenhower calm. A cover story of 'I Like Ike' father-figure contentment. . . .

Dad looked at his house and car and manicured lawn, and he

was proud. All of his material possessions justified his life. . . .
Elvis Presley ripped off Ike Eisenhower by turning our
uptight young awakening bodies around. Hard animal rock
energy beat surged hot through us, the driving rhythm arousing
repressed passions . . .
Elvis told us to *let go!*
let go!
let go! . . .
Affluent culture, by producing a car and car radio for every
middle-class home, gave Elvis a base for recruiting.
  While a car radio in the front seat rocked with 'Turn Me
Loose', young kids in the back seat were breaking loose. Many
a night was spent on dark and lonely roads, balling to hard rock
beat.
  The back seat produced the sexual revolution, and the car
radio was the medium for subversion.
  The next step was obvious. After merely appropriating products
of an affluent economy the young began to usurp processes too, to
explore and exploit new technology. The Beatles and Bob Dylan
used the pop music industry to articulate and amplify the concerns
of a section of the human race that had previously lacked a coherent
identity, let alone an international voice. Behind the ephemeral and
playful facade of Carnaby Street was a radical pragmatism: civilisation was to be redesigned, thoroughly and permanently.
  In the mid-1960s a huge populist upheaval, inchoate but for that
aim and a broad commitment to the principle of pleasure, spread
from the West Coast of America all the way across Europe. Nowa-
days the hippies are remembered as an anti-materialist movement,
devoted to mysticism and puritan agrarian values. They were tech-
nophobic: computers, bombs, wrist-watches and domestic
appliances were bad; the state itself was 'The Machine'. Theodore
Roszak makes their opposition to 'the technocracy' the centre of his
analysis of the cultural conflict. What is less obvious and less
appreciated is that this rejection was only one face of a technological innocence. There were nice machines as well as nasty ones:
motorcycles, vibrators, stereos and offset lithography were good.
To the urban radical, automation was liberation. Every job elimi-
nated meant another opportunity to drop out. The young, with the
leisure industries coming under their influence, looked forward to
an extended lease of childhood, which they idealised. Richard

Neville published the *Schoolkids' Oz* magazine and a guide to the revolution called *Playpower*. Farren wrote:[8]

> It is a technical fact that man need no longer be concerned to such an extent (that is, to the extent of eight hours a day plus) with the production of his own life support.
> The robots are coming – make way for the robots.

A second technological feature on the revolutionary programme was further reaching and even more alien to the preceding generation, and that was the issue of psychedelia, the sudden popularity of mind-altering drugs. One way the young proposed to enjoy increased hours of leisure was by consuming cannabis and LSD. Over and above enjoyment, they claimed that these drugs offered philosophical and moral benefits, in the liberation of the senses and imagination from physical and habitual restraints. Anyone who takes LSD undergoes intense reorganisation of his perception of matter, space, time, and identity. He makes a complete re-examination of the foundations of consciousness, not systematically but spontaneously, experientially. This in itself makes him different from someone who does not take LSD. The experience certainly involves confusion and evanescent hallucinatory effects that seem meaningless to him, but it is also characterised by broad and extremely lucid patterns of metaphysical thought which can survive the 'trip' and will bear comparison with the reports of visionaries and traditions of mysticism, especially those of the East. The whole experience can be coloured by a profound feeling of revelation and conviction. As Richard Neville put it, 'Non-acid takers regard the LSD trip as a remarkable flight from reality, whereas cautious devotees feel they've flown *into* reality. . . . After an acid trip, you can reject everything you have ever been taught.'[9] The sensory distortions produced by cannabis are easily assimilated to the loosened frame of reference provided by LSD, mescalin, or psilocybin.

There are the makings here of a complete social division: revolution in the head, along the highways of perception and understanding. The psychedelic experience, being entirely subjective, is self-authenticating. It sweeps away mundane distinctions and criteria and provides an altogether different vision, perfect material for a message. It gave its first advocates an inexorable sense of rightness in opposing their holistic, libertarian ethos to the discriminatory and repressive outlook of their elders. 'Grass teaches us disrespect for the law and the courts. Which do you trust: Richard Milhous Nixon or your own sense organs?'[10] They really were exclusive. In legislating against cannabis and LSD the governments of America and Europe were not only outlawing drugs that encouraged disaffection among the young but making a stand on a crucial problem of phenomenology. They were reaffirming faith in Western materialism and a single objective reality. Anyone who does not act in that faith is mentally unstable; any substance that promotes his disbelief is a poison. Nevertheless, there was no way for them to reconvert the children who had seen reality flicker and melt, could reproduce the experience at will, and felt themselves wiser for it. National economies might compromise with new tastes and demands, but to embrace a resurgence of solipsist philosophies was not in their interest.

Timothy Leary, prophet of psychedelia, preached that hallucinogenic drugs offered the best opportunity for coming to terms with a world transformed by technology.[11]

Human beings born after the year 1943 belong to a different species from their progenitors. Three new energies, exactly symmetrical and complementary – atomics, electronics, and psychedelics – have produced an evolutionary mutation. The release of atomic energy placed the mysterious basic power of the universe in man's hands. The frailty of the visible. The power of the invisible. Electronic impulses link the globe in an instantaneous communication network. The circuited unity of man. Psychedelic drugs release internal energy and speed consciousness in the same exponential proportions as nuclear and electronic space-time expansions.

Though coming from a follower of the other camp, Leary's rhetoric echoes Fiedler's. ('This is not a sociological trend. It's an evolutionary lurch. The generation gap is a species mutation.'[12]) He speaks like a comicbook professor, borrowing numinous phrases from science and from science fiction, where evolutionary lurches have already been described by Wyndham and Clarke.

Science fiction, essentially the literature of altered circumstances, is the obvious place to seek a language for the unprecedented, especially since it offers as many anxious images as utopian ones. Leary dreads 'the dead posturing of robot actors on the fake-prop stage that is called American reality.'[13] R.D. Laing feels doubtful 'whether my world is not a five-channel synchronized hallucination.'[14] William Burroughs habitually calls reality a movie, and a mediocre one at that. This is the vocabulary of dehumanisation, familiar to psychiatrists from the conversation of schizophrenics. Poets and orators do not always misconstrue their borrowings from the languages of science, or those of insanity. These new metaphors are not altogether arbitrary. Much of their vibrancy in the popular imagination is because they tremble on the edge of becoming literal. The distinction between man and machine is no longer as clear as can be. This fact is attested not only by the fantasies of Leary and Laing or by the sensations of prosthesis patients, but also by the existence of a science of cybernetics. Norbert Wiener founded it precisely in the overlap:[15]

I have spoken of machines, but not only of machines having brains of brass and thews of iron. When human atoms are knit into an organization in which they are used, not in their full right as responsible human beings, but as cogs and levers and rods, it matters little that their raw material is flesh and blood. *What is used as an element in a machine, is in fact an element in the machine.*

The pundits who turned to science fiction for a vocabulary did so because their students and children were doing so, though they expressed their alienation by identifying with the aliens, not like Laing with the machines or like Fiedler with the obsolete parents. In one of their songs the San Francisco band Jefferson Airplane quoted lines from Wyndham's *The Chrysalids*, while David Bowie seemed to have 'translated' *Childhood's End* in the way Fiedler recommended:[16]

Look out at your children,
See their faces in golden rays.
Don't kid yourself they belong to you –
They're the start of the coming race.
The Earth is a bitch,
We've finished our news;
Homo sapiens have outgrown their use.
All the strangers came today
And it looks as though they're here to stay.

Neil Young and the Pink Floyd were also to take texts from the book of Clarke. Dressing up as an alien certainly had its glamour, not to say menace, which Bowie later paraded as Ziggy Stardust.[17] But the image also covered some more drastic attempts at dissociation from civilisation, as Neville noted.[18]

'We want our son to be free, unprogrammed and completely unidentified with the state,' says one child's young father, who delivered the baby himself, and told no one except the Underground press. That means no birth certificate, no schooling unless the child wants it, no taxation, no official record of his existence. . . . And if [he] is ever discovered by the bureaucracy? 'He will tell them he's from another planet.' . . .

And in a sense, he will be.

The sense of fantasy in hippy doctrine, however dynamic and vital, was too large to be manageable. Juvenile egotism, militant against conformity, made the revolutionaries pursue desires rather than possibilities. Their reaffirmation of the force of subjectivity accomplished liberations on the way, but could lead only to division and dissent. After the first joyful fraternity of rebellion they could find no community of cause. Differences of attitude towards established society and its projected replacement were quickly revealed. The extreme, often fantastic solutions offered by instant mystics, acidheads and politicos proved generally incompatible. In the disintegration the number of private worlds multiplied. Confidence in the existence or nature of objective reality has not yet been consolidated again. Technology continues to grow in ambiguity; the future flickers ever more urgently. Science fiction is still very popular and, if the two are not the same thing, highly appropriate to our place and time.

Writing elsewhere, Fiedler suggested what the implications were for science fiction itself.[19]

Science Fiction . . . found . . . its real meaning and scope only after World War II. At that point, two things become clear: first, that the Future was upon us, that the pace of technological advance had become so swift that a distinction between Present and Future would get harder and harder to maintain; and second, that the End of Man, by annihilation or mutation, was a real, even an immediate possibility. But these are the two proper subjects of Science Fiction: the Present Future and the End of Man – not time travel or the penetration of outer space, except as the latter somehow symbolize the former.

This book deals in large part with a science fiction writer and the magazine he edited, into whose pages crowded a large number of writers concerned with those 'proper subjects', the end of man – indeed, the end of everything – and the place of the future in the present. While poets and orators were making free with old images of utopia and Metropolis, starmen and robots, these writers were occupied with a newer theme: entropy. They saw the degeneration of energy as a fit image for the disintegration of society and the individual consciousness. Brian Aldiss's *Barefoot in the Head*, serialised in the magazine between 1967 and 1969, is a perceptive chronicle of the hippies themselves, from the brilliant, ecstatic sunlight of the first Summer of Love to the confused moral chiaroscuro at the end of the decade.

Michael Moorcock and the writers he gathered about him were conscious, even self-conscious, about science fiction, its symbolism, its immediacy, its responsibilities, and above all its possibilities. They were the first generation in science fiction to consider and discuss their work principally as art, not as cult, didactic tradition, intellectual pastime, or anything else. Some of them, including Thomas M. Disch and Charles Platt, contributed to the leading article in issue 173 of *New Worlds* in July 1967. It was printed as an anonymous editorial statement on 'The Lessons of the Future'.

Man has changed, and is changing. The process, begun a century ago or more, is still accelerating. He has become, characteristically, an urban dweller who lives out his life in an environment of artifacts and artifices where he cannot avoid a consciousness of his own mutability (a theme of much of the best speculative fiction). The social sciences, imperfect as they still are, indicate this much at least: that a man's character (and soon, perhaps, his physical person) is as artificial and arbitrary as any accessory of his culture.

The article gives examples of 'artifacts and artifices' that alter our relationship to our world. The urban dweller lives in a controlled environment, impervious to 'basic rhythms of night and day and of the seasons', by virtue of everything from street lighting to frozen food. The erosion of 'the Protestant work-ethic' by automation means that he has to rearrange his priorities, while the mass media bombard him with random images from the whole spectrum of human thought and behaviour, thus broadening his awareness but modifying his choices. His identity is threatened by depersonalisation to one unit in a socio-economic mass; his sociality by the general arbitrariness of the city; his territorial sense by the geographical distortions of high-speed transport. Man is destroying and remaking himself, at best only semi-consciously: the argument is familiar, rehearsed by many in our time. This *New Worlds* version goes on:[20]

> It is our intention only to point out that literary art has characteristically lagged behind in dealing with these elements of modern life, even sometimes in recognising them. When our best writers *have* recognised them, it has too often been to renounce them and turn from them to a past that is viewed as somehow more congenial and 'humanistic'. Lawrence's primitivism and Eliot's orthodoxy represent two popular alternatives to an acceptance of the present world.
>
> There have been, since the time of Kafka, many writers who have made the effort to deal with the present on its own terms, though they have all suffered . . . from the common uncertainty of our age as to what exactly those terms are. So much of the significance of the present lies not in the past but in the future.
> . . .
> We all stand in need of the 'new sensibility' that can enable us to handle experiences and ideas for which nothing in our past lives has prepared us, and this sensibility can be won only by an act of sustained and informed imagination. It is to be hoped that this magazine can provide, in some degree, imaginative works that will fulfil this need.

As well as its useful symbols and flexibility of assumptions, science fiction offers two approaches to the present: through science and fiction. It encourages the interaction of intellectual analysis with literary imagination. Not all *New Worlds* writers would have offered such a utilitarian argument for the magazine, which soon became primarily literary, but their attitudes provided a counterbalance to the impracticality of the optimism of the 'new mutants'. Science fiction writers know best what all utopias come to. It is significant that of the principal contributors whose works I shall be assessing, J.G. Ballard and Brian Aldiss were ten years older than its average writer or reader, while Michael Moorcock's personal experience of the last days of the bohemians in Europe gave him a head start on many things the young revolutionaries thought they were inventing themselves. Strongly influenced by drugs, the magazine never became a platform for the psychedelic gospel.[21]

Leary's *The Politics of Ecstasy* received a brusque, dismissive review, and hippy extravagance elsewhere was observed with a jaundiced eye.[22] A copy of *New Worlds* looks rather different from (and much less dated than) its contemporaries *Oz* and *IT*, though it attracted many of the same readers. It looks even less like its erstwhile competitors, *Analog* or *Galaxy*. I shall describe and account for this divergence from the genre, discuss themes and attitudes taken up in *New Worlds*, and the transformation of style and prose design that accompanied them. Eventually we shall see how the literary movement that came to be known as 'New Wave science fiction' spreads far and wide across contemporary fiction; but first we must look at the origin of that movement, in the history of *New Worlds*.

Chapter Two

The 'field' and the 'wave'
the history of *New Worlds*

Perhaps the most characteristic volume of *New Worlds* writings did not appear as an issue of the magazine, but as an anthology edited by one of Moorcock's co-editors and regular contributors, Langdon Jones. Under the title *The New SF*[1] he collected pieces from almost all the principal writers – Moorcock himself, Brian Aldiss, James Sallis, Charles Platt, Michael Butterworth, John Sladek and Thomas Disch – and from other associates – Giles Gordon, Maxim Jakubowski and Pamela Zoline – with poetry by George MacBeth and D.M. Thomas, and an interview presenting J.G. Ballard at his most emphatic and enigmatic.

In his preface to the anthology Moorcock declared: 'If proof were needed of the contention that much of the very best modern literature is emerging from the SF field, this book should supply that proof'.[2] The notion of an 'SF field' and a modern literature 'emerging from it' is central to my analysis. Hilary Bailey's precise and witty survey of the 'field', 'this mysterious stretch of land, property no doubt of some worried farmer with many sons,'[3] demonstrates how uneven and populous it is, and how inadequate any generalisations about it must be. It is a task for the theoretical critic to say what science fiction should, and for the encyclopedist to say what it does, encompass. I shall do neither. As more critics turn their attention to it, the problem of defining science fiction is becoming more difficult, not less. I shall not attempt to contribute to the solution, since one of the few things the *New Worlds* writers shared was their impatience with the limitations of genre fiction. Their own fiction was intended to defy categorisation, and I shall follow that as far as possible. I may even end up contributing to the problem; though when I speak of 'the *New Worlds* writers', I am not instituting a new category, only stating that they all contributed to the magazine and so may temporarily be considered together. Similarly, the term 'New Wave', which is as misleading as most critical labels, signifies only that the writers *were* considered together, as a collective movement sharply distinct from and hostile to what they saw as the old order. This collectivity the writers themselves affirmed in editorials and in public. Though they now disclaim any artistic unanimity, they were associated at the time, and much, I think, may be critically induced from that association, however unstable it proved.

So, injustice is about to be done all round. I shall refer sweepingly to 'traditional science fiction', and more often to 'sf', the initials unexpanded as a reminder of their uncertain provenance. Many better read than I will probably take issue with my assertions and disagree with how I present 'the tradition', especially since I shall be looking at it over my shoulder and in contrast to the achievements of Moorcock and his dissenters. Attracted by the imaginative potential of sf and inspired by its best, they felt strongly that it was encumbered by its worst and struck out accordingly. They saw no reason why sf should be segregated from the rest of fiction, and resented editors, writers and readers who seemed to be in conspiracy to keep it insulated, governed only by low standards hardly changed for forty years.

Sf is popular fiction. Its public image as a trivial, sub-literary pastime was a product of the specialist sf magazines and their cultivation of a coterie audience. Magazines bring writer and reader closer than any other form of publishing. Serialisation can permit readers' reactions to influence a story during composition, and they will almost certainly have an effect on what revisions the author makes before publishing it as a complete novel. From month to month (or quarter to quarter), the magazine relies directly on audience approval for survival. An editor will often court readers by appealing to them not as isolated individuals engaged in the private act of reading, but as participants in a larger group, a society of like-minded people, to which the magazine is the entrée. Some of these groups actually exist. Of these, the sf enthusiasts are surely the most organised, vociferous and demanding. They have a nationalistic (though anarchic) conception of themselves as 'fandom', with hierarchical degrees of greater or lesser loyalty; they converse in their own jargon; when not gathering at 'sf cons' they gossip indefatigably about writers, and about each other, in 'fanzines'; they judge authors fiercely and possessively, idolizing favourites and heaping scorn on the rejected. No editor can ever remain in doubt as to their feelings about his policies. However, those feelings are those of an elite, and tend to be conservative. The period when specialist magazines dominated sf publishing is over, but fandom has survived the transition to paperbacks, intact.

New Worlds was itself created within this close collaboration. In the late 1930s the Science-Fiction Association, a group of fervent fans, keen writers and readers, met in London pubs and teashops to plot, if not the future of mankind, then fictional versions of that future. Their fanzine, *Novae Terrae*, was a typical cyclostyled newsheet, but E.J. Carnell, the Association's treasurer, had plans and material to develop it into a magazine of fiction and discussion, a British alternative to the American magazines that they all read and to which some of them had sold stories. After the war he was given the opportunity to do so. His magazine, now called *New Worlds*, was issued by Pendulum Publications in July 1946. The economic uncertainty of the period brought about the collapse of Pendulum in the following year, but not before three issues of *New Worlds* had been produced and the old Association had swollen from an itinerant board-meeting to a vast informal congregation that occupied the White Horse Tavern in Fetter Lane every Thursday evening. Carnell acquired the title and in 1948 he and five others set up Nova Publications Ltd to publish and distribute the magazine themselves.

NW was not the first British sf magazine, but it was the first to be 'home-grown' in this way, from the very capital of British fandom. The six directors met formally in the private bar of the White Horse while the fans and pilgrims overflowed the saloon. *NW* survived where others failed: *Tales of Wonder*, for example, and *Fantasy*, both edited by Walter Gillings, had already folded when he became a co-founder of Nova. *NW* came to be respected in America too. Nova Publications were taken over by a larger firm and brought out a sister magazine, *Science Fantasy*, which Carnell also edited. The company acquired a third title, *Science Fiction Adventures*, an American magazine which was dying in 1958; revived, it ran for another five years in England.

Nevertheless, the Americans still dominated the market in the early 1960s (with *Amazing, Analog, Fantastic, Galaxy* and *Fantasy and Science Fiction*), while Nova was running into difficulties. The parent company, faced with declining sales and dim prospects, decided to discontinue the remaining two magazines. Carnell's last issue of *NW*, no. 141 for March 1964, gave the results of a statistical survey of 350 readers. Limited though this sample was, it showed a fall in demand for specialist sf magazines of any nationality, and a corresponding rise in paperback purchasing. Import restrictions imposed in wartime had been lifted in 1958, causing a flood of cheap commercial fiction from America. Sales of *NW* had begun to fall off in 1959, and had never recovered.

The correspondence columns of *NW*, no. 141 included a letter from Michael Moorcock, a young fan whom Carnell had published in both his magazines. Moorcock deplored their demise; he was an adventurous writer, impatient of timid editors, who knew that Carnell, though essentially conservative, could be persuaded to print experimental work that the American sf magazines would not entertain and that did not conform to the specifications of magazines like *Argosy*, or *Playboy*. Together with J.G. Ballard, another unconventional author similarly frustrated, Moorcock put together a dummy issue of an ideal magazine, in a large format on good quality paper, intended to bridge the widening gap between experimental art and the general public. As well as popularising the work of artists already established in more exclusive circles (such as William Burroughs and Eduardo Paolozzi), it would offer an outlet for the different and the new by authors yet unrecognised (such as Michael Moorcock and J.G. Ballard); moreover, 'it would attempt a cross-fertilisation of popular sf, science and the work of the literary and artistic avant garde.'[4]

For the moment their idealism was only wishful thinking, stimulated by the death sentence on *New Worlds* and *Science Fantasy*. But just before his last issues appeared Carnell had written to Brian Aldiss telling him that 'Nova has sold the two magazines to ... Roberts and Vinter Ltd who plan to continue them immediately.'[5] David Warburton of Roberts and Vinter saw in the magazines some potential for publishing imaginative fiction of a higher standard than the American magazines maintained. This was a policy that Carnell had always tried to pursue, and the company asked him to continue as editor; but, as he told Aldiss, 'After a whole weekend of mulling things over, I turned down their offer and have recommended a 'certain person' to them as editor. He sees them today.' This was Michael Moorcock, whose name Carnell had advanced without his knowledge, though with sympathy for his aspirations and faith in his editorial experience – as well he might, since Moorcock had begun with a magazine devoted to the fantasies of Edgar Rice Burroughs, at the age of seventeen. Also interested in the Nova magazines was Kyril Bonfiglioli, a novelist and bookseller, and Warburton decided to give them one each. Moorcock explains,[6]

> Many people expected me to opt for the editorship of *Science Fantasy*, since most of my work had previously appeared in that magazine, but in fact I was interested in broadening the possibilities of the SF idiom and *New Worlds*, being a much more open title, seemed the best place to do it.

He had to shelve his ideal *NW* because of financial restrictions, so issue 142 for May and June 1964, Moorcock's first, came out in Compact Books as a cheaply produced paperback on familiar pulp paper. Its editorial announced that, however familiar the format, the contents of *NW* would be altogether new, 'a kind of SF which is unconventional in every sense.'[7] 'A *popular* literary renaissance', declared Moorcock, 'is around the corner. Together, we can accelerate that renaissance.' The new Renaissance Man would be William Burroughs – 'his work is the SF we've all been waiting for' – whom J.G. Ballard champions in the same issue as the 'true genius and first mythographer of the mid-20th century.'[8] The excitement and exaggeration aside, Moorcock proved himself as practical an editor as Carnell had hoped. Aware that too swift a transformation would alienate the habitual buyers of *NW* before it could build up a new readership, Moorcock changed the contents of the magazine much more slowly than he pretended to. Alongside Ballard's fiction and his own, 'taboo-breaking' stories by Langdon Jones and Hilary Bailey, and novelties by John Hamilton and David Rome, Moorcock continued to include plenty of traditional sf. In his first year on *NW* he published perfectly commonplace work by P.F. Woods, Donald Malcolm, Sydney J. Bounds, E.C. Tubb – even Arthur C. Clarke. The correspondence columns began to fill with altercation over the new versus the old. The unfamiliar fiction did not seem to have any corporate identity or even many common factors, but it was quickly lumped together under the label that now seems to be attached to surprising developments in any popular art, a label that may be useful historically but otherwise only compounds confusion: the 'New Wave'. Advocates (led by the eclectic American anthologist Judith Merril) and opponents began to convene.

There were many who completely misinterpreted Moorcock's policies. Carnell, editing his new series of anthologies, *New Writings in SF*, understood nothing of what was going on back at the old homestead. After three issues of Moorcock's editorship, Carnell wrote to Aldiss: 'The new *NW* . . . is degenerating into an imitation of Nebula – in fact, I think the salvation of my old magazines lies solely with Bonfiglioli and S-F.'[9] But Bonfiglioli had none of Moorcock's vision or skill. He lost circulation by changing his title from *Science Fantasy* to *SF Impulse* at a time when distributors were reluctant to handle new promotions. In 1966 he resigned the ailing magazine to J.G. Ballard, who took only a few days to realise he didn't want it after all. The amiable Harry Harrison caught it, knocked it back into a more traditional shape, and kept it alive until the end of the year when Thorpe and Porter, distributors for Roberts and Vinter, went bankrupt, owing £20,000. Cutting back, Roberts and Vinter decided to amputate sf, the less profitable end of their range.

In fact Moorcock had improved the sales of *NW* and was just getting into his stride. Brian Aldiss, who had been hesitant over Moorcock's reorganisation at first, but was now convinced that he had 'worked . . . wonders with the magazine',[10] began to look for someone to buy it from Roberts and Vinter. Aldiss, never having suffered from the disrepute that writing sf could often earn, had more influence in the republic of letters than Moorcock, who in any case had personal and principled disagreements with the literary establishment. He sought help from Kingsley Amis, Charles Osborne of the *London Magazine*, and Douglas Hill of Pan Books. In addition he approached a number of writers and critics to gather support for an application to the Arts Council for a grant for *NW*: 'a wild idea, but everything must be tried.'[11] Kenneth Allsop, Anthony Burgess, Edmund Crispin, Roy Fuller, Marghanita Laski, and J.B. Priestley all replied in favour, and on 11 January 1967 Aldiss wrote to Ken Slater and Doreen Parker of the British Science Fiction Association:

> I seem to have saved the day with New Worlds. I was up in London yesterday, met David Warburton, and we went round to the Arts Council. We had a brief discussion there, but it appears the Council has already made up its mind to move on our behalf . . . and . . . provide financial help for a year. . . . Although there is a 95% certainty we shall get the grant, this won't be confirmed yet awhile.

Moorcock, who had not been altogether in agreement with the application and had never expected it to be approved, found himself in receipt of a guaranteed £150 per issue. It was not enough to finance a whole magazine, but the award and the prestige it brought persuaded Warburton to continue his involvement. He entered partnership with Moorcock to produce *NW* themselves, though Panther and Fontana had already expressed interest in it. In the meantime a couple of bridging issues (nos 171 and 172) had been assembled from shelved material and special donations (including stories by Aldiss and Ballard which had proved too radical for other publishers), and personally guaranteed against loss by Aldiss and Warburton. With Charles Platt, responsible for the design, layout and later much of the editing of *NW*, Moorcock looked over the dummy magazine he and Ballard had originally compiled, and Warburton agreed to print it in that format. There was an unexpected delay in the certification of the grant – on 17 May Aldiss wrote to Judith Merril, 'The damned thing is still not official' – but in July 1967 *NW*, no. 173 came out as a large magazine, on glossy paper, with a cover that reproduced a picture by M.C. Escher. This was a clean break with the traditional sf 'pulps'; in neither form nor content did it now bear any resemblance to the magazine Carnell had left three years earlier, though its progress was to be no less uneven. Merril, writing to Moorcock in October 1967, was already referring to 'New Worlds' current difficulties'. While Moorcock was in America in November Warburton decided that the sales had not been good enough to sustain his interest. To Moorcock[12]

it seemed yet again that *New Worlds* was to fold. . . . David Warburton had decided to end his involvement with the magazine and had gone to Scotland, leaving me a note to tell me that the magazine was now mine to do with as I pleased

– and, of course, solely his financial responsibility. Unexpectedly Sylvester Stein of Stonehart Publications offered rescue; his firm had scant experience of dealing with fiction, much less the radical and *avant-garde*, but Stein had a liking for *NW*.

Before long there was trouble of a different kind. Norman Spinrad's 'Bug Jack Barron', an aggressive and tumultuous story of media and political corruption in a near future America, was serialised for most of 1968. It was intended to disturb, and did. A Member of Parliament dubbed Spinrad a degenerate and asked the Minister of Arts why taxpayers' money was being spent on an obscene publication. W.H. Smith and John Menzies refused to stock it, thus effectively crushing its circulation and consigning it to commercial obscurity. Stonehart began to regret their agreement. Moorcock had lost heavily by investing his own money in pay for contributors; contributors were not paid, and began to queue up; there were difficulties with the Arts Council grant; Stonehart delayed paying the printers; the printers refused to deliver; the press, enticed by bans and accusations of obscenity, gave *NW* some inaccurate and unwelcome publicity; the distributors grew nervous, secretly withheld stocks and pulped back numbers; the staff were to be seen selling copies on the street.

Despite all, the quality and aspirations of the magazine were upheld. In October 1968 Moorcock took over complete responsibility and published it himself. Since his energies were stretched between this and writing commercial fantasy to finance it, the magazine came to depend heavily on the commitment of everyone involved, each issue being assembled communally. The Arts Council seemed about to withdraw but renewed their grant; but in April 1970 Moorcock and Platt found they could stand the strain no longer. No. 200 was the last of the series; Moorcock made up a special farewell issue, containing an index, for subscribers only, and it seemed that this time *NW* really was dead.

In autumn 1971, however, the first *New Worlds Quarterly* came out from Sphere Books. Moorcock, determined that *NW* should continue, but avoid the troubles that had beset magazine publication, thought the answer was to return to paperback editions distributed and controlled as ordinary books (much as Carnell's *New Writings in SF* were). It was an excellent opportunity to relax a little and to reprint some material from previous issues that few people had had the chance to read, but the *Quarterly* never achieved the immediacy and vigour of the monthlies, and after only a year had contracted their endemic irregularity of appearance. A letter to Moorcock from the publishers mentions a contract for volumes 7 to 11,[13] but another breakdown intervened. Moorcock gave up editorial involvement again, handing no. 7 to Charles Platt and Hilary Bailey, 'experienced editors who have not become, as, frankly, I feel I have become, jaded!'[14] A disagreement with Sphere resulted in a change to Corgi Books for nos 9 and 10, and then a long silence. In 1976 Moorcock wrote, 'Plans are afoot to publish *NW* again in large size, probably through Quartet. Format will be reminiscent of the old *NW* under my editorship but even more lavish. Hilary Bailey will edit.'[15] Two years later, in spring 1978, an envelope of xeroxed sheets calling itself *New Worlds*, no. 212 was distributed to a small number of interested parties. Once again, Moorcock was responsible. Most of the material featured, by regular contributors, had first been printed in *Frendz* magazine.[16] A flyer for the next issue announced, 'There will be no conventional narrative fiction in *New Worlds* and little conventional criticism. The majority of the material will have a strong visual flavour.' This last series was irregular and short-lived. Moorcock edited two issues, David Britton a third and Charles Platt a fourth. The principle was that editorial continuity and conformity of design and schedule are unnecessary impositions: the material should dictate the magazine, not vice versa. Sales were hardly encouraging; plans for a fifth issue by Phil Meadley were not carried out; personal disagreements became divisive. Now Moorcock warns, 'If ever I start to talk about doing another issue, that's the time to send for the ambulance.'

The divorce between *NW* and the genre sf magazines was inevitable rather than intentional. When Moorcock's original bid to develop sf on its own terms met with misunderstanding and vehement resistance, he rejected those terms and committed the magazine to a broader range of imaginative fiction which might still acknowledge sf, but only as a point of departure.[17]

We were surprised by the lack of response from old guard sf fans, who we had assumed were as hungry for real imagination as we had been. Naively, we had honestly expected that these readers would be more open to new kinds of writing. It took me some years to learn that a certain kind of sf fan is about the most conservative reader of all!

The ventures that Moorcock proposed threatened the denizens of fandom. What the outsider may perceive as the limitations of genre the fan feels as the security of city walls. Commercial genres exist by exclusion, have specific functions, satisfy particular tastes. Some less parochial enthusiasts would be happy to open the gates and encourage visitors to enjoy the peculiar virtues of the region, its climate, geography, flora and fauna – the critical benevolence of C.S. Lewis and Kingsley Amis, for example. Others want to keep the walls closed, prize the esoteric delights of belonging to a clique, and relish exchanging conspiratorial grins while the outsider stands baffled – the nationalist zeal of Sam Moskowitz and Donald A.

Wollheim. Moorcock's programme amounted to knocking down the walls and trading local resources with countries far and wide. It met with much disapproval. Begun in a spirit of benign optimism, it was pursued determinedly, even aggressively. Editorial manifestos pounded a party line, belieing the fact that the party hardly knew where to draw one. Today it was a return to the values of H.G. Wells; tomorrow an advance to the innovations of William Burroughs; next month a sidestep to embrace Mervyn Peake. Meanwhile reviewers sniped at the sacred colossi: Heinlein, Asimov, Blish. *NW* broke the pulp taboos, kindling controversy, to challenge the reader's assumptions and stretch the limits of his acceptance. Nowhere was there more scandal, or more success, than in the areas of psychology and sexuality, two topics of much popular interest and excitement in the 1960s, and two respects in which science fiction, with its chaste and cardboard characters, was famous for its deficiency.

.

Chapter Three
Love among the mannequins
sex and science fiction

In *NW* no. 144 Moorcock published 'I Remember, Anita' by Lang-don Jones.[1] It makes dreary reading now: a neurotic music student falls in love with an older woman who has been victimised and damaged in just about every way available: born illegitimate, raped in her teens, exploited, impregnated and deserted to bear a child that does not survive. He and she are wonderfully happy and make love with great frequency until someone drops the Bomb. The story, as the title indicates, is all flashback delivered by Mike as he rants and vomits over the grave where he has just buried the bits of Anita's body. The style is atrocious, a mixture of protest poem, soft porn, and women's magazine romance (Anita worked for a women's magazine):[2]

'It's a funny thing about people,' I replied shakily, 'they always try to hurt those they love the most.'
  Suddenly my mouth was on yours and our bodies were pressed violently together. My tongue found the fever heat of your mouth, and my hands ran over your body. I thrust my hand up underneath your loose jumper, and found the warm flesh of your breasts.

That phrase 'fever heat' and those anatomical dislocations characterise the story: the writing is sick, and the story is about sickness – the sickness of those who corrupt and are corrupted, the sickness of men who drop bombs, and the sickness of Mike at Anita's grave. The sickness of society was often ruthlessly diag-nosed in protest writings of the 1960s, usually with the same effect on the reader or listener: disgust, disinterest, and disbelief, in var-ying proportions. Cataloguing the symptoms of disease ('I remember . . . and I remember . . .') is no way to arouse sympathy, especially if each term is adjectivally overloaded ('solitary sadness', 'grinding depression', 'convulsed ecstasy'). Sex is ostensibly Mike and Anita's escape from their inherited disease, as it was for Winston Smith and Julia, but Jones's ponderous, obsessive tone failed to distinguish the joys of loving from the agonies of living.

Jones has admitted that 'Anita' is a bad story and wants nothing more to do with it. But in 1964, to the sf fans who found it lurking in their favourite magazine, it must have been quite a different experience. Moorcock's editorial tag announced,

This story may shock you. It's meant to.

Apparently it succeeded. Readers were still writing in about it up to two years later. The primary shock they felt seems to have been from a clash between what they thought of as two incompatible things: science fiction and sex. 'Anita' was obviously sf (at least as far as, say, Nevil Shute's *On The Beach* was), being set in a near future before, during, and after a nuclear attack on London. On the other hand, there was a lot of sex in it. No one complained that the story was a failure *as a story*; either they praised it, sometimes with qualifications, or objected to it, on the grounds that one, Louis Van Gastel, does here.[3]

What youngster, with refined artist's feelings, would so blatantly over-stress his sexual relation with an adored and respected mistress! No, sir, it should have had a more delicate touch. The author should have passed more lightly on that point and don't you forget the circulation of this magazine among young eager readers, who want something else than trash just good enough to be sold under the counter. I think sex is all right in sf inasmuch it serves to give a little life to a plot. I won't squirm if it is a little spiced, *sometimes*, but . . . a *good* story don't need that. . . . Will sex rise its ugly head, since you took the desk over?

M. Van Gastel's last sentence is an intriguing one. Leaving aside its Freudian suggestiveness, and its reminder of the cliff-hangers in juvenile serials ('Will sex rise its ugly head? Don't miss next week's thrilling instalment!'), it is a cliché that is surprisingly appropriate for a consideration of sex and science fiction. The phrase conjures up a familiar scene: the bug-eyed monster leers over the helpless maiden as the space pilot leaps to the rescue, raygun blazing. (Anyone to whom the scene is *not* familiar should consult *Great*

Balls of Fire!) Harrison's study of sex in sf illustration.[4]) That tableau, if no other, is the contribution of sf to contemporary iconography, embodying a myth whose last Western manifestation was probably the legend of St George and the Dragon. It is interesting that in both examples the maiden is not really in any danger sexually, though the threat persists, since – as John W. Campbell pointed out – copulation between human beings and alien reptiles would probably be impossible. This most enduring of traditional sf images is exactly that, only an image: the essence of a thousand magazine covers, whose erotic implications never matched the stories they purport to illustrate.[5]

The old pulps always promised more than they delivered, and the contents were but a shadow of the garish cover. Not only were they fit for a child to read, but a re-reading . . . rapidly convinces one that they were *only* fit for children to read. . . . A little blood, a little torture, no sex and the hero always wins.

An excellent example is a copy of *Amazing Stories* from the 1950s.[6] The blurb on the cover claims,

Every lovely woman was a fragile toy to this MAD MONSTER OF MOGO

and gives in evidence a picture of a redhead, considerably déshabillée, swept aloft in the arms of a winged man, a veritable seraph, and nude (as far as we can see). The everyday world, healthy but hapless, is represented by the scene below: a picnic spread by a car parked in a green field, and hubby throwing up his hands in alarm. He is wearing slacks and a sweater; she is in *décolleté* evening gown and black stockings with flowers behind her ear. (Inconsistencies like this were rife in the artwork of the pulps, as in all cruder commercial art: the cover of *Amazing* no. 22 shows a woman wearing similar gear, including five-inch heels, on board a spaceship.[7])

Some readers, especially today, might be puzzled. Abduction by this Mad Monster from Mogo doesn't look such a bad option. Turning to Don Wilcox's story, they'd find the answer.[8] The seraph isn't the Mad Monster at all, nor is he even from Mogo. He is a Venusian social worker, Green Flash by name, rescuing rather than abducting the woman, from an internment camp. The picnic is a pure contrivance by the illustrator Walter Popp, as is the erotic innuendo. Each party is happily married, the woman to a burly space pilot, of course, and Green Flash to Purple Wings. The Mad

Monster of Mogo, incidentally, is an ogre called Faz-O-Faz. He has a great quantity of ears and fingers and spends most of his time eating or sleeping. It is true that 'every lovely woman is a fragile toy' to him, but then so is every express train and every skyscraper: Faz-O-Faz is a mile tall, and none too careful where he puts his feet.

This is a typical pulp magazine of the sort Harrison deplored. Others were more culpable: *Marvel Stories*, for example, and *Planet Stories*. Kelly Freas, one of the artists for *Planet Stories*, recalls[9]

There were more Wild, Wayward, Willing and Wanton Witch-Women in the cover blurbs than ever got into the stories, and the 3-B cover was an almost inviolable rule: Boob, Babe, and B[ug-] E[yed] M[onster]. . . . Anything else was purely incidental, and while the actual display of feminine flesh was usually minimal, the gender of spacesuits was always aggressively obvious. The objective, of course, was to suggest sex in every way possible, without the overt display which would have had us yanked off the newstands the moment we appeared – especially with those blurbs!

At the beginning of the 1960s *Amazing Stories* became the first American magazine to recognise the new generation of sf writers. Its editor, Cele Goldsmith, published the first stories by Thomas Disch and Roger Zelazny, and early work by J.G. Ballard. In the mid-1950s, however, when the field was dominated by policies like Freas's, it is no surprise to find that *Amazing* was still decorated with 'aggressively obvious' sex symbols.

John W. Campbell's *Astounding Stories* (later *Analog*) was an altogether more earnest production. Much has been said and written about the puritanical censorship practised by Campbell and his assistant Kay Tarrant, but, personalities aside, Campbell's editorial commitment to intellectual rigour forced him to rate the head above the heart, and therefore above the genitals too. The emotions could be seen only as a 'problem', sex as a distraction.

'People whose work lay in space had no business with marriage and children.'[10] And for 'people' read 'men', of course. Any survey of sf before 1970 would show that, by an overwhelming majority, it was written by men for men – or, some would say, adolescent boys. Female writers are memorable because they were exceptional, often using ambiguous names or male pseudonyms like women novelists of the nineteenth century. This is not to say that *Astounding* was a misogynist publication, but, in contrast to *Amazing*, a sample of twenty-five copies from 1959 to 1961 yields only one cover picture with a woman in it, and she is far away in the background . . . serving behind a counter. Whole issues can go by with scarcely a feminine pronoun. 'Good old sf,' marvelled Harrison, 'where the girls just don't come in.'[11] Campbell was too logical to regard women as dispensable; they had their place, but it was not usually in the stag preserves of Research and Development. The titular entity in Randall Garrett's 'A Spaceship Named McGuire' is a cyborg, a spacecraft whose control mechanism is a human brain transplanted from its body into an artificial life-support system. McGuire attracts the attentions of a teenage girl (called Jack!) who possesses a charismatic ability to influence people by projecting an 'emotional field'. The hero-narrator discovers her interference and lectures her about it.[12]

'You found that McGuire didn't respond to emotion, but only to data and logic.'

'You've always felt rather inferior in regard to your ability to handle logic, haven't you, Jack?'

'Yes . . . yes. I have.'

'Don't cry now; I'm only trying to explain it to you. There's nothing wrong with your abilities.'

'No?'

'No. But you wanted to be able to think like a man, and you couldn't. You think like a woman!'

Thinking and acting 'like a woman', projecting emotional fields, disrupts the masculine order of things. Women in space, like women at sea, are trouble. Some, like Jack, mean no harm but can't help interfering. Others, like Elissa Krand, ought to get a grip on themselves. When their space-liner is wrecked, Miss Krand's hysterical demands for attention infuriate and imperil the other survivors until one of the men comes up with a solution. They lobotomise her.[13]

The 'Mating Problems' in Christopher Anvil's story beset a team of colonists, gruff, dogged men called Bart, Ed, and Sam – frontier Puritans in space. They are caught between two feminine evils: the wiles of an oversexed wife in a male majority, and the interference of four female tourists. They solve their problems by preventing the sightseers from leaving and co-opting them to restore the sexual equilibrium.[14] Women are necessary but unfortunately random factors that need to be controlled. Their opinions are not consulted.

Not all women create such a disturbance, but even the most

logical of them can play havoc with a hero's good intentions: Milton's Adam all over again.[15]

> For a while that spring, deoxyribonucleic acid had begun to take second place in my heart. This is a painful admission for a biochemist to make – DNA should be the cornerstone of his life. But Shari was something rare – a gorgeous woman, if somewhat distant, who was thoroughly intelligent. She had already earned her doctorate, while I was still struggling with the tag ends of my thesis.

The flippant tone disguises the fact that sentiments like these were seriously maintained in the world of *Astounding*. The quest was all-important, but that old biochemistry. . . . Editor and writers knew that the girls just had to come in occasionally, so they made them take doctorates, put on white coats, and pass through the sterilisation chamber before opening the An Lab door. The resulting creatures, distant if somewhat gorgeous, are prodigiously cool, Nordic and steely, hyperefficient secretaries, field research assistants, or masters of extra-terrestial philology. Spacewomen are rare, and very brave, as Jane Calver explains to her husband when choosing to chance her life with him on the Rim of the galaxy.

> 'But it's just this, Derek. Women are different from men. Even though we are accepted in Space, even though we take the same risks as you, we still have that longing for security. One part of me hates to see the security that we have achieved thrown away. That part of me has spoken now. The other part of me wants to join in this crazy adventure.'

Derek, we are told,[16]

> did not, he admitted to himself, altogether like the idea of having Jane along, any more than little Brentano liked to see Tanya risking her life. But he could see that both the women were of the breed that prefers to meet danger side by side with their men. He loved them for it, and wouldn't have changed them for all the Universe.

Women of that 'breed' are prodigious because they are successful in what is obviously classed as a man's world. Woman, described by Jane Calver, has a split personality. One part is sexless, ready for adventure and danger in the eternal quest of the human spirit. The other is homeloving, wifely, the source of sexual and maternal urges. Women who qualify for duty in *Astounding* unsex themselves, like Lady Macbeth. When psychologist Siryl of the spaceship

Sépelora reports to her captain, 'Siryl's bearing was more military than his, in spite of her civilian blouse. . . . Under her professional pride lay the curious overdeveloped consciousness of being female possible only to women who wanted to be men.[17]

Sexual denial disinfects *Astounding* fiction. Even its erotic moments acquire a clinical flavour and scientific rationale. In Garrett's '. . . And Check the Oil', Brownie the linguist manages to get into the alien spaceship when all the male investigators have failed, simply by taking all her clothes off – not, however, to seduce the guards, but to prove that she is unarmed.[18]

Eroticism in *Amazing* is much less subtle though just as self-deceptive. At the hot end of the spectrum come descriptions of busty women that match the portraits on the covers. These sirens are quite often humanoid aliens like Nerissa, vestal in a Martian priest-cult: 'And what a woman! Full-breasted and red-lipped, with dark hair tumbling down across her shoulders. A clinging dress in the Martian style revealed rather than concealed the loveliness of a lithe body.'[19] This is the hostess in a galactic night-club:[20]

The blood-purple iridescence of her hair, cascading to the soft white of her smoothly rounded shoulders, stirred strange emotions. Her eyes, either through some secret of artificial pigmentation or some chameleon-like quality, were star-shaped pools of liquid, purple fire, that completed the almost other-worldly effect augmenting her natural body.

This mode of physical description, swathing a check-list of bodily attributes in a welter of adjectives, is a staple convention of commercial fiction, shared by sf with detective stories, men's magazines, and pornography. It is the same effect that vitiates Langdon Jones's 'Anita', as we saw. Usually applied to women, it robs their images of identity, even of life. The writer freezes them in an instant and dissects them at length, the rhapsodic fervour of his tangled prose contrasting oddly with the dismembered plastic mannequins it invariably evokes.

The purpose of these descriptions is obviously sensuous, titillatory, but to no good purpose. The rules forbid anything further. In 'Victims of the Vortex' by Clinton Ames, Craig, stranded in space, sees floating in the void outside his 'cosmicar'[21]

a girl whose beauty was beyond the ability of the imagination to conceive, with lips full and red, cheeks smooth and flushed, eyes large and covered by closed olive lids, forehead smooth and

sloping into a wealth of dark hair.
Her name is Ahla-ahloa and she is a native of a parallel universe, but
the dimensions are in close conjunction, so that Craig can see her.
She has an extraordinary emotional effect on him: he exhibits a
whole casebook of symptoms of extreme sexual frustration. The
page teems with verbs like 'sobbed', 'cursed', 'glared fiercely'.
He looked through the thick glass at her, yearning for her with
every fibre of his being. She returned his look from the blue
depths of her eyes with one that caused his heart to hurt with a
pain that was ecstacy [sic].
Then he finds that they can communicate by telepathy (true to sf
tradition), and starts to chat her up, beginning with a formal lecture
(true to sf tradition) on the history of Terran space mechanics, to
which she attends meekly.
'The next step was the bringing together of a Q charge and an
ordinary atom to produce a cosmic particle. This was finally
accomplished . . .'.
'It is as I thought,' Ahla-ahloa said.
Note that 'bringing together . . . to produce'. It must be inhibiting to
have to carry out preliminary mating rituals through the sealed hull
of a spacecraft, but the impression that author and character are
collaborating to keep sex at bay is curious and persistent. After
some inter-continual shuffling, largely achieved by abandoning
astro-physics for wishful thinking, Ahla-ahloa materialises on
Craig's side of the dimensional interface. The story ends with her
knocking politely on the door of his cosmicar.
As in *Astounding*, there are guest appearances by agents of sexual
repression.[22]
Frake eyed him sharply; 'Whatever you're thinking is no good –
understand that! We're not messing up this deal over a
yellow-haired skirt. Keep your needs in check until they don't
get in the way of more important things.'
The Governor of Mars exercises similar restrictions on a woman
who has stowed away on a transport ship to seek a husband in his
all-male colony. 'I forbid you to have any romantic dealings with
any colonist of Mars, on pain of imprisonment, until the time you
are due to blast off.'[23] There is general agreement among the heroes
that whatever those alien women may get up to out on the frontiers
of space, ordinary decent womenfolk don't do that sort of thing.
This is the cooler end of *Amazing*'s spectrum of femininity. Marcia

Frazer, for example, is obviously an ordinary decent woman: she has 'fine square shoulders and warm honest features' instead of those flushed cheeks and full breasts.[24] Interestingly enough, she is a first cousin of *Astounding*'s 'thoroughly intelligent' career-women, with a degree in English Literature. Larre, victim of the bunny-girl with the (geometrically) starry eyes, is a superhuman space-travelling secret agent; nevertheless, his preference is for Marguery,[25]

> as good a cook as she was beautiful. . . . She had laughed with
> him, and sang to him. She was a happy, delightful companion.
> She loved life, every small event was an adventure. . . . He
> caught her sweet woman scent and he wanted to kiss her. But he
> knew she wouldn't like that – not yet.

It is difficult now to isolate the origin of this syndrome of repression: abstinence, on the one hand, titillation, on the other. There was official censorship of publications; there were more rigid sexual taboos operative in society then than now ('Will sex rise its *ugly* head?'); there was the conservatism of the genre itself, as Moorcock was to discover. Complicating everything was the strong bias of the magazines towards the male reader, which permitted the perpetuation of the old and dangerous myth of female inferiority. Of course there were writers who did not hold themselves bound by these circumscriptions, who found subject matter for sf in the mysteries of sex, or who came upon sf from outside, with different preconceptions: Philip José Farmer, Theodore Sturgeon – and Wells and Huxley and Orwell. As Brian Aldiss recalls from his adolescent reading,[26]

> That was one great advantage of Wells over *Astounding*: he
> knew sex existed, which all the Simon-pure Asimovs and
> Heinleins demonstrably didn't; only Sturgeon acknowledged
> that sex existed, in the sf of those days. In the process of reading
> Freud and his popularizers, I felt that the heroes of *Astounding*
> falsified by admitting no worlds below the belt.

Other critics have done far more than I can here to expose and examine that falsification, and to indicate what authors must do to correct it.[27] I can only describe the state of prejudice when Moorcock took over *NW* in 1964, when many readers, not unreasonably, assumed that the historical development of sf showed its definitive and necessary shape. Hence the belief of Van Gastel that sex and sf are distinct, compatible only up to a point ('I think sex is all right in sf *inasmuch* . . .'). The conservative case was further illustrated in another letter to *NW*, from E. French Biscoe.[28] She claims that the proper business of sf is with 'non-human forces' and 'tremendous (and as yet unlived) imaginary experiences'. Intimate inspection of individuals and what they do with one another is not only distracting but inappropriate. This is the job of 'ordinary' fiction. Biscoe uses an analogy with painting. 'Ordinary' fiction is like portraiture, while sf depicts landscapes: it needs figures, but only small ones, in proportion.[29] Sf, she says, 'offers so much of absorbing interest that we should not ask for what is not in its nature to give – all this and sex, too.'

In his editorship Moorcock was not content to let the nature of sf be dictated by its history. Where cautious readers saw barriers, he saw hurdles. Other relationships of figures to background were available to the imagination, and therefore should be explored. From the very first he claimed, 'Sf is one of the most potentially flexible media for the presentation of the human drama there has ever been.'[30]

He meant to develop out of the 'sf field' 'a new literature for the space age' that could 'deal with the present on its own terms'. Such a literature could not excuse itself when sex was mentioned, certainly not in the 1960s, when mentioning sex was something of a mass compulsion, and especially not if it were to take its lead from William Burroughs, who sometimes mentions nothing else for pages on end.

As with other radical literary enterprises of the twentieth century, this one issue often drew attention away from the others. As one correspondent put it, 'There is also sex and Sex. *I Remember, Anita* was an attempt at capitalisation.'[31] Several writers who tried to adapt to Moorcock's regime from Carnell's 'capitalised', often mistaking the old *Astounding*-style titillation for frankness. Joseph Green's 'sociologists' travel to distant worlds to film 'beautiful nude savages', while John Baxter's hero and heroine wander periodically into places where it becomes inevitable for them to take off their clothes and pose for him.[32] When they drift off in a stolen boat his prose becomes rhapsodic:[33]

> Naked and brown, they were at once the pure essence of
> humankind and an extension of it, their physical appearance
> remaining the same, though purified and perfected, while their
> minds drifted into new lands of thought and dream.

Aldiss jocularly referred to the magazine as 'Lewd Worlds'. Moorcock's policy was certainly in tune with the 'permissiveness' of the
1960s, and it is hardly surprising that some of his contributors
showed considerable clumsiness in handling material that had previously been forbidden. It was a policy to permit everything rather
than emphasise anything, but it was not only uninformed authors
who thought fiction about sex had to be a kind of pornography.
Most if not all of the distribution problems that beset *NW* were a
direct result of rumours of obscenity, the stock public response
which had hampered the careers of Joyce, Lawrence, Miller and
Burroughs. Sexual explicitness suddenly became an issue in itself, a
platform on which Moorcock was required to stand, in defence of
Norman Spinrad's 'Bug Jack Barron'. Ironically, one of the reasons
for Barron's sexual hyperactivity was that Spinrad's story was an
attack on the exploitation and depersonalisation of sex in the mass
media – the charge then levelled against *NW*.

As well as the shock tactics of 'Anita', *NW* writers used other
approaches, more and less successfully, to the forbidden zone.
Hilary Bailey's 'The Fall of Frenchy Steiner', a tale on the much
used motif 'what if Germany had won the war?', is a competent
piece of traditional English sf; but she would not have been able to
sell it to any other magazine because the fulcrum of the plot is the
professional virginity of Hitler's personal prophetess and the collapse of his power when she surrenders it.[34] Bailey kept her story out
of the pornographic mode by upsetting the conventions of reader
identification and grounding it firmly in unromantic banalities:
Sebastian insists on cigarettes *before* intercourse, neatly inverting
the cliché Langdon Jones allowed into 'Anita', and afterwards *he*
starts to cry, which is definitely not in the canons of pornographic
machismo. Bailey's story is a modest and soft-spoken alternative to
Jones's breast-beating melodrama, demonstrating that an otherwise commonplace example of sf can accommodate a sexual theme
with ease, history notwithstanding.

This, however, was scarcely half of the *NW* plan. Exceptional
fiction was to be produced, breaking new ground for sf. The explo-
rations that had boldly gone to far Andromeda were now to brave
those unknown 'worlds below the belt'. Of this kind is David Harvey's 'Jake in the Forest', which appears to be a grand reverie on the
sombre mysteries and miraculous transformations of sex. It draws
on myth, symbol and dream, on the techniques of the nouveau

roman and the grave absurdities of Beckett's anti-novels to contrive a portentous atmosphere. Jake wanders through intensely allegorical terrain. Having passed between a pair of 'ancient burial mounds, built to nurture the modern memory in the food of the past', he nears another mound where[35]

> two huge stones jut upright out from the surface of the land and support a lintel stone of enormous dimensions. . . . As He approaches closer He sees that the summit to which he is progressing contains a long deep triangular hollow and it is within this hollow that the two upright slabs of stone are embedded. He descends at the long apex of the triangular depression. . . . He enters the shadow of the megalith and the sky darkens behind the three stones until they form an entrance to darkness. His muscles are tense, His lips are dry, His movement sparse. . . .
>
> In the centre of the cavern entrance there is a pool of water, and here He briefly moistens his hands and face before He strides along the well-defined path. . . . This leads downwards into the earth. . . . He commits Himself with every leap downwards until the darkness makes each progression an act of faith.

The solemnity is strenuous and often sounds hollow, but Harvey is experimenting with style and effect, taking us into areas of critical uncertainty. Is the leaden tone intended or not? However we rate 'Jake', it was a decisive step towards a new sf, a probe into different regions, in the direction that Ballard had indicated when he announced, 'It is *inner* space, not outer, that needs to be explored.'

> Tired of life I lay down for the night. I looked up at the stars. I was a microscope with an infinite resolving power. Something was using me to observe the universe.[36]

Michael Butterworth's 'Girl' is another story designed to turn sf inside out. The principle of looking at the universe through the individual is exactly what Ballard was recommending. The phenomenological universe is referred back to its origin in the percipient consciousness, which is therefore said to contain it; a microscope, not a telescope, is needed to observe the stars. In the pictorial terms of Biscoe's analogy, this new sf is neither portrait nor landscape, but something in between: a Surrealist painting. Butterworth's style deliberately blurs the narrator's perceptions so it is difficult to separate literal from metaphorical, outside from in. The eponymous Girl does not appear in the story, which relates the encounter between two male survivors of some unspecified catastrophe, but her absence is specifically evoked, in a sex scene of the most extraordinary casualness.

'We'll do it here,' he said softly, slowly and thoughtfully. His eyes grew as big as a doll's. He looked exactly like a doll now. 'Now,' he said.

I fell in his eyes. 'Now,' he muttered (round and round in the swirling flotsam pools of his eyes): 'Now.'

We did it there on the sand, in homage to the vanquished goddess, Girl.

'Right,' he said. 'Let's get this barn done up . . .'

The boldness of Butterworth's venture in this, his first published story, is apparent: to provide for the sexuality of the survivors, even though homosexual intercourse is their only option; and to do so with both the minimum of pornographic sensation and the maximum of symbolic resonance. However, his style, like Harvey's, is not altogether under control, with the result that the sex of the narrator is never actually stated. Ironically, this story, which is a remarkable attack on one aspect of sexual repression in sf (the refusal to mention sex at all), works only if the other aspect (the exclusion of female primary characters) is taken for granted: sf is about men.

NW featured unusual and adventurous fiction by Pamela Zoline, Carol Emshwiller, Eleanor Arnason, Gwyneth Cravens, and Joanna Russ, but there were not many other female contributors, though it was edited for four issues by Hilary Bailey. The magazine showed no specific awareness of feminism and did not do much to advance the improvement of the image of woman in sf which was beginning elsewhere. It could be argued that the mechanical women which appear in many of its stories are actually only the old stereotypes of sf in a new guise, but that would be ignoring the extent to which they are themselves a comment on those stereotypes. For the predominant theme in *NW* was the overlap between humanity and machines: sex in terms of technology, and technology in terms of sex. The elements were all there, in public fantasies broadcast by the mass media. Advertising encouraged the male consumer to consider his sexual partner as a possession, and his possessions as sexual partners.[37]

Now, slide into foam-padded comfort. Peel back the top and

feel the freedom of the great outside. Touch the array of
controls to answer every command. . . . Now you know how it
feels to ride under the sun and stars, secure in the knowledge
that the 360-hp engine and Super-Turbine transmission will
respond to your needs, instantly. This is integrity in a fine
automobile. This is cushioned comfort. This is romance on
wheels. . . . Wildcat pulses with response and agility.

Sf was clearly the mode to work out the possibilities of this sinister
new alchemy. Granville Hawkins's 'Playback' pursues them into a
future England tyrannised by a neo-Calvinist dictatorship, which
has killed the narrator's wife. He keeps a forbidden three-
dimensional recording of her and makes love to the projection.

She dances naked on my worn carpet and then kneels,
beckoning.

The disc ends and she fades and vanishes. I take the disc
carefully. My fingers tremble. I reverse it. She fades into view,
the music returns. . . . She raises her buttocks from the floor,
and like an acolyte at the altar I kneel before her and plunge
into her. Sometimes I vary things at this point and kiss her
instead but tonight it will be straight and we move together with
the perfect synchronism of recorded sex.

Hawkins's narrator begins to realise the ambiguities of the new
fetish.[38]

I don't know whether I could make love to a live woman now.
Every motion I make is matched exactly to the rhythm of the
recording. To have a live girl in my arms! The thought excites
me and terrifies me. . . .

What was it like when Margot was alive? I cannot truly
remember. Maybe then, as now, all the novelty was in my own
mind. Perhaps all our kisses were controlled by the track of
domesticity. And if so, maybe the disc has encapsulated not a
fraction of our sex, but the totality. . . .

Margot was never anything but a tape, a record, a film. I
could have changed it if I had known.

'Playback' exemplifies attitudes crucial to the British New Wave. At
first, technology provides the dream-machine, which transcends
human limitations and realises human ambitions. But the relationship between the narrator and his machine seems to exclude human
vitality, while apparently reproducing it enhanced to perfection.
Before long the machine completely supplants the dream. Now it

reveals secret dimensions of mechanisation within humanity itself. The actual instruments of technology recede to a metaphorical function in 'Playback', but this is not so much a narrative device as a commentary on our attitude to technology. The more we extend our limbs and senses, the more we isolate ourselves, from each other and from our planet, within the cocoons of extensions. Or, to look at it another way, in 'Playback' both technology and sex are used metaphorically, as paradigms in the logic of human desire.

NW writers reiterated this apprehension in many ways. Though (like the Vorticists and Futurists) they pressed for images and a fiction of the future, they seemed to fear the technology that is shaping that future. They mistrust the machine and suspect that mechanisation is a corruption of the human. Like Leary, Laing, and Burroughs they used electrical and mechanical imagery to evoke what they felt were unreal aspects of contemporary life, to denounce the depersonalising effects of systematic social conditioning and overdependence on technology. Sex is private and intensive, connecting one human being as closely as possible with another; technology is public and extensive, connecting one human being as closely as possible with the rest of the world. Between the two the individual identity and its sense of reality may be in danger.

Jack Barron is a tv star. The medium has inflated and extended his personality by transmitting his voice and image at prime time all across America. He takes groupies as they come, enjoying them arrogantly: the magnetism that draws them to him keeps him aloof, polarised from them. The casual partner who lasts longest is Carrie Donaldson, a secretary with Barron's tv company, devoted to her profession.[39]

> Good old Carrie, he thought, favourite all-business no-bullshit
> network watchdog All-American lay. He stared at her tight cool
> face, hard-edged, composed even under rat's nest morning-after
> long black hair, wondered what went on in that network-flunky
> head of hers. Too good a fuck to fake it, he thought, but where's
> the connection between her cunt and her head at, anyway?
> What's she really getting off me? No better balling than she'd
> get from anyone else could keep up with her one for one, he
> knew realistically, and all the emotion of an anaconda. Head
> filled with open-secret network orders, box with plenty of heat
> for anyone can cut it, and no gut-connection at all between. Just
> once, Miss Carrie Donaldson, I'd like to *really* fuck you, fuck

with that so-called mind of yours, that is. But how do you mind-fuck network-programmed electric circuitry computer with sexy long black hair?

The steely, perfect women of *Astounding* and the soft, plastic women of *Amazing* failed to convince because they were insufficiently lifelike and all too obviously symbolised anti-sexual notions. Spinrad's 'network-programmed' men and women, his 'secretary-robots', exploit those older images to make social comment through exaggeration, a primary function of sf. The comment is one which becomes more and more familiar, not only through the pages of *NW*: that a society dependent on high technology dehumanises its members. Spinrad plays ostentatiously on the ambiguities by presenting these lifeless people in a very lifelike environment. This is not sf describing a future after drastic change, a disaster like Ballard's *The Drowned World* or Aldiss's *Greybeard*, but sf plotting the future most likely to come about if nothing changes. A reader of the mid-1960s would have had no trouble believing in Spinrad's future America of commercial marijuana, black senators, cryogenic suspension for the rich, and colossal leisure industries. The escalation of technology has continued unchecked. In this increasingly mechanised society humans are forced more and more into the roles of simulacra, incapable of autonomous activity, completely reliant on artificial equipment and programmed information. They think of themselves within these conditions and relate to each other from them. The insistent, monotonous mechanical jargon of Spinrad's metaphors is deliberately obtrusive.

The logic of futurism ensures that sf stays at least one jump ahead of prevailing conditions. Thus, while John Landau's non-fiction article 'Does Sex have a Future?' seems hardly speculative at all in predicting robot sex partners and mechanical waldo genitals that can reproduce the recorded movements of a human lover,[40] Ian Watson's story 'The Sex Machine' goes further along with reification, into the mind of a public sex-vending machine that believes itself to be a woman.[41]

> It had been a busy day. The salarymen had received their summer bonuses. They flooded into the store to spend and formed long queues outside afterwards to use me. My slot hardly had time to close. I was tipped backwards and forwards like a roller-coaster rider. I felt butterflies fluttering in my belly.

And, as usual, J.G. Ballard was going further than anyone else. His imagination was not engaged by the tension between an authentic, organic sexuality and an intrusive, artificial technology. For him the invasion was already complete, and artificiality had become our natural mode of being. It was unrealistic and unhelpful to separate the two, or wish for any lesser degree of dependence. Ballard was in search of a new sexuality, man embracing machine to celebrate our entry into the post-human condition.

In the 1960s, while advertising and design were persuasively eroticising the automobile and everything else, new looser codes of socio-sexual behaviour were in formation. Advances in the technology of contraception facilitated careless and casual sex, detached from love as from reproduction. Sex became a game, played for minimum risk and maximum gratification. No longer the most private and significant form of human intercourse, it emerged everywhere, trivialised, public, at large. Ballard was among the first to doubt that this was liberation. To him it seemed merely another aspect of dehumanisation. He reviewed a manual of sexual instruction:

> The lengthy description of acts of intercourse couched in detailed narrative terms are much more reminiscent of erotic fiction than they are of any handbook. . . . Sadly, the conceptualisation of sex which has taken place along with everything else leads us away from precisely those idealised sexual encounters. . . . To a large extent this book, like so many others, is a nostalgic hymn to a kind of sexual Garden of Eden, whose doors Havelock Ellis, Marie Stopes and numerous other pioneers tried for so many years to re-open. Alas, the original tenants are no longer interested.

He concluded, 'Sex does not exist, only eroticism.'[42] In the absence of true sexual relations between people, he observed a sexualisation of things, of our interaction with our environment. 'After Freud's exploration within the psyche it is now the outer world of reality which must be quantified and eroticised.'[43] This he saw as the task of sf, traditionally a thing-obsessed genre, much weaker on characterisation and personality. His fiction of the period attempts it. The anonymous characters in 'The Summer Cannibals' inhabit a surreal landscape where concept melts into object, an affectless zone void of the intermediate term, personality. Violence seems appropriate.[44]

He looked down at her body. Humped against his right shoulder, her breasts formed a pair of deformed globes like the elements of a Bellmer sculpture. Perhaps an obscene version of her body would form a more significant geometry, an anatomy of triggers? . . . Through the apartment window the opalescent screen of the open air cinema rose above the roof tops. Immense fragments of Bardot's magnified body illuminated the night air. . . .

    An enormous neutral ground now divided them, across which the little left of their emotions signalled like meaningless semaphores. If anything, her voice formed a modulus with the perspectives of wall and ceiling as postural as the design on a detergent pack. . . . What act between them would provide a point of junction?

    'Sex is now a conceptual act, it's probably only in terms of the perversion that we can make contact with each other at all. The perversions are completely neutral, cut off from any suggestion of psychopathology – in fact, most of the ones I've tried are out of date. We need to invent a series of imaginary sexual perversions just to keep the activity alive.'

The women in *The Atrocity Exhibition*, robbed of their erotic attributes by the illusory hyperboles of billboard and cinema screen and the trivial reductions of packaging and commercial design, begin to resemble the nightmare dolls in pornographic illustrations.[45]

Her naked body was held forward like a bizarre exhibit, its anatomy a junction of sterile cleft and flaccid mons. . . . Already she had the texture of a rubber mannequin, fitted with explicit vents, an obscene masturbatory appliance.

As the humans turn into mannequins, the mannequins become more human. In the same issue of *NW* as 'The Summer Cannibals', an article describes one.[46]

Simulator One, a robot that can blink, breathe, cough, vomit and even die on command from its computer is an American development to help train doctors to administer anaesthetics during major surgery. . . .

    The scientists, by converting physiological responses to mathematical equations, programmed the dummy to simulate an individual undergoing an operation.

The irony of the word 'individual' is apparent.

Photographs chosen by Ballard to illustrate 'Cannibals' remind us that we also use mannequins as our surrogates in laboratory car-crash tests, and to wear our clothes to best advantage in shop-window displays. For him the 'simulator' is a sign of our changing attitudes towards ourselves; he and other *NW* contributors were convinced that 'converting physiological responses to mathematical equations' is a much more widespread activity than one might think, and that a competent contemporary literature must acknowledge it.

D.M. Thomas's narrative poem 'X' is based on 'The Cold Equations', a traditional sf story by Tom Godwin.[47] It exemplifies not only the complete detachment of *NW* from the sf magazines amongst which it originated, but also the unexpected use it made of its dubious inheritance from them. 'The Cold Equations' is the story of a space pilot on an urgent errand of mercy who discovers a young female stowaway aboard. The calculations on which his flight depends allow no tolerance for an extra person. She has to be jettisoned or they will both die.

> Her weight would crash them, metalflesh deep in soil.
> No one wanted it this way. No one. No one.
>
> Man flew, harnessed to drives beyond control.
>
> He forced himself to look at her. Emotions
> He buried deep along the frontier, stirred.
>
> . . . As if, somehow, she understood
>
> His search for miracles to make her end
> Bearable, she rose and stood by him. . . .
>
> One thing, she said, that he could do, that he had sought
> To do for so long. Now she was prepared.
> She was his bride, his nun. Under the weight
> Of his kisses her lips forced open like an air-
>
> Lock closing for the last deep opening.
> The room spun in her head like a space-top.
> Ungravitied she rose, observed the swing
> Of a red iron cauterize tongue, lips,
>
> Breasts, loins. Blue petals flowered under
> His teeth. From an alp of love she watched tissues

Explode in poignant tenderness and wonder.
Her ribs and diaphragm crushed, her lungs issuing

From her mouth stretched wide to its limits like
Space-debris.

Deep-frozen catafalques, her lids
Opened after two million years that took
An instant. He clambered from her, slid

His right hand from her buttock to her left
Breast, squeezed it lustlessly once, and lay
Still, eyes closed. He readjusted the soft
Penis that had ridden up like a skirt. Furtively

His eyes flickered toward the chronometer.

Down the left-hand margin of the poem figures tick off the minutes
to her ejection, and, as a kind of commentary on the story, another
column sets out words spoken by a schizophrenic, Julie, as recorded
by R.D. Laing –

I was born under a black sun. Everyone pretends to want her,
and doesn't want her. . . . I'm a no un, a noun, a nun, a no one.
. . . I wasn't born I was crushed out. You're leally lovely lifely
life, you destroy me with a red hot iron, burn my heart, cut out
my legs, hands, tongue, breasts. . . . I'm wasted time . . .
– and so on.[48]

What Thomas has done in introducing love and sex between
Godwin's astronaut and stowaway is not just heighten the poig-
nancy of the story in a popular way, nor merely violate inhibiting
conventions. Like Spinrad with his secretary-robots and circuitry
creatures, he has developed metaphors latent in the earlier work:
the astronaut as man ruled by machine, sacrificing to it the innocent
woman, no chance companion but his beloved.[49] Like the narrator
of 'Playback' his compact with the machine comes to forbid the
intercession of another human life. What Thomas has also done,
unintentionally, is to provide an ironic complement to Ames's
'Victims of the Vortex'. Craig's nervousness at encountering Ahla-
ahloa, his frustrations in attempting to bring her into his spacecraft,
the author's refusal to continue the story beyond her entrance, all
seem vindicated by the experience of Thomas's pilot. He discovers
that the cold equations do not admit the unknown quantity, the x of

humanity. They have time, fuel, and oxygen enough to make love, but then she must die. He can relieve his frustrations, but only at expense of her, and he cannot relieve his guilt.

Julie is another victim of the vortex, whose apocalyptic utterances employ science fictional imagery that authorises Thomas's metaphorical reading of Godwin's story. Julie is a real woman who has suffered her own disaster in space and time, her own ejection from the life-support systems of human affection. She has been reified, her identity destroyed. Metaphors of floating and of physical disintegration are often used in romantic expressions of the sensations of orgasm. Here Thomas exaggerates them as a presentiment of the explosion the girl will soon suffer, and as images of split personality. Throughout the poem he mixes vocabularies of the organic and mechanic to evoke the cold, hard, 'masculine' urge that compromises itself with machinery, realising too late that it is sacrificing the warm, soft, 'feminine' urge that complements it. Intuitively Julie knows 'Deep in me somewhere is the bright gold, the pearl at the bottom of the sea.' Is there an inner treasure, or is that another schizoid delusion? The way to find out was to turn the spacecraft round and get back to Earth.

Chapter Four
Pulling out of the space race
anti-space fiction

In the 1960s the myriad proud star-fleets dispatched in fiction since the 1930s started heading home. J.G. Ballard was one of those pressing the recall button.[1]

> I think science fiction should turn its back on space, on interstellar travel, extra-terrestial life forms, galactic wars and the overlap of these ideas that spreads across the margins of nine-tenths of magazine s-f. . . . It is these, whether they realise it or not, that s-f readers are so bored with now, and which are beginning to look increasingly out-dated.

Brian Aldiss and Harry Harrison compiled a retrospective anthology, *Farewell, Fantastic Venus!*[2], and Aldiss decided that the last chapter of his history of sf should be called 'The Stars My Detestation'.[3] While the hardcore sf fans waited breathlessly for the NASA heroes to step onto the moon, Ballard declared that the Space Age was in fact already over, and celebrated it in elegiac stories of wrecked spacecraft and rusting gantries, where the last idle tourists gaze up at new comets: dead astronauts, still orbiting in their burnt-out capsules. His prophecy was not just arrogant perversity, but a genuine mistrust for the sub-genre which had sponsored more clichés and inanities than any other, and which unfortunately typified sf to those who never read it. Humanitarians were querying whether expenditure in space was justifiable while people starved below; Ballard posed an analogous question of literary economy. Should writers send so much imagination spiralling upwards into vacuum, leaving the new dimensions of daily life on Earth unexplored? Besides, as the actual progress of spaceflight was proving so grey and routine, the colour and excitement of the fiction that had 'predicted' it seemed more and more misplaced. Ursula Le Guin, a leader of the movement to humanise sf, found no room for the writer of fiction in the cramped confines of the space capsule. 'The humanity of the astronaut is a liability, a weakness, irrelevant to his mission. As astronaut, he is not a being: he is an act. It is the act that counts.'[4]

What space fiction Moorcock did publish in *NW* only demonstrated the failure of the act, and of writing about it.[5]

> In the drive chamber, John Sumpter squatted beside an explosion-torn casing, probing a cavity with an oil smudged hand. Without effort, he smoothly unfolded to stand erect and stretch his tall frame. . . . His black curly hair struggled in an unruly tangle allowing one curl almost to reach equally black eyebrows. . . .
>
> Orlando Rees stood beside him and contemplated the visible damage with a worried scowl. Thrusting hands deeply into the pockets of a stained jacket, he switched his stare to the other man and in a controlled gruff voice said, 'Out with it, John, what's the verdict?'
>
> John shook his head. 'This is the end of the line.'

Their ship is crippled, repair impossible, help remote, death inevitable. Engineer and Captain prepare for it by telling each other the more depressing portions of their personal histories. These prove to be as hackneyed as their physical descriptions. The relentless clichés eventually convince us that these are not individuals talking but the fictional types themselves – the last of the spacemen, spokesmen for the entire genre. We are eavesdropping at the last rites of a minor literary convention.

What follows, however, is far from commonplace. The starship is visited by a sphere of 'bluish radiance' which suffuses the pair in a 'flood of glorious intelligence . . . forgiveness and love.' God (though they are too awestruck to name Him), engaged nearby in the continuous toil of maintaining Creation, has heard their confessions, absolved them from sin and guilt, and incidentally repaired the control crystal. 'Crewed by two whole men, in less than an hour the ship was heading for base.'

Startling, not to say ludicrous, though this mixture of banal and divine may be, Ralph Nicholas's 'Clean Slate' illustrates much of what the new writers were saying. In the first place, it is a devastating display of the exhaustion of the language of traditional sf.'

Worried scowls, controlled gruff voices, even 'an aura of forbidding sorrow', do nothing but depersonalise John and Orlando, even though Nicholas's intention here is to expose the private, human agonies which stigmatize them as individuals. Adjectives and nouns work against each other. Neither ship nor crew nor author can function at all.

Nor is there hope of aid from within the provisions of the genre: no passing repair-ships, no flashes of technical ingenuity, no kindly telepathic aliens. That Nicholas had to stretch back beyond science and logic, beyond even narrative trickery to secure rescue for his damaged heroes shows a high degree of desperation. Technology is failing; the god must come not out of but into the machine.

In 1969 Charles Platt observed that once again the dream evaporates as soon as machinery is devised to attain it.[6]

Readers of 1950's science fiction will remember with nostalgia the vignettes by Arthur C. Clarke which described, with strict attention to fact and logic, the steps that would be taken in the exploration of space. Somehow, despite the dry, matter-of-fact description, Clarke's near-future stories could never be read merely as journalism. They seemed more like romantic visions than views of a believable, everyday world.

With the fulfilment of the visions, their romance has vanished – displaced by the pragmatism of astronauts, the vocabulary of space hardware, the somehow unimaginative mechanical processes of Cape Kennedy.

The satellite launch which would have rated headlines ten years ago is not even reported today.

An American public information film stated, 'The Moon belonged to the poets as long as it was out of reach.' After 1969, not only was it within reach, but it had already been processed, converted into a golf-course, and littered with the remains of disposable gadgets.

The development of terrestial exotic tales and romances of exploration was limited by the history of Western cartography, beginning with the sailing-ship and ending when there was no more *terra incognita* left to locate fantasies in. In the same way the achievements of the Russian and American space programmes systematically deprived the poetic imagination as they supplied the need for knowledge. The new Mariners and Vikings extinguished the myths of Mars and fantastic Venus, and 'the Moon had become real estate.'[7]

NW satirists made much of the banality of spaceflight. In John Sladek's 'The Poets of Millgrove, Iowa', the Astronaut makes a homecoming speech to the proud citizens of his birthplace.[8]
'All the pigs**t you hear about astronauts is so much f**king – uh – s**t. What the f**k, a guy goes up inside this little metal room, see, it don't mean a f**k of a lot. Any f**king body could do it, you see what I mean?'
Kenneth Harker's 'Cog' is set in a busy remedial centre for similarly disenchanted space-pilots who find the tedium of planet-hopping demoralising. 'Clip an atmos-corrector on my helmet; and a grav-adjuster on my suit-seat – and they're all alike to me.'[9]
The possibility that astronauts could suffer worse than boredom from the unprecedented stress of spaceflight was among objections voiced when the American space programme was first designed. Three astronauts who fronted a NASA public relations lecture in 1968 asserted,[10]

Environmental hazards and the effects on man appear to be of less magnitude than originally anticipated. . . . No abnormal psychological reactions have been observed, and no vestibular disturbances have occurred that were related to flight.
Although much remains to be learned, it appears that if man is properly supported, his limitations will not be a barrier to the exploration of the universe.

Alongside those sf writers who use outer space as virgin territory for frontier heroics, there have always been others (Clarke, for instance) who have shown it as the vast perspective it really is, to point up the relative tininess and isolation of man. *NW* writers started to apply that to the individual spaceman, imagining how he might feel.[11]

Up on the outside of the hull is a piece of apparatus that keeps automatically fixed on the sun. It is part of the old navigational equipment and on the console it registers by a small red light on a map of the starfield.
It is a reassuring thing. I did not realise how much we depended on it. Yesterday I had to manoeuvre the ship slightly, to compensate for the jettisoning of two more used tanks. The ship turned over due to a fast reaction on the part of one of the steering rockets, and for a few moments we lost the sun. . . .
When we lost the sun it was . . . like forgetting one's name. It suddenly struck us that we were in a void with nothing below us

but an infinite fall and there was no point to anchor our senses. We were in the centre of the universe, and it was cold and empty and hostile. When the red light flashed on again Brewer was unconscious. The shock lasted several hours.

Considering the 'abnormal psychological reactions' of astronauts Buzz Aldrin, Edgar Mitchell, James Irwin, Bob Grodin, and others, it seems that Terry Pratchett's 'Night Dweller' may have estimated the limitations of humanity rather more accurately than NASA. Michael Butterworth quoted from 'a letter found in a dead astronaut's possessions':[12]

> Space is a vast church, though no people have any connection with it, or if they had they would fall out of time.
> Space is a matrix of avenues, cold planes of continuity.
> Human feature is blurred by the spiralling patterns of space, rendered insignificant by their continual cone formation and wave within wave fluctuation.

'No Guarantee' by Gordon Walters illustrates the changing fortunes of the astronaut.[13] It takes the form of a personal account by one Frank Webb McCaffrey, an amateur author, of his attempt to write a fictional version of the first moon-landing while listening to the actual event being broadcast on radio. (Since 'No Guarantee' was published in 1966, that 'actual' moon-landing is itself a fiction by Walters.) What McCaffrey writes coincides with what happens on the moon. His wildest imaginings come true as he listens, until he feels he is somehow creating the event. As he predicts, O'Brien, the solo astronaut, starts to experience extreme dissociation. His communication circuits fail temporarily, and then he reports auditory and tactile hallucinations. McCaffrey, trying to keep everything within the structure of his story, wonders how to account for these. The explanations he considers cover a range of traditional sf: O'Brien is growing smaller under the effects of an unknown kind of radiation; he is dreaming it all, having blacked out at take-off; he is not on the moon at all but in an experimental simulator, having hallucinations fed to him as part of his training; or 'mysterious Lunar forces' are mutating his nervous system and synthesising extra neurons.

Walters's style is predominantly awkward and immature, unable to lift the story above the triviality of most of these formulae; but his preoccupation with complexities of fiction and non-fiction gives it a highly modern ambiguity. Having provided his selection of rationalisations, McCaffrey avoids choosing among them. He realises that the whole experience has grown too large for the limitations of commercial fiction. 'Personally, I think it would be better left without an explanation. But if I was submitting this to an editor instead of publishing it myself, I'd have to put one in.' Any logical explanation, conforming to the editorial conventions of sf, would reduce his story and falsify the inexplicability. As he says, 'I *know* it's the only bit of invention in the whole thing.' Nor does he wish to hear the official diagnosis of the experts who will examine O'Brien when he lands. In the same way Walters himself provides no explanation for the bizarre correspondence between McCaffrey's fiction and O'Brien's ascent into madness. 'No Guarantee' juggles with the genres – fantasy, comedy, supernatural, science fiction, horror – without confining itself to any of them. O'Brien's flight from Earth to Moon takes him out of the orbits prescribed for fictional characters, out of reach of reason itself.

New Wave sf writers have come close to establishing a new fictional stock type of their own: the Mad Astronaut. As Butterworth explains, 'His suit protects him from the real cold and the real vacuum. But his confused mind (accustomed to a keen perception of space/time) flips.'[14] His ravaged features eclipse the plucky grins of Buck Rogers, the Grey Lensman, and Dan Dare. He is Ryan in Moorcock's *The Black Corridor* and Newman in *The Final Programme*;[15] the anonymous stranger in Ballard's 'You and Me and the Continuum' and 'Journey Across a Crater', and the missing 'fourth pilot' who provides one of Trabert's alternative identities in 'The Death Module'.[16] Barry Malzberg's *The Falling Astronauts* and *Beyond Apollo* are the classic novels of this anti-hero.[17]

David Bowie, whose use of sf in music represents an independent but exactly parallel development to the New Wave in fiction, wrote the Mad Astronaut's elegy, 'Space Oddity'. Major Tom aborts his mission and sets himself adrift in space:[18]

> 'Ground Control to Major Tom –
> Your circuit's dead, there's something wrong,
> Can you hear me, Major Tom?
> Can you hear me, Major Tom?
> Can you hear me, Major Tom?
> Can you –'
> 'Here am I floating round my tin can

> Far above the Moon.
> Planet Earth is blue
> And there's nothing I can do.'

Angst in space, detestation of the stars, were not simply affectations of the new writers, but disenchanted expressions of their feeling that sf and mankind were both travelling in wrong directions. Anyone still seeking to 'justify' sf on its score of accurate scientific predictions might take ironic pleasure from observing that its writers pulled out of the Space Race before the competing powers themselves did.

Chapter Five

Footholds in the head
inner space fiction

> The biggest developments of the immediate future will take
> place, not on the Moon or Mars, but on Earth, and it is *inner*
> space, not outer, that needs to be explored.[1]

The reason for the great withdrawal from outer space was not only
fear of the void and distrust of the escalating technology so
dramatically exemplified by space rockets, but also a feeling that
Earth and Earthmen were strange enough, no need to look further.
When Ballard said, 'The only truly alien planet is Earth,' he was
pushing the Existentialist concept of alienation as far as it would go
towards the sf concept of the alien; and it stuck there. Young
radicals in *NW* adopted expressions of psychosis. They wrote of
estrangement not from parents, political regimes, or nations, but
from reality itself. Their sympathies were with Julie in Thomas's
poem, with the Mad Astronauts of inner space.

That phrase has been so current that it is not easy to trace its
origin: Rilke, for example, was concerned with 'Innenraum'. Most
prosaically 'inner space' has been used to distinguish earth and its
atmosphere from outer space, which lies beyond.[2] It has been much
more common as a psychological metaphor, denoting the landscapes of dream and memory; and, by extension, of the subjective
world: that is, the external world as transformed and encoded by the
individual consciousness. In 1961 the Scientific Book Club offered
its members a travelogue by one 'Jane Dunlap' called *Exploring
Inner Space: Personal Experiences under LSD-25*. If taking a hal-
lucinogen is a 'trip', then inner space is where the tripper goes.
Commercially produced, a badge bearing the phrase and a picture
of a spaceship made out of a psychedelic mushroom enciphers the

concomitant notions of inner space in one emblem.

Since italicising it in his 1962 *NW* guest editorial, Ballard has often been credited with introducing the phrase to sf, but J.B. Priestley had already done that, in 1953. In his essay, 'They Come from Inner Space', he explained the popularity of UFO legends and the growth of sf as alarm signals from the neglected unconscious mind, 'the myths and characteristic dreams of our age. . . . They may be the first rumblings of the volcano that will overwhelm us.'[3]

> We prefer to think of ourselves travelling to the other side of the sun rather than sitting quietly at home and then moving inward, exploring ourselves, the hidden life of the psyche. All this comes of trying to live a dimension short, with infinite length and breadth, from here to Sirius, but with no depth, without the spirit.

Priestley distinguished three kinds of science fiction: 'corny short stories, on the gangster or Western pattern . . . trade rubbish'; utopian surveys of the future by 'the cybernetic public relations team' which none the less 'cannot communicate their enthusiasm. . . . Their plastic, electronic, atomic-power-run cities seem to be inhabited by stale ghosts'; 'the third kind, still sparsely represented, differs from the other two in being genuinely imaginative and having some literary merit', and seems to be all by Ray Bradbury.

> His stories use the familiar properties of science fiction . . . but . . . to express some of his own deepest feelings. It is significant that he lives in Southern California. . . . Here, on this sign-post to the Future, sits Mr. Bradbury, telling us his dreams.

That Bradbury should be discerned at the head of the crusade back to inner space is not surprising. Ballard's editorial too notes that Bradbury 'can accept the current magazine conventions and transform even so hackneyed a subject as Mars into an enthralling private world.'[4] In the 1950s Bradbury was writing with a contempt for technology and astronomy equal to any demonstrated later in *NW*; heedless of scientific accuracy, he ignored the manifest content of sf and worked up its latent symbolism to inform a peculiar, stylised vision of his own. The vision was a tacky, elegiac version of pastoral in which Bradbury idealised the American mid-west and mourned the lost elfin tribes of Mars. His sentimentality and relentless nostalgia altogether separate him from the more cynical and appalled visionaries of the 1960s. Nevertheless, the literary sophistication of his symbolic and lyrical prose endeared him to contemporary intellectuals like Christopher Isherwood, brought him to the notice of J.B. Priestley, and at least created a public illusion of the reconciliation of literature with science fiction. Sf could be interpreted, with some condescension, as a new Gothick, the popular expression of the Modernists' Angst. It is noticeable that all Priestley's examples are drawn from the darker, more horrific strain of Bradbury's work. Priestley even provides a premonitory glimpse of the Mad Astronaut when he says that modern man 'cannot come to terms either with this good earth or his own soul, he is rootless, destructive, insane, so goes hurtling and screaming, a lost spirit, into endless black space.'

'They Come from Inner Space' expresses a very literary psychology and romanticises the unconscious mind. The imagination's description of itself in spatial terms has a long history, especially in literature. The location of this space *inside* the mind gives the notion a greater fixity and permanence. Earlier metaphors concerned a place of dreams which we visit nightly and leave every morning, and transient insubstantial things which visit us: phantasms, figments, vapours. These metaphors are combined in that of inner space, which we carry around with us, inside us, a permanent 'level' (another spatial metaphor) of mentality and therefore of personality.

The spatial description of mind (as distinct from phrenology and cerebral anatomy) was formulated early in the development of psychoanalysis. Freud divided the mind horizontally, into conscious and *sub*conscious. Jung went further, even drawing diagrams of the psyche showing 'where' the various faculties reside in relation to one another. 'Beneath' the personal unconscious he located the collective unconscious, a luminous primeval tract that he would identify with anything that man had ever said about the soul, and virtually deify. 'The Unconscious is surely the Pammeter, the Mother of All . . . the matrix, the background and foundation of all . . . we call psychical.'[5]

This assertion of an extra aspect of mentality which, though concealed, is in fact larger and more important than any other, is implicit in many of the earlier inner space stories. The spirit if not the substance of Jungian psychology was amenable to writers who wished to continue the sf tradition of describing new worlds, but felt that the subjectivity of their vision was more important than objective correspondence with the laws of probability, astrophysics, or, even logic – the conviction that Frank Webb McCaffrey voiced in Walters's story 'No Guarantee'.[6] Moorcock's 'The Golden Barge', David Harvey's 'Jake in the Forest', Norman Brown's 'House of Dust', Michael Butterworth's 'Girl', and Reg Moore's 'High in Sierra' are all classic Jungian fictions.[7] A dream-like atmosphere displaces the reader as it does the central character; removed to an unfamiliar and unpredictable world, we share his enlivened awareness of its contours and climate. Details assume the quality of omens, signs, annunciations. Incidents seem portentous, decisions irrevocable: the hero is engaging the events of his destiny. This is from 'High in Sierra':

> I walked until my feet were sore, and the laughing voices of the indians in the reservation had been replaced by the singing of birds above me, in trees shading the road. They were all colours of the rainbow, and following them, they led me to an open city, with a high marble cathedral. All of the streets were marble, but empty; I realised the new world lay behind me in the reservation.
>
> There would be no way, now, of leaving the island.

When Aldiss published his story 'The Source' in 1965, stating that it was written according to the theories of Jung, the implication was that this was an original and interesting venture.[8] The common reader might have been puzzled by this. Even apart from the works of Miguel Serrano and Hermann Hesse, and David Stacton's *Kaliyuga*,[9] which are virtually Jungian scriptures, mythical dramatisations of private, specifically 'inner' worlds had been made in fiction many years before. He might have thought of James Joyce, at least; of D.H. Lawrence and Virginia Woolf; of the similarities and differences between the mental landscapes they depicted and the models proposed by Freud and Jung, of whom each was well aware. That Jungian ideas could still be a new influence on it in 1965 suggests that sf had become isolated not only from the rest of literature but also from developments in science – an ironic fate for a fiction that prided itself on its scientific acumen and alertness to present and future.

The creation of a subjective sort of fiction was counter to previous trends in sf, with its deliberate emphasis on objects and objectives, mechanics and materials. The tendency of the more intellectual writers had been to admit the subjectivity of all perception; the task of creating authentically alien races, for example, contributed to a relativistic understanding and an appreciation of how mentality is conditioned by culture. However, the general consensus was that there is a single, objective, external reality which our minds have difficulty grasping (emotion and imagination 'twist' or 'colour' facts, according to this view), and that the function of science is to secure it for us: whether physics or anthropology, science deals in clarification of the relative and distinction of the absolute. This was John W. Campbell's doctrine. He maintained an odd belief that a large proportion of the human brain was normally unused, and that faculties of titanic mental power lay dormant there, like the submerged enormities of an iceberg. The cause of our partial, disordered perception was that we were only three-tenths awake. The right exercise of moral and scientific capabilities, he believed, would unlock that forgotten powerhouse and open our atrophied minds to the fullness of objective reality. Campbell devoted much thought and column space in *Astounding* to the possibilities of Dianetics, L. Ron Hubbard's 'science of mental health', and was passionately interested in telepathy, one of the lost faculties, which could unite human beings mind to mind and end misunderstanding and discord forever.

Though not derived from it, this theory resembles Jung's. Jung had a great respect for the uniqueness of every mind, but made self-realisation only a phase of the psychotherapeutic process. Like Campbell he considered that the unconscious operations of the mind were more important than the conscious ones. Apart from the activities, both conscious and unconscious, that constitute the individual personality, the human mind seems to show other unconscious habits that are not specific to individual, race, or epoch. Jung decided some collective principle was responsible. All his cross-cultural indexing of symbolic and mythic 'types' was to provide evidence for this covert unanimity. Jung believed most strongly in a unified world, if only people would wake up and harmonise with it.

Later psychologists have abandoned this positivist faith in favour of more immediate concerns. The sf writers of *NW* also went beyond Jung, and abandoned the Campbellian quest for the objective. Though they did not seek authorisation from scientists, or from anyone else, they recognised that the trend in physics as in psychology had been away from absolutes towards the relative and contingent, even in Campbell's day. Norbert Wiener wrote in the 1950s:[10]

One interesting change that has taken place is that in a

probabilistic world we no longer deal with quantities and statements which concern a specific, real universe as a whole but ask instead questions which may find their answers in a large number of similar universes. . . .

[We] consider not one world, but all the worlds which are possible answers to a limited set of questions concerning our environment.

If psychiatrists no longer found Jung's 'Unus Mundus' helpful and even the physicists felt it necessary to multiply the universe, the time had come for sf to re-emphasise the subjective imagination, to turn from hard science to soft speculation. 'Realism', however defined, was outdated; just another pose. Moorcock declared in a 1965 editorial,[11]

As the sciences reveal increasingly the ambiguity of our nature, so the essential subjectivity of 'realism' becomes apparent. To look at it another way – if you assume that only so many things are 'real' sooner or later you begin to run out of possibilities.

An extraordinary claim, but one which applied widely at the time. 'Possibilities', like 'alternatives', was a word much in vogue: the new imperative was to realise as many as you could. Respect for authorities declined as more of them – the physicist, the psychologist – admitted they did not know what was absolutely real or right. Perhaps man did not have to be governed by history; perhaps things did not have to be as authorities said; perhaps they could be some other way, or every other way. In any case, the culture over which the authorities presided was so dependent on fiction, in advertising and the mass media, and so full of the ersatz and processed, that it detracted from their own credibility. For the artist realism was out of the question because reality was losing ground, to possibility. Conspiracy theory became popular; schizophrenia, it seemed, was now useful.

Nor was it necessary to be an idle young acidhead to hold these views, as readers of *NW* found out.[12]

The fictional elements in the world around us are multiplying to the point where it is almost impossible to distinguish between the 'real' and the 'false' – the terms no longer have any meaning. The faces of public figures are projected at us as if out of some endless global pantomime, they and the events in the world at large have the conviction and reality of those depicted on giant advertisement hoardings. The task of the arts seems more and more to be that of isolating the few elements of reality from this mélange of fictions, not some metaphorical 'reality', but simply the basic elements of cognition and posture that are the jigs and props of our consciousness.

Ballard, of course, with a policy we shall hear again, advocating a return to the teachings of the Surrealists who brought a bemused world the first documents from inner space. For Ballard reality is a very degraded (though very important) concept. As we see, it signifies only 'the basic elements of cognition and posture', the lowest common denominator of perception and action, discovered at the few crucial points where there is interchange between the energy of the individual mind and some figment of externality. Inner space is the hunting ground for reality; everything beyond is fiction.

Behind Ballard on this issue is William Burroughs, who states that the reality of the Western world is just another movie.[13] The director of the 'reality film' is Bradly Martin, Burroughs's corrupt god. Bradly Martin is an alien stranded on Earth by accident; he has infiltrated himself into society as a supplier of addictive fictions, like money and political power. Like the heroin supplier, Martin is both supported and enslaved by the addiction of his clients.[14]

Martin's reality film is the dreariest entertainment ever presented to a captive audience. . . . Martin's film worked for a long time. Used to be most everybody had a part in the film and you can still find remote areas where a whole tribe or village is on set. Nice to see but it won't do you much good. . . .

The film stock issued now isn't worth the celluloid it's printed on. There is nothing to back it up. The film bank is empty. To conceal the bankruptcy of the reality studio it is essential that no one should be in position to set up another reality set. The reality film has now become an instrument and weapon of monopoly. . . . Work for the reality studio or else. Or else you will find out how it feels to be *outside the film*. I mean literally without film to get yourself from here to the corner.

Burroughs, who has called himself 'an explorer of psychic areas . . . a cosmonaut of inner space', achieved this extreme alienation by being 'outside the film' himself, a physical wreck and social outcast with the frozen insights and horrible handicaps of heroin addiction. The literature of narcotic imagination has come a long way since Coleridge and De Quincey when this forced schizophrenia can be presented and received as social commentary.

The unspecified disaster rumbling in the background of so many *NW* stories is an image of this devalued, damaged reality. For Ballard it may be the invention of the atom bomb and the 'communications explosion of the 1960s'; for Aldiss the Acid Head War;[15] for Moorcock the consecutive failures of orthodox religion and science. Whatever the exact nature of the catastrophe, it has disrupted the continuity of history and left a world of arbitrary fragments from which the survivors must piece together their own realities, according to subjective values. In their own ways and with their varying degrees of confidence, Traven, Charteris, and Cornelius are all occupied with bridging the gap between inner space and a derelict external world.

The alienation of inner and outer worlds, with the impoverishment of the outer, which proves to be malleable and chaotic – these are the qualities that distinguish the inner space fiction of *NW*. An interesting prologue is provided by E.C. Tubb's story 'New Experience'.[16] Tubb, one of Carnell's associates from the earliest days, was a frequent contributor to *NW* throughout the fifties; 'New Experience' represents his attempt at crossing into the sixties. The new experience is a step into inner space, assisted by new drug X113 which incapacitates the memory, deleting the dimension of time from thought and perception and reducing the mind to a state of infantile fugue. Fendor, the chief research chemist, tries it out on himself, and, as far as Tubb can see, the trip's a singularly bad one.

He didn't understand.

He was lost and alone in a world he didn't understand.

A world of sheer nightmare. . . .

Before his eyes the world changed and changed and changed again and, each image that he saw was new and different and unpredictable.

Grass . . . trees . . . a path . . . the sky . . . Green, brown, grey, blue, singly and in combination, a chaotic whirl of colour without sense or meaning, constantly altering with each passing second and, all the time, the mounting need within him to know, to understand, to quell the mounting terror.

Eventually Fendor calms himself by deciding he must be God, the same conclusion reached in similar circumstances by Colin Charteris in Aldiss's *Barefoot in the Head*. Fendor's assistants exert themselves to bring him back down to normality. When the drug wears off they do their best to negate his experience and its metaphysical implications by reinforcing the claims of objective reality: ' "It was just a dream," ' they say, lining up with Alice's elder sister. Tubb's story demonstrates how the mental set of a traditional sf writer resists invasion from inner space.[17] His precision instruments will not register in flux. His training is all for prediction, not for discontinuity. Tubb predicted, accurately, that the prime agent of dissociation would be a mind-altering drug.

Most NW writers did not share the alarm of Tubb's scientists. A weakened respect for reality only fed their imaginations, and they expressed it with conviction as well as anxiety. A story headed, 'Which is more real: the daydreams, the acid trips, or the 9 to 5 jobs?' does not provide an answer to its own question.[18] In Chris Lockesley's 'Travel to the Sun with Coda Tours', Lyautey proclaims the autism his name perhaps suggests, and it is the external world that seems to be threatened.[19]

So Lyautey closes the door behind him and starts to walk down the road, warmed by the sun. Yet he is still cold inside from a source which no sun can penetrate, where alien trees partition the green sky and eggs are split from within by ragged machines and headless antelopes which ride the clouds while hiding, escaping from the tiger-sun emerging from the depths of despair contained within him like a flaking onyx.

'I'm within a foreign planet' he cries out into the warmth, and in the distance a dull concussion congealing on the air gives his words for one minute a taste of truth.

If there is this tendency to feel that, when it comes to a choice, the daydreams and acid trips are more real, and the only alien planet is Earth, that is not just decadent romanticism, but a reaction to the previous imbalance in favour of materialism. Sf favours extremes. It also dramatises that apprehension that modern man is busy making his '9 to 5' environment increasingly unreal, multiplying its fictional elements, in Ballard's words.

Jack Barron's sense of ontological priorities is already awry because his role on television is his most significant activity and consists mainly of manipulating images and half-truths. As he tells Sara Westerfeld, he believes the rest of the world to be just as malleable, and the purpose of life is to bang it into a shape you like.[20]

'It's all out there, every dream, everything anyone wants. But you don't get it by talking about it or dropping acid and wishing.

You gotta get out there in the nitty-gritty and grab it, take as much of what's out there as what's inside you can get you. *That's* reality, not what's inside or what's outside, but how much of what's inside you can make *real*.'

This philosophy of competitive consumption is a cruder version of Ballard's theory of inner space, with a technical emphasis: reality consists in the correct application of money and technology. Jack's apartment is a masterpiece of expensive kitsch simulation. His bedroom is an air-conditioned replica of the Californian beach-hut where he lived with Sara in their days of hippy austerity. The sound of surf washes from concealed speakers, the floor is carpeted with plastic grass, and real ivy trails across the control panel set in the headboard of the bed. Visiting him there for the first time, Sara sees

his externalised head like a cornucopia before her – or just as like some silly-ass Hollywood set. . . .

Yet it's *real*, real fantasy playpen, no interior-decorated calculated baloney, straight from Jack's head to reality, with nothing inbetween. It's *him*, it's his dream – Berkeley, L.A. California candy-store window, unafraidly naked garish conscious-subconscious Jack Barron day dream, sugarplum reality that money made real.

The means are gadgets and gimmickry; the motive power is money; the implicit faith is that technology is the genie of desire. The more perfect the machinery, the closer Barron approaches his ideal of reality – and the more he surrounds himself with substitutes and fakes.

Sara's identification of the mediated environment as 'L.A. California' echoes a correspondence drawn by Priestley in his essay, between present-day California and the brash technopolis envisioned as the future city in so much science fiction. This identification has also been made by Ballard in his Vermilion Sands stories, and by Pamela Zoline:[21]

Until we reach the statistically likely planet and begin to converse with whatever green-faced, teleporting denizens thereof – considering only his shrunk and communication-ravaged world – can we any more postulate a separate culture? Viewing the metastasis of Western Culture it seems progressively less likely. Sarah Boyle imagines a whole world which has become like California, all topographical imperfections sanded away with the sweet smelling burr of the plastic surgeon's cosmetic polisher; a world populace dieting, leisured, similar in pink and mauve hair and rhinestone shades. A land Cunt Pink and Avocado Green, brassiered and girdled by monstrous complexities of Super Highways, a California endless and unceasing, embracing and transforming the entire globe, California, California! 'The Heat-Death of the Universe', Zoline's first story, is one of the best things ever published in *NW*. For a critical anthology Brian Aldiss introduced it as follows:[22]

> With her pruned and clawed prose, Pamela Zoline makes the connection between private and public, between physical and metaphysical, between the Big Outside and the Big Inside. And she makes the connection that lies at the kernel of all art: the connection between the thermodynamics of biochemistry and an individual death.

Sarah Boyle sees a vision of California not as Jack Barron's kingdom of reality, but as a zone of advanced entropy, a collapsed, undifferentiated environment where the extension of leisure has actually meant the surcease of available energy.[23]

> Sarah Boyle is a vivacious and witty young wife and mother, educated at a fine Eastern college, proud of her growing family which keeps her happy and busy around the house, involved in many hobbies and community activities, and only occasionally given to obsessions concerning Time/Entropy/Chaos and Death.

Despite the sunny assurance of the clichés, the language of the *Ladies' Home Journal*, perhaps, Sarah is losing her grip, sliding into her obsessions. Even this sentence decays as it proceeds. As a housewife Sarah is a heretic. She 'realizes that the dust is indeed the most beautiful stuff in the room', but struggles to uphold the law, buying one of every cleaning product in the supermarket and emptying them all over her kitchen. She labels everything, anxious to secure its identity and function, but her inner preference is for surreal assemblages (like those made by kindred victims in Ballard's stories) and she considers 'ordering a household on Dada principles'. The artifacts that surround her efface her, like the vanishing housewife in Richard Hamilton's portrait *$he*; her identity is one of the 'topographical imperfections' that California polishes away. Sarah fails to fulfil her function and, like a faulty appliance, has a breakdown.

At least since Euripides' *Bacchae*, literature has often presented a strong case for the matter in madness. Typically, the madman in fiction reaches a deeper, more magical awareness (like Agave, and Catherine Linton), or else his alienated perspective and its privileges grant him a cynical, more acute insight than common sense (like Pentheus, and Hamlet). If the fool would persist in his folly, Blake declares, he would become wise. Sanity, meanwhile, appears as a deadly compromise of the imagination, and civilised mentality as a maze of pretence and partial comprehension. Contemporary fiction, with its apprehensions of crisis in society and in the individual mind, has restated the case more emphatically. The mental breakdown is frequently presented as an authentic existential act, the most honest response to an impoverished and obsolescent environment. Inner space may be a richer, more primitive, less corrupt world – the Mars of 1950s sf, but one which resists colonisation by Earth. A plunge into this region may be a desperate but therapeutic trip. Doris Lessing's *Briefing for a Descent into Hell* is the classic novel of the kind, which she labelled '*Category*: Inner-space fiction'.[24] Charles Watkins, a psychiatric patient, is the mythic hero in the adventure of himself, a quest abruptly curtailed by his 'cure' at the hands of the impersonal villains Dr X and Dr Y. Stories in *NW* develop the same themes. In Katherine Maclean's 'The Other' the child Joey has a voice in his head, a paternalistic superego that supervises his behaviour. The 'Other' tells him,[25]

'I am part your mother and your father and little parts and feelings of anyone who ever worried about you and wanted you to stop doing things so that you would be all right and strangers would not be angry at you.'

Society, the parents and strangers who enforce this anxious conditioning, endangers the precious inner vision.

Outside-people do not know the roads and paths inside the world of image, memory, and dream: they stumble, blunder and destroy among the fragile things. Joey decided that he should not have listened and replied. When time came around to return from darkness to the world of light, he would be silent.

The story's revelation that the psychiatrist is also ruled by an Other is no shock. Dr X is a victim as well as a villain, perpetuating the tragic split.

In 'Mr. Black's Poems of Innocence' D.M. Thomas intercuts as Lessing does the clinical observations of the anonymous 'operant conditioner' with episodes from the inner quest of the autistic Jimmy Black.[26] His dreams and fantasies blend personal memories with mythic treasure from Blake and Rider Haggard, but the external world to which he is being readjusted seems to consist entirely of the commonplace: combs, pens, cups, cigarettes, names and addresses, itemised in the interminable catechism of therapy. The 'conditioner' employs a professional detachment and crude masks of emotional pretence: approval, disdain, etc. Mr Black identifies her as the Queen of Sheba, infinitely desirable but spiritually corrupt. Her technique is 'the harlot's promise'. It is unclear who should be saving whom.

A similar ambiguity is at work in 'The Squirrel Cage' by Thomas M. Disch. The story is written as the journal of a prisoner of unknown beings who is kept in a padded cell and supplied with food, a daily copy of *The New York Times*, and a typewriter whose printout he cannot see. Disch develops the concept of inner space beyond the dichotomy of consciousness and unconsciousness.[27]

One of my theories is that they (*you* know, ungentle reader, who they are, I'm sure) are waiting for me to make a confession. This poses problems. Since I remember nothing of my previous existence, I don't know what I should confess. I've tried confessing to everything: political crimes, sex crimes (I especially like to confess to sex crimes), traffic offences, spiritual pride. My God, what *haven't* I confessed to? Nothing seems to work. . . .

I have another theory . . . that I'm being kept here by people. Just ordinary people. . . . They read the things I type on this typewriter as it appears on a great illuminated billboard. . . . When I write something funny, they may laugh, and when I write something serious, such as an appeal for help, they probably get bored and stop reading. Or *vice versa* perhaps.

The prison is the boundary of selfhood. The writer tries to communicate beyond it by typing 'just about every password there is', but in the absence of any authoritative direction or even a guaranteed public response, why write anything rather than anything else? He accuses us 'ordinary people' of keeping him in prison – we, after all, have access to the output of his keyboard and so must be part of the conspiracy – but ultimately he needs his prison to survive. 'The only thing that could terrify me now is if someone were to come in. If they came in and said, 'All right, Disch, you can go now.' That, truly, would be terrifying.'[28] The prison in Langdon Jones's 'The Time Machine' is time itself, history, the constraint enforced by previous choices and actions. Jones's story ends with a similar startling, alarming proclamation of release.[29]

Disch continued to work on the metaphor of the prison in *Camp Concentration*. This is the journal of another incarcerated writer, Louis Sacchetti, an involuntary participant in an experiment to heighten intelligence artificially. The director of the programme, General Haast, promises:[30]

'The real excitement won't start until certain officers in certain Pentagon offices hear about what I've accomplished. No need to name names. It's common knowledge that for twenty years a small but powerful clique in Washington has been burning up millions and billions of taxpayers' dollars to get us into Outer Space. While all of *Inner* Space has yet to be explored.'

The location of the research centre in Camp Archimedes, a subterranean prison complex, adds to the irony of inner space as a zone for military exploitation. Out among the stars, deep under the ground, or inside the privacy of the mind, nowhere is safe from the systems of aggression.

When sf writers of the 1960s turned back from the stars to search inner space, it was already very late. Whether they found a land of symbolic treasure, like Thomas, or a concrete desert occupied by obscene phantoms, like Ballard, they described it as a desolate place, ravaged by the all-pervasive disaster of twentieth-century history. On the way there they overtook the pioneers. Jung was working at a time when mass communications had less power over the psyche, with theories that largely omitted mass psychology from the interactions between the individual and eternity. He was naturally less pessimistic about social and personal fragmentation than later thinkers have become. Modern man, he saw, was divided, self in search of a soul, but proper psychological guidance could bring him to individuation.[31]

The individuated person . . . through his acceptance of the unconscious has, while remaining aware of his unique personality, realized his brotherhood with all living things, even with inorganic matter and the cosmos itself.

Living in the reverberations of the cultural explosion of the 1960s, we may feel that our uniqueness is at best an ambivalent asset and that the cosmic brotherhood is probably a fictitious organisation.

Priestley's expressly Jungian essay looked wistfully for a future when the world would be united, space travel abandoned, and science fiction obsolete, as an expression of the outgrown neurotic desire to go 'hurtling and screaming' 'from here to Sirius'. Perhaps, suggest the writers of *NW*, we should not try to wish away our perverse but continuous multiplication of worlds, but learn to accept it and use it as a basis for revising our concept of the human condition.

'No one can begin to think, feel or act now except from the starting point of his or her own alienation.'[32] The new spokesman for the divided self is R.D. Laing. His work in orthodox psychiatry (the British Army, the Glasgow Royal Mental Hospital) served only to convince him of the futility of trying to pull the fragments together. 'Humanity,' he wrote, 'is estranged from its authentic possibilities.'[33] Not only can we no longer hope for elfin Mars and fantastic Venus; even the Earth, planet of our inheritance, has slipped between our fingers. Laing turned his attention to the fragments. 'I am a specialist, God help me, in events in inner space and time . . . Observing day in and day out its devastation, I ask why this has happened?[34] An urgent disembodied voice repeats the same question in Moorcock's fiction, from *The Black Corridor* through the Jerry Cornelius stories: 'What is the exact nature of the catastrophe?'[35] It is the voice of officialdom, of computers requesting data, of government inquiries, of Ground Control and the military; it is never to be satisfied. The sf writer can, however, supply models, analogical explanations like those tried out by McCaffrey in 'No Guarantee'. Laing uses many:[36]

We are living in an age in which the ground is shifting and the foundations are shaking;

Long before a thermonuclear war can come about, we have had to lay waste our sanity;

Orwell's time is already with us;

In . . . Heidegger's phrase, *the Dreadful has already happened*.

Sf passes out of fandom's walled city and into general circulation, with exchanged values. Its unknown landscapes, alien races, robots and gadgets, global disasters and ruptures in space and time provide extreme symbols for elusive aspects of our situation. Earlier, unsophisticated fictions in the tradition now appear to have a mythological force unsuspected by their authors. The imagery is suitably cheap and glossy, uncontaminated by official authorisation, ready to be dismantled and reconstructed by artists and theorists who have lost faith in orthodox models. In the same way Laing has reinterpreted the speech of some schizophrenic patients, seeing their words not as incompetent distortions of a 'proper' social language, but as special, personal languages, to which the victims necessarily resort to express a condition the social language cannot name. In Thomas's poems, Jimmy Black's therapist reproves him for talking 'garbage', but Julie's words prove extraordinarily eloquent descriptions of her state, rich in verbal cunning and poetic sense that have largely passed from everyday social conversation. Though the messages are of doom, disaster and entropy, the images that carry them show an imaginative vigour and creativity no one could have predicted.

In the 1960s old frontiers of both outer and inner space were breached, by two very different venturers: Neil Armstrong and Ronald Laing. The contrasting attitudes of the scientific establishment to the two breakthroughs gave little encouragement to the popular imagination of the day. Sf writers began to demystify two of their stock characters, the astronaut and the psychiatrist. *NW* contributors inflicted them with insanity and put them to death; they sabotaged the theories and technology that had backed them up; they insisted on the impossibility of their missions and disparaged their ideals. Stripped of their masks of heroism and authority they stood revealed as two highly vulnerable human beings, overcome by awe and anguish at their confrontations with the alien within and without.

The development of the British New Wave shows a shortening of imaginative focus, from the inconceivably remote to the inescapably present, from outer to inner space. While the romantic heritage of fantastic fiction, temporarily enhanced by the ambiguous glamour of psychedelic drugs, caused some to write of the beauties of dream-worlds, the general tone was of disenchantment, depression and doom. Nor was there any propagandist intent, like that of the young utopians who had commandeered the stored wealth of sf to express their own longings for a new world, populated by star-browed aliens. The trend of *NW* was scrupulously negative, describing the disease, but leaving the individual reader to decide whether a cure was possible, and if so, what it should be.[37]

Each sometimes sees the same fragment of the whole situation differently; often our concern is with different presentations of the original catastrophe.

Laing's *The Politics of Experience* also borrows from sf and presents the same retreat, from doctoring to doubt. The more understanding you accord schizophrenics, the less credibility adheres to psychiatrists. It begins with scientific lectures and ends with a document from inner space, 'The Bird of Paradise', which could easily appear in any issue of *NW* and exhibits strong traces of the influence of Burroughs.[38] It acknowledges the same obsessions: the catastrophe, the madness of the official solution, the infinite number of private realities, and the dissolution of certainty.

Tidal wave one million miles high moving at the speed of light. Impossible to go above or beneath, to run away, to get round to left or right. The Government fires the land with massive flame throwers, earth to desert, to absorb the water. Fire against Water. Don't panic. . . .

City lights at night, from the air, receding, like these words, atoms each containing its own world and every other world. Each a fuse to set you off. . . .

If I could turn you on, if I could drive you out of your wretched mind, If I could tell you I would let you know.

The new sf writers share this intention: to let us know, despite failing communications and disintegrations of language, where and what we are now. They have brought home the devices and effects of a fiction previously devoted to other times and places where by definition we are not. If their landscapes are bleak and their portraits more like robots and madmen than normal sane human beings, we may no longer dismiss them as wayward trivia. Those images are reflections from an urgent and highly disturbed vision. They express opposition not only to the dogma of sf – that all things must yield to technological or intellectual inventiveness – but also to fiction of the mainstream, because of its assumptions about the nature of identity and its inability to express the new aspects of the human condition, the relationship between man and machines. As Leslie Fiedler noticed, the objections and new models put forward by sf writers were quickly taken up by others who had no prior connection with the genre, while some of the sf writers, by expanding their areas of concern and their techniques, began to receive attention outside the fan community. In the next three chapters I shall examine the work of the three most prominent contributors to *NW*, Brian W. Aldiss, J.G. Ballard, and Michael Moorcock, three very different, very idiosyncratic writers. All of them have sustained a high level of popular and artistic success while working outwards from their origins in sf to achieve a new, non-generic imaginative fiction. I shall survey the work of each by reference to first book publication of novels and collections, without mentioning the complicated network of sf magazines and anthologies through which each story may have passed in its earlier stages, except where it seems necessary or especially interesting to note dates of first publication. For the sake of congruence, however, I shall confine the three chapters as much as possible to the main period of Moorcock's *NW*, 1964–76, and focus them upon major works of sf first published serially in the magazine.

Chapter Six
The Works of Brian W. Aldiss

1 Many compartments

In 1966 Brian W. Aldiss wrote to Judith Merril, anthologist and 'priestess' of the New Wave:[1]

> It's great to be even a splash in a new wave. But even the newest wave gets cast upon the shore. One feature of this particular wave (which I suspect to be a journalistic invention of yours and Mike Moorcock's, ultimately of no service to any writers willy-nilly involved . . .) is a strong tendency to abolish plot. Plot, I mean, in the grander sense of structure. . . . But I'm strongly against the abolition of structure in fiction: or at least in long fiction; for you will find most fiction to be a history of a process. . . . I'm for structure in fiction because I believe fiction must mirror and/or shape reality and because I believe the external world has structure: a different sort of structure from fiction's, but fiction is only an analogy for the external world, and we must use what we can. . . . I feel I am no part of the New Wave; I was here before 'em, and by God I mean to be here after they've gone (still writing bloody science fiction)!

Among the *NW* writers Aldiss remained an ambiguous figure, both more and less adherent to their cause. Older than most of them, rarely participating in their crowded, communal editorial meetings, his books published by Faber and acclaimed in the *Times Literary Supplement*, he sustained an image of thorough respectability at odds with the rebellious and defensive poses of his 1960s' confederates, in the view of the general reading public as well as the more jealous eyes of fandom. Nevertheless, his dedicated support in mounting the 1966 rescue operation for *NW*, donating free material during its financial crises, and negotiating the Arts Council grant, give him a special and important place in the history of the British New Wave, while his writings of the time include *Report on Probability A* and *Barefoot in the Head*, two polar masterpieces of the new sf.[2] Unexpectedly, the classic novels of both entropy and exhibition were written by the same man.

The abundance and diversity of his work, the ease with which he changes direction, make it difficult to be altogether confident in any discussion of Aldiss. Generalisations obscure the discouraging frequency with which another story will provide a contradictory example. Disdainful of passports and frontiers, he has written poetry, criticism, social comedy, travelogue, and essays roaming the cultural world at large. Even within his science fiction, his topic is as likely to be Holman Hunt or the character of India as time-travel or adventures on other planets. As a whole, his career has no discernible periodic structure, neither the deliberate symmetry of Ballard's nor the meandering progress of Moorcock's. There is nothing in the ample, stately *Greybeard* that would lead the reader to expect that Aldiss's next novel would be as exhausted and misanthropic as *Earthworks*. Nothing in the encroaching horror of *Frankenstein Unbound* prefigures the jolly extravagance in *The Eighty-minute Hour*.[3]

We can, of course, secure a basic continuity by accounting for an author's work biographically. *Earthworks*, for example, was written towards the end of Aldiss's long and tedious efforts to obtain legal termination of his first marriage. Nevertheless, accidents of publishing can scramble the evidence (*The Eighty-minute Hour* was written before *Frankenstein Unbound*), and books may, like dreams, compensate for circumstances instead of expressing them directly, especially books with a high fantasy content, such as sf. Unlike some contemporary authors, Aldiss is not trying to be elusive, to avoid the pain of committing himself. He insists on commitment, but also on change: in his work he returns to previous conclusions and re-examines them. The continuity of his fiction is not the linear movement of a biography, but the turning of a single, large, ruminant personality. That is how he presents himself in his essay in autobiography, *The Shape of Further Things*, and in a letter to Charles Platt: 'I have always discovered many compartments in myself, all of which need an airing occasionally.'[4] He is not the chameleon artist, devoted to creative anarchy and the strategies of surprise. All the compartments are in one writing-desk, boldly labelled with the author's name. Perhaps we should begin with what Aldiss told Merril was the first and last compartment: bloody science fiction.

No author of any ambition can be always in love with the mode he has chosen to write in. Aldiss once praised Ballard for managing 'to escape from the tedious clichés and conventions of our teacupful of genre.'[5] In a moment of despair, he wrote to Harrison,[6]

Really, Harry, I think I hate sf. . . . I have tried to avoid this conclusion, but I wouldn't care if the whole operation sank, apart from you, Blish, Ballard, Dick and who else, really? So I must act on my beliefs and try to make my writings in future more *extreme*, as PROB A will be.

Another letter written during the composition of *Barefoot in the Head* records,[7]

Just at present, since the beginning of this year, I am learning to write fiction anew. The result will gradually be purged of the clichés and tired gimmicks of sf, but I hope it will be forward-looking and more modernistic in style than it has been. . . . Perhaps it won't even count as sf any more.

Aldiss was the only one of Carnell's star contributors to retain his status in Moorcock's *NW*, but he did not achieve that distinction by renouncing the traditions that had governed his previous work. Unlike his new colleagues he had already spent ten years at the craft; that gave him a security in the genre which they neither had nor wanted. It is hard, for instance, to imagine anyone else from Moorcock's *NW* even wishing to write a history of sf, let alone one as cordial and generous as *Billion Year Spree*.[8] If *Barefoot in the Head* does not 'count as sf', it is because it is too wide to find a home in any category. Set in the future after another World War, it is thus sf in its origin, but not in its scope. The issues it engages are too major for us to assign it to any particular genre of fiction. Aldiss, as he prophesied to Merril, continues to write sf after the 'New Wave' has dispersed. He remains in 'the field', but his catholic reading habits and his training as a reviewer ensure that he has never been uncritical of sf, or considered it self-sufficient. His first sf novel, *Non-Stop*, was already a critical act.[9] Its setting, a failed interstellar expedition whose members, several generations on, have forgotten they are inside a spaceship, is directly taken from a pair of stories by Robert Heinlein, 'Universe' and 'Common Sense'; but Aldiss's version of events is quite different from Heinlein's.[10] Where Heinlein shows the conditions stimulating heroism, Aldiss objects that they would be more likely to expose human frailties.

It was exactly this critical attitude, this commitment to enlarging the capacity of the fiction at the expense of the tradition, that brought Aldiss into alliance with Moorcock, Ballard, and the other *NW* writers. What kept his work distinct from theirs, however, were the conservative principles he mentioned in his letter to Merril, when he referred to the 'strong tendency' of NW writers 'to abolish plot. Plot, I mean, in the grander sense of structure.' Aldiss goes on,

I'm for structure in fiction because I believe fiction must mirror and/or shape reality and because I believe the external world has structure: a different sort of structure from fiction's, but fiction is only an analogy for the external world, and we must use what we can.

Casual as this declaration is, it does indeed set its author against Ballard, Butterworth, Jones and the rest, philosophically as well as formally. Aldiss's mimetic prescription would find little favour with them, first because it makes use of an old-fashioned aesthetic, with nothing 'new' about it, and second because the new writers were professionally sceptical whether there was anything out there to mimetise. Aldiss's principle, so explicitly deferential to the external world, is out of line with their preference for inner landscapes and unstable structures. This is Aldiss doing the background in *Greybeard*:[11]

The van Allen belts, those girdles of radiation encircling the Earth, and in some parts much wider than the diameter of the Earth, were thrown into a state of violent activity by the nuclear blasts, all of which were in the multimegaton range. The belts had pulsated, contracting and then opening again, and then again contracting to a lesser degree. . . . The biosphere received two thorough if brief duckings in hard radiation.

Long-term results of this ducking could not as yet, barely a year later, be predicted. But the immediate results were evident. Although most of the world's human population went down with something like a dose of influenza and vomiting, most of them recovered. Children suffered most severely, many of them – depending on how much they had been exposed –

losing their hair or their nails, or dying. . . . Most of the women pregnant at the time of the disturbance had borne miscarriages. Animals, and in particular those animals most exposed to an open sky, had suffered similarly. Reports from the dwindling game reserves of Africa suggested that the larger wild animals had been severely hit. Only the musk ox of Greenland and the hardy reindeer of Scandinavia's north (where earlier generations of the creature had presumably reached some sort of immunity to cosmic and other fast-travelling particles) seemed to be almost entirely unaffected. A high percentage, some authorities put the figure at 85 per cent, of domestic dogs and cats had been stricken; they developed mange or cancer, and had to be put down.

Aldiss reports from the disaster area with his geiger counter, his statistics and press releases. He focuses on the causes of the disruption, its effects, and the parties responsible. Compare the equivalent passage from 'The Ash Circus', one of M. John Harrison's Jerry Cornelius stories:[12]

London was in a mess.

The marshes had returned: the sunken housing estates of Deptford and Plumstead had become a flat tract of khaki mud, pocked by the glassy craters of low-yield nuclear explosions . . . Here and there Jerry picked out the blistered facade of a *Chez Nous* or *Dunroamin*. Off to the west, the hills of the city were dark misty heaps . . . like most things, the old geomorphology no longer held. . . .

Things went from bad to worse. There were rumours of the Second Coming; a Dutch woman gave birth to triplets without showing previous indications of pregnancy.

The process of dislocation that had begun during the late fifties accelerated.

There were intimations of entropy everywhere: an avalanche trapped a hundred members of the Greek Orthodox Church in a mountain ziggurat in Capadocia where they were praying for revelation; two thousand people threw themselves into the sea off Scarborough after sighting a large green and gold hemisphere protruding from the base of a low cumulus cloud; the accidental detonation of a 'Thanksgiving' class orbital hydrogen device in the Van Allen belts severed global radio communication throughout the month of October; the

> Astronomer Royal reported a shift in the orbit of Halley's
> Comet and, operating from a jury-rigged radio telescope at the
> summit of Ben A'Choirn, declared the Millenium and the Age
> of Saturn.

Harrison's surrealist catalogue of unease is a parody of Aldiss's
report, or rather of the conventions Aldiss uses in setting out the
connections and implications of his disaster. There are no connections between Harrison's examples: this is merely 'the process of
dislocation', the unnamed catastrophe that features in so much *NW*
fiction. The passage from Harrison would stand close textual comparison with Aldiss's for style, assumptions and effects, and what
each reveals of their contrasting attitudes. Aldiss is explaining; he
wants us to understand these fictional conditions and their significance. Harrison is describing; he offers no explanation even when
he seems to; there are no certain connections between these
phenomena, but they tantalise us to find some. Aldiss is appealing
to our intellects; Harrison is exploring the absurd, toying with the
paranoid vision of a disintegrating reality.

Aldiss has written surrealism too, but his principle that 'fiction
must mirror . . . reality', substantiated here by his concern for
measurable detail, is closer in spirit to the traditional assumptions of
science fiction than to the anarchy of the New Wave, though far
more aware of the aesthetics of writing. Authors like Asimov and
Clarke, whose fiction contains most science and least fantasy,
champion science fiction on the grounds that it is instructive, a
healthy gymnastics for the intellect. This presupposes a direct,
mimetic relationship of art to life. Though the worlds of traditional
sf are imagined, beyond the known in time and space, their details
are extrapolated from our world. Their locations, though virtual,
appear to be actual: nobody has been to Andromeda or 1999, but
everyone accepts their existence, can point to where they lie.
According to the 'hard' sf writers, science fiction is a branch of
science, subservient to actuality, which it imitates by conforming as
precisely as possible to the laws of nature. It is in this persuasion that
Poul Anderson, giving directions for designing imaginary planets
and their satellites, recommends: 'Algebra and trigonometry are
the best tools for jobs of this kind. But failing them, scale diagrams
drawn on graph paper will usually give results sufficiently accurate
for storytelling purposes.'[13] By adopting protractor and graph paper
as tools of the writer's craft, Anderson assigns to science fiction a

degree of literalism far higher than that required by any other area of fiction. He is proud to do so, distinguishing this as the essential delight of sf and the factor which keeps it distinct as a genre. Aldiss, more aware of the gulf between art and reality and of the needs of science fiction as a branch of fiction, would not go so far. The instrument he chooses is not the protractor but the mirror borrowed from Hamlet and from the theory of a pre-Romantic critical tradition analysed by M.H. Abrams.[14] In this theory mimetic accuracy is the ideal; the perfect work of art would be a frictionless medium through which some portion of the external world could be transferred to our minds uncontaminated by the author's personality or the imprecisions of language. The purpose of the exercise is an educational or moral one. The mirror enables the reader to dress himself properly.

Aldiss similarly has designs on his reader, but while the terms and assumptions of his scrap of aesthetic theory are classical and conservative, what he wishes to communicate is a highly modern uncertainty: the complicity of personality and other imprecisions in all things. Fiction is not a transparent medium for the external world, but 'only an analogy . . . we must use what we can.' He writes of characters who advance, with difficulty, to an understanding and a momentous moral decision – Complain in *Non-Stop*, Gren in *Hothouse*, Noland in *Earthworks*, de Chirolo in *The Malacia Tapestry*. In a traditional sf structure the function of such an eventual understanding is to solve the problem the story poses, thereby resolving narrative tensions into equilibrium. Aldiss's 'resolutions' only enable the character to stand up straight and face the enormous future, awful or unknown, which is just about to start.

2 Software

'And indeed, what is the external world? Since we can only know it through our senses, we can never know it undiluted; we can only know it as external-world-plus-senses. What is a street? To a small boy, a whole world of mystery. To a military strategist, a series of strong points and exposed positions; to a lover, his beloved's dwelling place; to a prostitute, her place of business; to an urban historian, a series of watermarks in time; to an architect, a treaty drawn between art and necessity; to a

painter, an adventure in perspective and tone; to a traveller,
the location of drink and a warm bed; to the oldest inhabitant,
a monument to his past follies, hopes, and hearts; to the
motorist −'[15]

It is significant that the eloquence of this observation is entirely lost
on its hearers. Sir Mihaly Pasztor, director of the London Exozoo, is
addressing two of his specimens, the first (arguably) intelligent
extra-terrestial aliens to be brought back by a space expedition. On
their cluster of homeworlds the utods, large, two-headed, bovine
creatures, live in a society organised on immemorially established
religious precepts; they enjoy an elevated strain of philosophical
discourse and are adept at spaceflight. Nevertheless, they maintain
a natural *participation* so basic that it hardly even qualifies as
mystique: their principal ritual is wallowing in their own excrement.
So alien are these aliens that there is no prospect of communication
with them. Hardly any two humans approach agreement about the
'rhinomen': hence the argument (which grows furious) as to their
intelligence. Hence also, of course, the irony of Sir Mihaly's homily.
To the utods, the external world (which involves symbiosis with a
small reptile, seasonal alternation of sex, and a planetary system
that regularly changes suns) is quite simple, naturally. To humans,
who have lost the ability to identify physically with their own
environment, daily life on planet Earth is confusing enough without
considering the alternatives elsewhere.

The Dark Light Years is the most thorough statement of New
Wave disenchantment with interplanetary expansionism. Aldiss's
shabby heroes miss the chance to learn from the utods and gun them
down instead. Only Hilary Warhoon, an academic observer, even
glimpses the true nature of utod civilisation and why humans cannot
appreciate it. 'Mrs. Warhoon . . . saw that . . . mankind could not
fail to misunderstand this lifeform. . . . It retained humanity, or the
quality humans call humanity; and it was something that mankind
had lost and might have retained.'[16] Awareness, like this epiphany
to Mrs Warhoon, is permitted rarely, in flashes, and is not trans-
ferable. The various odd dances of misunderstanding performed by
a large cast of characters are by turns absurd, pathetic, tragic, erotic,
and beautiful, and the book ends with a deftly ironic report that the
humans have almost succeeded in annihilating themselves and their
planet, taking most of the utods with them in 'the hazards of war',
but that 'everyone is reconstructing like mad.'[17] Embittered and

depressing as his lapsarian image of man may sound, Aldiss's comic method and surprisingly gentle touch are those of a man who accepts humanity, and an author who is not ready to write it off. Aldiss is not eager for the 'post-human future', now or to come. He is similarly forgiving towards the clattering bulk of sf tradition. While revealing unsparingly the idiocy of some conventional devices – 'translation machines', aliens who speak English or, worse, communicate telepathically with Terrans[18] – he accepts the formalities – lift-offs and light years, starships and their troopers. The utods, though they embody an ideal, do not lose their bodies in the process; they are not symbols but autonomous creatures, given significance by their author as well as solidity. Indeed, they function in the book by realising something demonstrably unreal, the myth of Natural Grace. The humans around them cannot see that, much less accept it, because the expression is so disconcertingly physical. Aldiss's sole crime against orthodoxy in *The Dark Light Years* is to bring on the shit, unwelcome to traditional sf writers as to the keepers of the Exozoo. Even so, he introduces it in precisely the orthodox way: what if there were aliens who . . .?

This is the character of Aldiss's science fiction. He maintains the traditions, but is impatient of their exclusions. Adept at the special operations of the genre, he refuses to confine himself to being only a specialist; outside his specialisation he is a writer, and outside that a human being, and he works to bring what is outside in. While relishing the effortless pleasures of traditional sf, he understands that its habit of simplification has delayed its literary maturation.[19]

The fatal error of much science fiction has been to subscribe to an optimism based on the idea that revolution, or a new gimmick, or a bunch of strong men, or an invasion of aliens, or the conquest of other planets, or the annihilation of half the world – in short, pretty nearly anything but the facing up to the integral and irredeemable nature of mankind – can bring about utopian situations.

This is the familiar New Wave denunciation again, disparaging robots and Lensmen and reinstating an ordinary human figure as the proper study. Elsewhere Aldiss complains, 'Too much hardware, too great a lack of respect for human software!'[20] Respect for human software is what Aldiss has in abundance. The key story here is 'The Girl and the Robot with Flowers', a piece of fictionalised autobiography first published in *NW* in 1965, and something of a turning-point in his fiction. Brian and Marion, amid plans for a picnic and problems with their aging refrigerator, discuss Brian's latest idea for a story, about robots. He admits he is disappointed with it; it seems formulaic, especially in its pessimism, and 'so far divorced from real life.' Marion asks,[21]

'How do you mean, divorced from real life? We may not have robots yet, but we have a fridge with a mind of its own.'

'Exactly. Then why can't I get the fridgw into an SF story, and this wonderful sunlight, and you, instead of just a bunch of artless robots? . . . Wouldn't it be a change if I could make a story about just this transitory golden afternoon instead of centuries of misery and total lack of oxygen, cats, and sexy females?'

She laughed . . . 'Go ahead and put these things into a story,' she said. 'I'm sure you can do it. Pile them all in!'

Though she was smiling, it sounded like a challenge.

In a way typical of contemporary fiction, his account of the conversation and the challenge actually becomes the story Aldiss desires, a story of science fiction humanised. He refers the imaginary 'centuries of misery' back to the moments of despair in which they originate. He overrules the genre's simplistic tendencies by sketching behind and around the sf story the complexity of the actual day of its composition and the psychological and poetic intricacy of the process by which experience is made into fiction. Aldiss annuls the 'divorce' of sf from real life by marrying the story back to its author, while 'The Girl and the Robot with Flowers' is also his public celebration of the hard-won termination of his miserable first marriage and the optimistic beginning of a new partnership. At the same time, the short story 'Robot with Flowers', ostensibly abandoned for its formulaic inadequacies, is paradoxically contained intact, a powerful image at the heart of the new story.

'The Girl and the Robot with Flowers' is a precise and passionate description of science fiction as fiction, showing the symbolic and expressive possibilities of the genre from the writer's point of view, and offering an example for its development beyond the traditional formulae. It is a triumphant affirmation of the values of subjectivity, quite apart from the need for objectivity stated in the letter to Merril. Statements of subjectivity, even solipsism, recur in Aldiss's work. Sir Mihaly Pasztor is joined by Edward Bush, the mind-traveller in *An Age*, an artist whose mode is a kind of mobile

sculpture. He says,[22]
'My spatial-kinetic groupages try to . . . oh, identify the spirit of
a moment, an age. Sometimes, I used to work in mirror-glass –
then everyone saw a SKG differently, with fragments of their
own features lurking over it. That's the way we see the universe.
There's no such thing as an objective view of the universe – ever
think of that? Our features look back at us from every quarter.'
Wattol Forlie in *The Interpreter* has a similar understanding:[23]
Thought. Thought: that field of force still to be analysed.
Thought: as inseparable from a higher being as gravity from a
planet. It wraps around me, as my senses go about their endless
job of turning all the external world into symbols. I can know no
external thing without its being touched – perhaps in some
unguessable way transmuted – by my thought.
In the first dislocations of *Barefoot in the Head* Charteris notes the
spaces between people. 'Then stand there half-inspecting each
other in the semi-dark you do not see me I do not see you: you see
your interpretation of me I see my interpretation of you.'[24] It is
through these spaces that everyone must wander for the rest of the
book. Aldiss is as conscious as any other *NW* writer of fragmentation. Organised activity disintegrates in *Barefoot*: 'All the known
noon world loses its old staples and everything drops apart.'[25] The
fabric of space and time tears in *Frankenstein Unbound*, throwing
mankind onto separate historical tracks.[26] Many novels and stories
concern the human race divided into tribes or factions, small and
unco-ordinated groups who live by differing principles, each
endeavouring to survive catastrophe according to its own
responses.[27]

In a sudden moment of detachment he saw the four of them,
each pursuing an elusive thread in his own being, conscious of
the others only as interpretations or manifestations of his own
fears. They were isolated, and every man's hand was against his
neighbour.

Aldiss prepares himself a large canvas to work on and a large
commission to fulfil. He admits the relativity of perception, the
predominance of private fixations in determining an increasingly
incoherent world; yet he will not resign his belief in a solid external
reality to which the artist has a primary obligation, however hard it
is to locate. Unlike his predecessors, he will not subscribe to a
convenient materialism; unlike his contemporaries, he will not

allow his imagination to disdain matter, or ignore its claims. Yet nor will he reject any ideas and techniques of either party, if he feels they may be useful to him. He does not submit to conventions just because they are conventional; nor does he avoid them for the same reason. For example, we have seen his insistence on the causes of his catastrophes. Unlike Ballard and Moorcock, or Harrison in the passage I quoted earlier, he had not decided to abandon rationality for the sake of imagistic resonance. He writes our scientific extrapolations, as traditional as those of a Wyndham or a Christopher, from our present to his futures. In *Greybeard*, the human race is sterile as a result of nuclear tests in the atmosphere. The ravaged society in *Earthworks* is suffering the effects of overpopulation, pollution, and the exhaustion of natural resources. Again and again Aldiss secures the origins of disaster in a time of human folly and apathy. In *An Age*, England's decline into totalitarian gloom is inevitable because expenditure on the time-tourism known as 'mind-travel' has bankrupted the government. That the central character, Bush, is addicted to the process is a symptom of moral failure both personal and national. *Frankenstein Unbound* also condemns the self-indulgence of nations, for more of the careless missile-juggling that began *Greybeard*. It damages space and disrupts time – an effect which Aldiss could have employed simply as a convention, with ample precedent not only in Philip K. Dick's *Martian Time-Slip* and Fred Hoyle's *October the First is Too Late*,[28] but also in the discontinuous worlds of Michael Moorcock. Instead, he preferred to justify it, even at the risk of sounding trite.

The extrapolations that provide background information in sf build bridges to the imaginary worlds from the one we know. For most authors this is a matter of respect for physics or politics, or else merely of securing the reader's patience: logical futures seem to have more cogency, less of the dreaded escapism, than the illogical confections of the fantasy writers. For Aldiss, however, it is a matter of morality and the definition of human responsibility in proper proportion. Acts of God or accidents in space diminish humanity. Upstart Triffids pose moral problems, but don't threaten our self-esteem: we couldn't help it, we were all blinded at the time. Aldiss would have put in some man-made mischief instead of the blaze of the comet, and exploited the blindness for its full metaphoric value. He may not want to scourge mankind, but his interest in us includes, as he demonstrated in *The Dark Light Years*, acute perception of our limitations. He offers what he calls his 'precis-definition of sf: Hubris clobbered by Nemesis.'[29] The disaster overtakes man because of his over-confidence, in solipsism just as in materialism. The inadequacy of man is the inadequacy of much science fiction: small-mindedness, especially in enormous enterprises; insufficient respect for human software; the failure to extend imagination into sympathy.

We could object that a strict focus on morality may itself constrict imagination, and therefore narrow literary reference. At worst delicate issues may be crudified; in any case an insistence on Man's perennial disobedience and the fruit of various forbidden trees may be an artistic over-simplification, as undesirable in its way as the pusillanimities of less considerate sf authors. There are other issues than blame and praise, especially in an age when the infinite intricacy of the moral web and the ultimate inadequacy of all solutions are the themes of much discussion and more art. To specify and denounce villainy, even if it turns out to be 'the integral and irredeemable nature of mankind' that is at fault, is the job of minor fiction: fairytales, westerns, Victorian melodramas. The belief that complex problems, moral or otherwise, evaporate under the concentrated glare of rationality is virtually dogma in traditional detective fiction, and has been in sf. Brian Aldiss is of course aware of the discrepancy between this and the irregularities of life. He recognises that the very ingenuity of traditional sf, the professorial expertise of its narration, tends to detach the fiction from experience; the thoroughness with which it is scientifically proven renders it imaginatively unimportant. He replies to a reviewer,[30]

> I believe you are too used to sf, where all has to be explained in the last pages, everything made clear down to the last sword-stab, as in a detective novel. I am now trying to find my way into a true philosophical novel, where such things remain unresolved if they are to stand in any way as an equation for life.

Over and above the moral structures in which we must confine ourselves, Aldiss continues to express a 'true philosophy' which embraces good and evil. Human life is conducted at a lower level where we tread the moral and political mazes of our own fabrication, but in the cosmic view the distinctions on which we insist do not exist. There is no Almighty Judge, no Hand holding a Cosmic Balance – only the flow.[31]

For Jandanagger was talking of many things at once, shifting
things that could not be spoken of in terrestial tongues,
dissolving mental disciplines never formulated through
terrestial voices. Yet all these things balanced together in one
sentence like jugglers' balls, enhancing each other.

For Jandanagger was talking of only one thing: the thrust of
creation. He spoke of what the synthesizer had demonstrated:
that man was never a separate entity, merely a solid within a
solid – or better still, a flux within a flux. That he had only a
subjective identity. That the wheeling matter of the galaxy was
one with him.

There are no gods, even from outer space, though aliens are often
credited with this high vision of wholeness that man has lost. It is the
vision of Jandanagger the Galactic Minister, of the mutant morel in
Hothouse, of the utods as shown to Mrs Warhoon; even, in a way, of
the unhappy tummy-belly men. That was Aldiss in 1958. In 1967:[32]

He saw the world – Europe, that is, precious, hated Europe that
was his stage – purely as a fabrication of time, no matter
involved. Matter was an hallucinatory experience: merely a
slow-motion perceptual experience of certain time/emotion
nodes passing through his brain. No, that the brain seized on in
turn as it moved round the perceptual web it had spun, would
spin, from childhood on. . . . Matter was an abstraction of the
time syndrome, much as the television had enabled Charteris to
deduce bicycle races and military parades which held, for him,
even less substance than the flickering screen. Matter was
hallucination. . . .

Charteris sat unmoving. . . . What was he?

Terrible though the answer was, it seemed unassailable. The
man he called Charteris was merely another manifestation of a
time/emotion node. . . . Only the perceptual web itself was
'real'. 'He' was the web in which Charteris, Metz, tortured
Europe, the stricken continents of Asia and America, could
have their being, their doubtful being. He was God.

It is dangerous to seem to identify any character's beliefs with his
author's, but I think we are not meant to disagree with Charteris –
yet. The hallucinogenic origin of this revelation in no way devalues
it. Charteris's error is in the way he applies what he has learnt.
Anticipating Charles Manson, he repersonalises this knowledge,
reinstituting on a grandiose scale the ego he has just successfully

dissolved; he mistakes this Buddhist Godhead, identical with all being, for a Christian God, separate, wielding power and authority. He violates the vision of Tao by not realising that respect and concern for others is necessary *because* of the arbitrary and fluid nature of existence. Because man (as distinct from everything else) does not really exist, it is necessary continually to invent him, and his morality too. Accepting that matter is illusory, as Charteris does here, does not permit us to ignore it or treat it wilfully. To do so is to invite and promote the sudden collapse of the illusion: in material terms, the extinction of oneself and others, the onset of nihilism. Charteris's disciples steer their crazed motorcade perilously near this edge; so, implicitly, on paper, do some of the more extreme contributors to *NW*.

This at least is how Aldiss sees it, and hence his own position, firmly held in the exact middle of the furious, confused hostilities waged between Old Guard and New Wave during the late 1960s.[33]

I felt they [*NW* writers] had given up on man, or on civilisation. I did care. I had a quarrel with them. At the same time, I had a quarrel with the standard sf stuff, forever producing disasters yet riding along with a too-easy optimism and faith in technology and capitalism. Don't forget my precis-definition of sf: Hubris clobbered by Nemesis. I believed in catastrophe okay; but the old guard didn't believe in Hubris, while the new wavers didn't mind about the nemesis. . . .

Platt and Moorcock and Ballard delighted in the thought of catastrophe actually being upon them; it 'turned them on' – there's a sixties phrase. If they were vague about the catastrophe and its nature . . . it was because they welcomed catastrophe, and it didn't matter where it came from – from the States . . . from a bottle, or from a dosed lump of sugar. My interest was in the catastrophe, in who was to blame. I preferred philosophy to acid fantasy.

Without expecting him to hold still under the label, we can consider Aldiss a humanist writer. He has a devoted, irascible concern for the species as it leaps and stumbles its way across the universe. Yet he appreciates that man is himself only one among many manifestations of the universe, and in the last analysis it may be that his identity is merely a Cartesian side-effect of his consciousness, since he is of no greater or lesser importance than anything else. Therefore Aldiss's is not a geocentric universe, as so many sf cosmologies seem to be; nor, for all his love of man, is it an anthropocentric one. Many of his stories incline to attribute a natural majesty to humanity – 'Amen and Out', for example, or the perennially reprinted 'Who Can Replace a Man?'[34] – but others present a different quality: man as seedy, squalid and stupid, the spoiler of planets. *The Dark Light Years, Earthworks*, and *Frankenstein Unbound* all urge us to look on our own humanity and weep. Aldiss does not always indulge man in his notions of his own supremacy. Some stories, especially the excellent 'Old Hundredth', are set in post-human worlds;[35] in *Greybeard* it is made fairly clear that the ecology of Earth may actually be improved by the removal of man.[36]

> Wild life swarmed back across the Earth as abundantly as it had ever done. In its great congress, there were a few phyla absent; but in numbers the multitude was as rich as it had ever been . . . The ascendancy of man had only momentarily affected the copiousness of this stream.
>
> Now the stream was a great tide of petals, leaves, fur, scales, and feathers. Nothing could stem it, though it contained its own balances. Every summer saw its weight increasing as it followed paths and habits established, in many cases, in distant ages before *homo sapiens* made his brief appearance.

The irreducible variety of Aldiss's work is not only the exercise of an agile and energetic mind, but also the expression of a broad and deep imagination which considers it dangerous to look from any viewpoint, even the human one, exclusively. 'With every novel I write, I grasp something, and then don't wish to repeat it; there's always something else to do.'[37] Suspicious of satisfaction, Aldiss has turned continually from compartment to compartment. Having come to prominence and high esteem in science fiction, he resisted any temptation to relax. There was something else to do, something more to be said than the prevailing definitions of sf allowed. This attitude endeared him to the revolutionaries of the New Wave, while their vigour and impulsive originality was highly congenial to him. *NW* offered exactly the place for his experiments, a place which was not open in the genre magazines that preserved the conventions to protect themselves from the commercial risks that Moorcock was taking daily.

3 Towards an unresolved equation

Whatever Aldiss's disagreements with 'the new wavers' and particular affinities for older ideas and methods, in the 1960s he wrote two emphatically modern novels, classics of the new fiction. Hitherto, as we have seen, his allegiance had been to sf as the literature of causality. Man's departures and disasters could be attributed to certain sins of omission and commission, and he did so, adding to the tradition of 'sf, where all has to be explained in the last pages, everything made clear down to the last sword-stab.' By 1969 he was 'now trying to reject all such models and find my way into a true philosophical novel, where things remain unresolved if they are to stand in any way as an equation for life.' *Report on Probability A* and *Barefoot in the Head* offer two ways towards the unresolved equation. In the first, many things are probabilities, nothing certain. 'The Congressman said, "All we are after is facts. We don't have to decide what reality is, thank God!" '[38] Facts we have, plenty of them, as do all the other observers of Mr Mary's house and the figures in his garden. Aldiss's meticulous attention to detail in this sf anti-novel intensifies from cold objectivity to paranoid hyperaesthesia; at times the two are indistinguishable.[39] Shapes and sizes are measured; the specifications replace adjectives. The most trivial actions of the exiles G, S and C are described with the fascination sf writers have generally reserved for the marvels of the ion drive. What this plethora of uncompromising facts conceals is significance. The novel forces us to add our own assumptions, to fill in the blanks left by those initials, while demonstrating how easy it is to be entirely mistaken in such endeavours. 'The Impaler rose and gathered his robe about him. "I believe we have all heard enough to draw our own conclusions, eh?" '[40] Yes; but we can never hear enough to be certain our conclusions are correct. We must go over the evidence again and again, have repeated to us the description of Holman Hunt's 'The Hireling Shepherd', a reproduction of which is owned by every one of the three men,[41] before we realise, unlike Midlakemela and the Governor, that the Hunt we remember may not be the right man. Parallel to Aldiss's brilliant explication of the painting as an unresolved moment in time, a waiting which will never end, the *Report* presents no conclusions, only data. Life – and the disaster which has stopped it – is always elsewhere, like the bizarre accidents from which survivors keep trailing past the house, carrying a blood-stained bicycle or riding with their hands over their eyes. A possibility: Mrs Mary is the key to the mystery; everyone seems convinced of that. The catastrophe may have been sexual. We know that C desires her. Perhaps S may have been caught seducing her. This is S, studying the compromising position of the girl in the painting:[42]

The situation was possibly as challenging for the shepherd to resolve as it was for the onlooker. If the girl was married to the shepherd's employer, the situation might be even more difficult. For it was possible that under her heavy lids she was looking at him in a way which he was at liberty to misinterpret as encouraging; he might then run his hands through that tawny hair, so soft about the nape of the neck; he might even attempt – half succeed! – to kiss that plump underlip; and she might then go to her husband and reveal what had taken place, thus involving the shepherd in a number of troubles; or, once in that difficult position, he might be unsure whether it had been brought about because the girl had told her husband voluntarily, or whether, in his plodding way, the husband had forced a confession from her. He might be dismissed from his post, to hover for ever after like a troubled spirit about the scene and the cause of the disaster.

For S read Shepherd . . . or Secretary. . . . Why should he begin to assume the dallying girl might be married to the hireling's employer unless he is projecting his own story into the painting?

– And likewise why should we? For that is what such interpretation amounts to, though the conclusion leaps to us rather than vice versa. We repeat S's idle, unfounded speculations at one remove. Our curiosity inflamed by all those subjunctives, we force the dilatory equation to a premature solution – by inserting our own expectations into a tentative explanation concocted by a character whose identity we don't know for a painting we can't be sure we've ever seen. Such intrusive reading, which would rather have a theory, however conjectural, than the uncertainties experience actually provides, is akin to the failing of those over-rational sf authors, who believe in total explanation. The 'liberty to misinterpret' is not just a trick of art but a flaw of consciousness; without even referring to it, Aldiss has expanded the convention back to its original impulse in human nature, forward to our complicity with it as readers, and, outside that, as human beings. In *Report* as never before in Aldiss, the catastrophe has disappeared. We long to have it back, and are reduced, when the dissatisfaction persists, to substituting a catastrophe of our own invention (which Aldiss manipulates cunningly). We need the simplistic, just as the humans in *Light Years* need to degrade the highly advanced utods to the status of inferior rhinos, dissecting what is in front of us until it is just a pile of bits, and then throwing the bits away.

One metaphor in *Report* is the circle of vision, taken from the telescope through which S spies from the coach-house. In the circle everything is focused, but outside it everything is obscure, and what it encloses is only a part, indecipherable except in terms of the whole. Through his telescope S sees the empty milk bottle on the doorstep; later he looks again and lo, the full milk bottle – but he misses altogether the milkman and the process by which the first intelligibly becomes the second. 'At the same time a dead leaf whisked through the circle of vision, over the step, and was gone into the darkness that always surrounded the circle of vision.'[43]

That sentence is repeated in *Barefoot in the Head*, where it is followed by a qualification: 'But none of the watchers any longer cared for the old movements.'[44] In *Barefoot* the catastrophe is very precisely delineated; it even has a name, the Acid Head War. The Arabs have bombed the industrial West with PCA missiles – Psycho-Chemical Aerosols. The war lasts only a few hours. Hallucinogenic fallout lingers, to be inhaled, ingested in food and water, absorbed through the skin. There is no further news from Kuwait, no sign of an invasion. Presumably the Arabs have achieved their objective in knocking out the control centre of civilisation. The brisk finality of the bombardment reminds us that the principal effect of disasters is the disruption of past from present. 'Like the man said, there had been a war, a dislocation.'[45] The chapter entitled 'The Serpent of Kundalini' emphasises the irrelevance of the past. To live in England now, Charteris must discard his previous notions of the country, stylised images 'culled from dozens of Saint books', while the English bourgeoisie must give up the cultural conservatism by which they have excluded time, their radios perpetually tuned to Glenn Miller, the sunsets arrested in their wrought-iron gates. 'The waiting man' in his Pear Tree Palace, with his absent daughter an eternally distant erotic possibility, is neighbour to Mr Mary and his tantalising wife in their inert estate.[46]

'Believe me, the old world has gone, but its shell remains in place. One day soon, there will come a breath of wind, a new messiah, the shell will crumple, and the kids will run streaming, screaming, barefoot in the head, through lush new imaginary meadows. What a time to be young!'

This prophecy of psychedelic pastoral is warped in the fulfilment, in *Barefoot* as in Britain in the 1960s. The crusade of barefoot kids becomes a rambling motorcade, and for their lush meadows they have only grey highways and grim decaying cities. Instead of their Brussels festival to première a film of Charteris's 'resurrection', there is a manic mass-hallucination, no film, while cholera-stricken fans are crushed in the crowd; instead of the new messiah, only a second-hand saint.

But it is not only that the present is disconnected from the past, and from past versions of the future. Everything is disconnected, the present divided against itself.[47]

He hoped his new-found mental state would enable him to see the future with increasing clarity; but, when he made the effort, as if, it might be, his eyesight misted over at any attempt to read small print, the endeavour seemed bafflingly self-defeating: the small print of the future bled and ran . . . until, trying to grapple with the muddled images, he finally even lost the *direction* in which his mind was trying to peer.

The dislocation is complete. The cause hangs back in the 'predelic' era; we may understand it, but it is no guide to what happens now. All the factors in the new equation are variables.[48]

'The times themselves, I mean, talk nonsense – but the sort of nonsense that makes us simultaneously very sceptical about the old rules of sanity.'

'There were no rules for that sort of thing. There never were. You make them up as you go.'

The disaster should have been a new beginning. By destroying all former structures and expanding the minds and senses of the human race it should, as Charteris claims, have opened all possibilities. The forced demolition of her frigid, obsessive past, the 'over-furnished/Years' spent sitting in her fully-automated house watching nothing on 'omnivision', should have liberated Marta Koninkrijk.[49] Instead she is caught anew, the third party in a sexual conflict, and dies unnoticed on a broken chair, hallucinating the rape of her mind and body by toads. The opening of all possibilities has in fact rendered nothing practicable, because there is no dependable connection between this moment and the next. The ultimate disaster dissolves not only the old equations but also the new. To insist then on moral circumscription and the Newtonian mechanics of single-value logic, as Angeline does, is to invite scorn from those who see the multiplication of alternatives, the 'fuzzy set', as an advance on the old restrictions.[50]

'Do me a fervour! I try to work on this document of human destiny and you want to know whether or not I took in the slack with Marta last night. Why not trip out of needling my alternatives? Get from me!' . . .

'Oh entropise human detestiny!' Angeline was washed and white like concentrate campallour, still calculating against the aftermaths of warcalculus, still by the chemicals not too treblinkered. 'I don't want to know if you slacked because I know if you slacked you slackered Marta tonight last night every night and I just damned won't stand it, so you just damned fuzzy-settle for her or me! None of your either-whoring here!'

'All that old anti-life stuff snuffed it with your wesciv world – from now on it's a multi-vulval state and the office blocks off.' . . .

'Colin – you need me! You need someone near you who isn't – you know – hippie!' . . .

'That was yesterday. . . . I need only the many now,' he said.

In *Report* we are helpless because we cannot know the nature of the catastrophe and have no way of apportioning significance amongst the data. In *Barefoot* the nature of the catastrophe is plain, but it is such that the data are all equivalent, everything simultaneously visible from all sides. We want the freedom of choice that Charteris preaches, but we want to hang on to love and devotion and importance, and all the other 'loot' that this freedom makes worthless. We want openness but we want privacy. We want the inconceivably complex truth but we want the security of our private simplifications. Ultimately, as Charteris says, we want it both ways. 'Things remain unresolved if they are to stand in any way as an equation for life.'

Aldiss gives it to us both ways, in the agonising simplicity of *Report on Probability A* and the intolerable all-inclusiveness of *Barefoot in the Head*. Fiction is an analogy of the external world just as subjective experience is an analogy of objective reality. In *Report* he shrinks life to the scanty dimensions of the page, eschewing the artificial flavour and colour that fiction normally adds. In *Barefoot* he expands and inflates the page, superimposing text on text, to approach the true multiplicity of life. He will not pretend that the pause between the two can be anything but uncomfortable. *Report*, an eternal time-starved hesitation like those observed by Harold Pinter and Alain Resnais, depicts man frozen by his own previous actions and inactions, self-condemned to the prison of his own precautions. Each observer attributes great significance to the probability on his particular screen, but nothing happens: the watchers form their own vicious circle of vision, from which all life has escaped, a dead leaf whisked away. It is a scene of contemporary despair, as empty and entropic as any of Ballard's terminal zones. *Barefoot*, in contrast, is so full that no reader can absorb it all. Incidents like Herr Laundrei's conversion are so rich with implication, allusion and ambivalence that the facts, so blankly prominent in *Report*, can elude detection. The flamboyance of the crusaders' appearance and behaviour is as eclectic and confused as the style in which Aldiss evokes them.

> Fearsome in our feathers brutally flowered
> We warn the predelics we're powered[51]

They are supercharged, like the words on the page, which use too much energy, and break at random into song and verse, puns and jokes and wordgames, as if Aldiss intends to push his language through all permutations, all the alternatives in one book. The author is ringmaster of a verbal circus, or, like Charteris, leader of a carnival procession. *Barefoot* is the apogee of New Wave exhibitionism, cavorting in the wake of Finnegan.

Aldiss being who he is, he climbs down from High Point X and has his hero turn back deliberately to ancient ways, predelic and preindustrial too, prehistoric even. Man the Driver becomes Man the Drover.[52]

> All you must have within is outside among verdance Christ and
> the westering thing supposited the inside out
> > Never imagined where all the roads would lead
> > Here
> > The eternal position
> > You have to have been there first

Many theres
For the here no multernatives
His thought chewed deeper and deeper into the ruralities as
the herding greentides lipped them
For Aldiss in this book the answer to the modern agony of living
at the end of time is to return to the beginning, to submerge the
dissociated individual consciousness in the natural flow, 'in eternal
recurrents and eddies of beening and borning.'[53] ' "You are more
merged each than you believe," ' Charteris assures the people of the
little rural settlement where he and Angeline finish up.[54] Again and
again Aldiss affirms continuity in time, co-existence in space. All
life is a 'multibrood'; man is inextricably part. Very often Aldiss's
illustration is ecological, as here; elsewhere it is more cosmic,
redeeming the disparities of form with the unity of being, in the
whirl of electrons as in the waltz of galaxies. He approaches wholeness gladly. Of his New Wave contemporaries, lost in the depths of
their cities, alienated from past and future, conjuring chaos with
dismantled prose and fragmented characters, few are in sympathy
with Aldiss's faith or artistic objectives, believing the healing
impracticable, an option closed to modern man. Nevertheless,
Aldiss shared the most intense and important phase of his career
with the entropy exhibitors, demonstrating the possibilities they
sought and setting standards that every one of them acknowledges
but few have matched.

Chapter Seven

The works of J.G. Ballard

1 The terminal man

At Columbine Sept Heures it was always dusk. Here Halliday's
beautiful neighbour, Gabrielle Szabo, walked through the
evening, her silk robe stirring the fine sand into cerise clouds.
From the balcony of the empty hotel near the artists' colony,
Halliday would look out over the drained river at the unmoving
shadows across the desert floor, the twilight of Africa, endless
and unbroken, that beckoned to him with the promise of his lost
dreams. The dark dunes, their crests touched by the spectral
light, receded like the waves of a midnight sea.[1]

J.G. Ballard is unmistakable. His habit of introducing a story with a
tableau, meticulous and stylised, proclaims his hand no less distinc-
tly than a name signed in the bottom right-hand corner of a canvas
or flashed in capitals across a screen.

Pictorial comparisons are the first that come to mind: the morose,
emaciated figures of a blue Picasso; the luminous spectres of a
Delvaux, half madonnas, half mannequins; a background of mysterious shadows or the oppressive clarity of noon, de Chirico's
colonnades or Dali's feverish sunlight, the livid clouds and brilliant
sand of Port Lligat. Repudiating eager attempts to find him literary
ancestors, in or outside science fiction, Ballard acknowledges his
debt to painters, especially the Surrealists. Story after story contains
a prominent image of this kind, figures in a landscape strangely lit;
and, after the narrative has led us around and away, still the initial
tableau seems to resolve it all.

Characteristic too are the scenes he depicts, places of dereliction and decay. Empty hotels, vacant resorts, abandoned construction sites, rusty launching platforms – former centres of human activity now deserted. But there are still people present, a few who have stayed on, or others who have deliberately sought these locations for purposes of their own. This is the special preserve of a sub-genre especially favoured by English sf writers: the catastrophe story. The world is destroyed by fire or plague, pollution or geophysical upheaval. The established order goes down with all hands. Clinging to the wreckage are a small group of survivors. The story commonly relates their attempts to resume human civilisation in a post-human environment.[2] Having already used them in several short stories, Ballard borrowed the conventions for his first novel *The Wind from Nowhere*.[3] Written at top speed during a fortnight's holiday, this was principally a commercial effort to earn Ballard enough money to leave his job and start writing full-time. The effort was successful. Ballard moved on immediately to a second novel, *The Drowned World*, which was artistically as fruitful as its predecessor had been financially.[4] Praise from Graham Greene and Kingsley Amis guaranteed his reputation as a novelist of note emerging from the dubious undergrowth of sf.

In *The Drowned World* rising temperatures and melting icecaps have caused worldwide flooding and inverted the balance of nature. Swamp conditions encourage the proliferation of reptiles and tropical flora, while mammals are in decline. It is as if time were turning back to the Triassic. Dwindling humanity gathers at the poles, from which the U.N. sends out scientific expeditions to explore the new coastlines and monitor biological developments, with a view to resettlement when the climate stabilises. Listlessness, apathy, and strange nightmares among the crew of his expedition indicate to Dr Bodkin that this official reaction is naïve at best. He relates his speculations to Kerans, the senior biologist.[5]

'Is it only the external landscape which is altering? How often recently most of us have had the feeling of déjà vu, of having seen all this before, in fact of remembering these swamps and lagoons all too well. However selective the conscious mind may be, most biological memories are unpleasant ones, echoes of danger and terror.'

Bodkin's putative science of 'Neuronics', the study of cellular memory, links man back into the ecology as a participant, even a victim, not an overlord. No longer dominant, he will find himself beset,

Bodkin suggests, by increasing fear and disturbance, his genetic inheritance from the lower mammals that were his Triassic ancestors. This supports Kerans's own observation that the 'growing isolation and self-containment' of the members of the survey team resembles[6]

the slackening metabolism and biological withdrawal of all animal forms about to undergo a major metamorphosis. Sometimes he wondered what zone of transit he himself was entering, sure that his own withdrawal was symptomatic not of a dormant schizophrenia, but of a careful preparation for a radically new environment, with its own internal landscape and logic, where old categories of thought would be merely an encumbrance.

This is a development against the trend of the catastrophe story, which has usually been concerned with the continuation of the human identity despite inhuman conditions: wit and will pitted against time and evolution. Kerans deliberately abandons the mission and deserts the cause of civilisation.[7]

The tacit assumption made by the UN directorate – that within the new perimeters described by the Arctic and Antarctic Circles life would continue much as before, with the same social and domestic relationships, by and large the same ambitions and satisfactions – was obviously fallacious, as the mounting flood-water and temperature would show when they reached the so-called polar redoubts. A more important task than mapping the harbours and lagoons of the external landscape was to chart the ghostly deltas and luminous beaches of the submerged neuronic continents.

Since the logic of the time demands the capitulation of humanity, Kerans complies, heading south into the uninhabitable tropics on a 'neuronic odyssey', and disappears in jungle.

Early editors objected. Why no happy ending? Cross out 'south' and put 'north'; have the hero rejoin his fellow men and survive. But Ballard insisted, and wrote two more novels on the same pattern. In *The Drought* Ransom (another doctor) avoids the official evacuation when the world's water evaporates.[8] Several years later he refuses to join a tribal community of survivors and remains aloof and starving in his shack on the salt beaches. After a final pilgrimage back inland he is last seen heading alone into the desert.[9]

To his surprise he noticed that he no longer cast any shadow on to the sand, as if he had at last completed his journey across the margins of the inner landscape he had carried in his mind for so many years.

Ransom seems to disintegrate completely. The disaster in *The Crystal World* is even stranger.[10] Jungle around Mont Royal in Central Africa begins to crystallise. The glaciation affects everything in range, animal, vegetable, or mineral.[11]

> They were soon within the body of the forest, and had entered an enchanted world. The crystal trees around them were hung with glass-like trellises of moss. The air was markedly cooler, as if everything was sheathed in ice, but a ceaseless play of light poured through the canopy overhead.
>
> The process of crystallization was more advanced. The fences along the road were so heavily encrusted that they formed a continuous palisade, a white frost at least six inches thick on either side of the palings. The few houses between the trees glistened like wedding-cakes, their white roofs and chimneys transformed into exotic minarets and baroque domes. On a lawn of green glass spurs a child's tricycle glittered like a Fabergé gem, the wheels starred into brilliant jasper crowns.

The effect, as described by Ballard in an impenetrable explanation, is attributable to increasing entropy. As the time available to it runs out, the universe begins to replicate itself, crystallising out in space like salts in a saturated solution. Irreversible, the process will run on until it fills all space, and time and motion cease. Realising that this is a transubstantiation to equal the most transcendental vision of Christian apocalypse, Sanders (Ballard's third doctor) deserts his practice and partner.[12]

> 'It seems to me, Max, that the whole profession of medicine may have been superseded – I don't think the simple distinction between life and death has much meaning now. Rather than try to cure those patients you should put them into a launch and send them up-river to Mont Royal.'

That afternoon Sanders himself takes the journey he prescribes, to seek eternal transfixion in the crystal zone.

Some critics joined the doubtful editors in objecting to this ruthless current of submissiveness. A hero, even one overtaken by events, ought to pursue a course of action, but Kerans, Ransom and Sanders, instead of motivating the plot, seemed to be preventing one from developing. Especially habitués of sf were puzzled, being used to stories of speed, momentum and conflict that grows more aggressive as opposition mounts. In a review James Cawthorn attempted to describe the essential situation of these books and distinguish it from what was expected of the catastrophe story. The author had established his own conventions, indeed his own territory,[13]

> the heartland of Ballard country where small communities crouch on the fringes of ancient deserts, interminable landscapes of repetitive geometrical forms burned and scoured of all irrelevancies, the naked bones of Time. Looking outward, the eye sees not Space, but deepening time-layers like Pythagorean shells of crystal. The two-fisted technologist of *Astounding*'s heyday is replaced, in this setting, by a figure it is tempting to label The Dissolving Hero. Faced with the breakup of the Universe he does not fight, but instead seeks, literally, to be absorbed.

In the traditional scheme Ballard could be accommodated only as the kind of cautionary writer who insists on belittling man in the cosmic perspective and enlists natural forces to overrule his presumption. But according to an interview in 1973, this is not how Ballard sees his own work. Asked why he had used the catastrophe form, he replied,[14]

> 'I wanted to deal with a large canvas. I was interested in events, if you like; systems, of a very large area. The entire biological kingdom viewed as a single organism, as a single continuing vast memory. In fact I've never thought of them as being disaster stories, because I don't see them as having unhappy endings. The hero follows the logic of his own mind; and I feel that anyone who does this is, in a sense, fulfilling himself. I regard all those novels as stories of psychic fulfilment.'

The grand scheme, though predominant, was not paramount. Even when not 'faced with the breakup of the Universe', Ballard's heroes tend to withdraw and dissolve. Seven of the twelve stories in *The Terminal Beach* and seven of the nine in *The Disaster Area* involve or imply the mutilation or destruction of the central character, deliberately sought if not self-inflicted.[15] Several of these are personal, domestic tales: Richard Maitland blinds himself in order not to be disturbed from his preoccupation with dream-memories of his childhood;[16] Charles Gifford, an archaeologist with an infected leg, prefers to stay and die near the Toltec ruins where he injured it than rouse himself to accept the ministrations of English civilisation.[17]

Charles Gifford remained silent and withdrawn, sinking more deeply into the interior landscape emerging from the beaches of the delta. His wife and Richard Lowry sat with him in the evenings when they returned from the terrace city, but he was barely aware of their presence. By now they seemed to move in a peripheral world, players in a marginal melodrama. Now and then he would think about them, but the effort seemed to lack point. His wife's involvement with Lowry left him unperturbed; if anything, he felt grateful to Lowry for freeing him from Louise.

In Kerans's room at the Ritz, above a flooded London, Strangman picks up a volume of Donne and improvises a pastiche: 'World within world, each man an island unto himself, swimming through seas of archipelagos . . .'[18] Stranded in his houseboat as the rivers drain, Ransom has a similar apprehension. 'Each of them would literally be an island in an archipelago drained of time.'[19] Whether the disaster is global or private, Ballard continually presents a fractured society filled with failed relationships, characters who never interact. The hero's retreat from the 'peripheral world' reflects a marked social decadence. Marriages drift apart, liaisons both sexual and professional are makeshift affairs, arranged to pass the time or fulfil some covert, selfish purpose. Groups of exiles – Kerans, Bodkin, and Beatrice Dahl in *The Drowned World*, Bridgman, Travis, and Louise Woodward in 'The Cage of Sand'[20] – find nothing in common though prisoners by choice. They take on no group identity and often avoid each other. The disintegration is hastened by the central character's increasing introversion: Gifford's wife and assistant become unreal to him, 'players in a marginal melodrama'. By contrast, his own experience is of a super-real realm, 'the world of absolute values'.[21] The 'growing isolation' and 'biological withdrawal' that Kerans notices in himself continue when he leaves the survey team. By the time Col. Riggs returns to rescue him, Kerans finds himself 'unable to accept wholly the idea of Riggs' reality' and remarks 'a similar lack of physical validity about the rest of the crew.'[22] Escaping from his first venture into the crystalline zone, Sanders has the same experience.[23]

After the endless glimmer of the vitrified forest the trees along the road, the ruined hotel and even the two men with him appeared to be shadowy images of themselves, replicas of illuminated originals in some distant land at the source of the petrified river. Despite his relief at escaping from the forest, this feeling of flatness and unreality, of being in the slack shallows of a spent world, filled Sanders with a sense of failure and disappointment.

These might be stories of failing minds, chronicling breakdown after breakdown, studies of the tolerance of the human brain. Their author provides vivid descriptions of the schizophrenic moment, when the mind ceases to balance itself and social communication is paralysed. But Ballard, the foremost explorer of inner space, redirects our attention. We watch the hero's dissolution from inside, and share his impatience with his wife and colleagues who cannot appreciate it. The beckoning spectres of deep psychosis, 'the twilight noon', seem far more alive and urgent than these awkward puppets who interrupt his meditations with mundane remarks. Ballard draws them sketchily, without interest, often with implied distaste, and always seems to endorse his hero's criticisms of their impoverished world.

Lowry's meticulous neutrality and good manners seemed to Gifford an attempt to preserve a world on which Gifford had turned his back, that world . . . where events moved on a single plane of time like the blurred projection of a three-dimensional object by a defective camera obscura.

Gifford, on the other hand, has access to three dimensions and more. 'All the while he moved through ceaseless dreams sinking from one plane of reverie to the next, the great mandalas guiding him downwards, enthroning him upon their luminous dials.'[24] His private phantasmagoria proceeds in measured cadences of hallucinatory splendour.

It seems that all the activities of the present are distractions from the eternal. The hero is right to renounce them and other people as blocks on his energies. 'It was almost as if the barriers between the deepest levels of the nervous system and the external world had been removed, those muffling layers of blood and bone, reflex and convention. . . .'[25]

The reappraisal of schizophrenia is complete. The victim becomes a hero, bound on a quest through solitude and death for a reality larger than we can perceive: the true nature of the external world. Separate from it, man feels a deathwish for total immersion in it. Ballard, convinced that reality itself needs psychoanalysing, has no place for novelistic conventions of verisimilitude, whether of things or people.[26]

'To be honest the relationship between my characters don't interest me very much. There is only one character I am interested in by and large. All my fiction is in a sense about isolation and how to cope with isolation. I'm talking about man's biological isolation in relation [to] the universe, his isolation in time, the sense of his finite life in the face of this panoply of alternatives from which he is excluded, and latterly the isolation between man the individual and this technological landscape, which offers more hope perhaps.'

Ballard parades his disregard for characterisation and turns it into a game by deliberately repeating names in his writings. The hero of his first book, *The Wind from Nowhere*, was called Maitland; Ballard used the name again in 'The Gioconda of the Twilight Noon', and a third time in *Concrete Island*.[27] An exceptional number of women are called Judith or Judy. There is no suggestion that these are in fact the same people (unlike similar repetitions throughout Michael Moorcock's fiction); nor does Ballard make much attempt to differentiate them. Characters are flat and functional, their humanity subordinated to their values as roles or signs. Some, such as Dr Bodkin, and Dr Nathan in *The Atrocity Exhibition*, are undisguised mouthpieces for Ballard's current ideas and whimsies.[28] Dr Nathan previously figured in an even smaller part, in 'The Impossible Man'.[29] The phenomenon of fluid identity becomes critical in the central character of *The Atrocity Exhibition*, the most dissolved hero of all, who may be a teacher, an astronaut, a rock singer, an assassin, a film extra, a bomber pilot, a doctor, a patient, or the new messiah. From section to section of the book he retains only his obsessions and his initial: I shall call him T–. T– can be traced back to 'The Waiting Grounds' as Tallis, 'The Thousand Dreams of Stellavista' as Talbot, 'The Cage of Sand' as Travis, and of course 'The Terminal Beach' as Traven.[30]

Ballard's early catastrophe novels, *The Drowned World, The Drought*, and *The Crystal World*, present physical, global disasters which disrupt history and society and leave everyone alone to come to terms with an altered reality. Everyone assumes a new role as hidden factors of the disaster expose latent forces in and beyond individual personality. More often than not, these forces are destructive. The anti-social impulses that are suppressed for social living take over when society itself is destroyed. In *The Drought* Rev. Johnstone observes, ' "There are too many people now living out their own failures, that's the secret appeal of this drought." ' Not long after, Ransom can tell that it is not so much a 'secret appeal' as a necessity. 'After the events of the previous days, he already felt that in the new landscape around them humanitarian considerations were becoming irrelevant.'[31]

At the same time Ballard was also writing short stories in which the disasters are private and mental. The hero-victim retreats from a fully functioning society to a point from which he sees that social life is an arbitrary and superficial pretence. It can be maintained only in denial of the true depths of mind and time, the enormities of existence. The altered reality, an ancient rather than a new arrangement, demands the mutilation or destruction of his physical identity. The catastrophe is the collapse of his own personality.

In both these kinds of story the physical catastrophe, according to Ballard, is more apparent than real. It is man's isolation which is the real disaster, and these emergencies, global or personal, offer a chance to break down the barriers, 'those muffling layers of blood and bone, reflex and convention'. The destruction of the self liberates a purer, inner being that flies straight to another plane, the reality beyond the catastrophe. Whether Ballard describes this release in terms of religion, psychology, or biological atavism, it becomes apparent that the notion is principally romantic.

In the stories that comprise *The Atrocity Exhibition* the strains converge almost to vanishing point. Society is no more than a conspiracy of postures; the 'flat' secondary character is reduced to a mere name and a set of mannerisms. Dr Nathan is simply a lecture punctuated by draws on a gold-tipped cigarette. Between Vietnam and the mental hospitals, the world is as devastated as in any geophysical upheaval, but the hero is in mental fugue as well. Mutilated and destroyed, unable to be found inside his own conceptual labyrinths, his identity fades. His predecessors in Ballard's fiction had to strive for their absorption, be crucified like Gifford and Maitland, or make a long quest for it like Kerans and Ransom. T– is born dissolved. Ballard spends a book accumulating and rearranging his fragments. He has no soul, no romantic inner self, but consists entirely of gestures, a few photographs, sections of electronic circuitry.

Such a mad idea would be disturbing enough, but Ballard, as ever, insists that T– is somehow right, that his state is the appropriate one for his catastrophic environment – and his environment, from Dealey Plaza to the reservoirs of Staines and Shepperton, is our own.

2 Revising reality

In a deserted Europe Richard Forrester meets the enigmatic Dr Gould in the Dali museum at Figueras.[32]
> Beside him on the divan were three canvases he had selected from the walls, and which he later took back to decorate his hotel rooms.
> 'They're a little too close to the knuckle for me,' Forrester commented. 'A collection of newsreels from Hell.'
> 'A sharp guess at the future, all right,' Gould agreed. 'The ultimate dystopia is the inside of one's own head.'

Ballard expresses an enthusiasm for the Surrealists which is shared, unsurprisingly, by many of his characters. Beatrice Dahl, Charles Ransom, Halliday, Dr Nathan, and Dr Gould all have small collections of Surrealist painting to which they attach much significance. I have remarked how the strange tableaux set up in many of the stories recall the work of Dali and de Chirico, Delvaux and Magritte; further reading shows that Ballard is indebted to Surrealism not for images only, but also for methods. In an interview he was asked whether there was a direct connection between his stories and the paintings mentioned in them.[33]
> 'The connection is deliberate, because I feel that the surrealists have created a series of valid external landscapes, which have their direct correspondences within our own minds. I use the phrase "spinal landscape" fairly often. And here, in these spinal landscapes, which I feel that painters such as Ernst and Dali are producing, one finds a middle ground (an area which I've described as "inner space") between the outer world of reality on the one hand, and the inner world of the psyche on the other.'

Ballard perpetuates the Surrealists' assertion that their art discloses contents of the unconscious mind. The dislocations and ambiguities in their pictures radiate an extraordinary power of emotional and imaginative conviction, as if bypassing the frontal intellect and striking chords in more remote regions of the brain. Violating our expectations of continuity, every painting, every collage is a metaphysical disaster area. The Surrealists assaulted 'the barriers between the deepest levels of the nervous system and the external world'.

Ballard remains highly sceptical as to what is actually in the external world, especially now that so much of it is our own creation, or at least shows signs of our interference. Our proliferating technology gives us unprecedented rations of power to act out inner fantasies and fulfil secret impulses. Psychology has reduced human mentality to terms of its most base drives, and so degraded all intentions and achievements. Rational accounts of what we make and do are dubious, ultimately irrelevant. The meaning of a multi-storey car park is not the parking of cars, not in Ballard's epistemology; and if the car park is a cipher in a code, what of the car, whose ambiguous emotional effects are much more evident?

Ballard's choice of the catastrophe mode for his first four novels was a wish to destroy the manifest form of the external world and release the deep desires latent in it. He suspected that the desires would be anti-social, selfish, aggressive, exploitative, ultimately self-destructive. In this respect *The Drowned World* is indeed closer to Golding than to Wyndham, and it is easy to see why critics thought Ballard had been reading Conrad, though he extends a heart of darkness to the entire human race. As Ransom admits, 'Mr Jordan, I daren't be honest with myself. Most known motives are so suspect these days that I doubt whether the hidden ones are any better.'[34]

Ballard has always shown a keen eye for motives. His writings are dotted with minutiae of kinesics, the analysis of gesture and posture popularly known as 'body-language':

> I expected to see a look of fury and outrage on her face, but instead her unmoving eyes showed the calm and implacable contempt of a grieving widow insulted at her husband's funeral.[35]

> Louise Peret . . . still wore her sun-glasses, screening off some inner sanctum of herself . . . but already he sensed from the slight movement of her hands across the table towards him that she was searching for some point of contact.[36]

Radek placed his hands palm-downwards on the metal desk as if trying to draw some kind of resolution from its surface.[37]

Trabert watched the young man pace at random around the pitch, replicating some meaningless labyrinth as if trying to focus his own identity.[38]

Ballard insists on this subtlety with such conviction that it is difficult to detect where and when it becomes absurd.[39]

'Lomax told me to follow you; tell him everything you did.'
'Interesting.' Ransom pondered this. The frankness could be discounted. No doubt these were Lomax's instructions, but the real point of Quilter's remarks would lie elsewhere.

Yet absurdity especially must be pursued, since it is an escape from the reasonable and expected. Randomness and surprise call into play the associative faculties of the brain, and undiscovered connections spark: the Surrealists' purpose, and Ballard's, precisely. He reproduces their effects, the bizarre juxtapositions which enshrine an enigmatic, irreducible authority. This device illuminates many incidents in his earlier work. In *The Drought* Quilter menaces Ransom with a cheetah he has stolen from the zoo: 'With a smile, as if decanting a pearl from his palm, Quilter let the leash slide off his hand into the road.'[40] As in the writings of Lautréamont and André Breton, the vehicle of the conjunction is a special kind of simile, a comparison which mystifies instead of elucidating. Thinking back to his capture by Saul and the fishermen, Ransom remembers 'the nets closing around him in the hot airless road, like the capes of bull-fighters called out to the streets behind their arena to play a huge fish found leaping in the dust.'[41] Later, and more obscurely, 'Laing had not been particularly interested in Melville, this ex-pilot who had turned up here impulsively in his expensive car and was now prowling restlessly around the solarium as if hunting for a chromium rat.'[42] Why a *chromium* rat? This is a pseudo-simile, one in which there is no discoverable parity between the terms. Ballard's version of it employs a literary sleight commonly used by ironists: he keeps the relation but blurs the distinction, so that the two halves of the simile, the actual and the virtual, can be swapped over. Charles Gifford, dying slowly on the drained delta, sees thousands of snakes emerge from the mud each evening.[43]

The nearest creeks were three hundred yards from the camp, but for some reason the appearance of the snakes always

coincided with Gifford's recovery from his evening fever. . . .
He would sit up in the stretcher-chair and find the snakes
crawling across the beaches, almost as if they had materialized
from his dreams.
'Almost as if. . .' – in fact, they have. No one else can see the snakes;
they are phantoms projected from Gifford's mind. But Ballard's
play upon the simile accomplishes more than this casual narrative
finesse. The ambiguity he contrives allows the point that the hal-
lucinated snakes are real, more real than the closed minds of Lowry
and Louise can admit. The snakes on the beach introduce Gifford to
the 'world of absolute values', the apprehension of eternity encoded
deep in his unconscious. As he says, reiterating a favourite idea of
his author's, 'The only real landscapes are the internal ones, or the
external projections of them, such as this delta.'[44]
   Later, when Ballard was submitting his 'condensed novels' to
NW, he included juxtapositions of a bolder kind than these similes,
as if listing the elements of a collage.[45]
Junction Makers
Dr Manston indicated the items: (1) Photograph of partly
constructed motorway cloverleaf, concrete embankments
exposed in transverse section, labelled 'Crater'; (2)
Reproduction of Salvador Dali's *Madonna of Port Lligat*; (3)
500 imaginary autopsy reports of the first Boeing 747 air
disaster; (4) Sequence of perspective drawings of corridors at
the Belmont asylum; (5) Facial grimaces, during press
conference, of Armstrong and Aldrin; (6) List of pH levels of
settling beds, Metropolitan Water Board Reservoir, Staines; (7)
Terminal voice-print, self-recorded, of an unidentified suicide;
(8) The market analysis of a new hemispherical building-system
module.
The Surrealist techniques that Ballard has used involve deliberate dissociations and mystifications. The object is taken from its
usual context and dismantled, or put in a new context, or confused
with other objects. But the result of the process is not mere nonsense, but a revaluation. The elements acquire new significance
from the reorganisation, so that we sense more about the object
than we knew or felt before. Surrealism can thus be said to have
both a synthetic and an analytic aspect; it consists not only of
inspiration, but also of inquiry. This duality Ballard has inherited. It
can be seen operating in his most characteristic writing. 'Mutating

kelp, their gene shifts accelerated by the radio-phosphorus, reared up into the air on either side of the road like enormous cacti, turning the dark salt banks into a white lunar garden.'[46] This sentence is what we might call techno-mysticism, a style in which Ballard can present scientific accuracy and evocative rhapsody at the same time. Again it is constructed around a simile: 'mutating kelp . . . reared up . . . like enormous cacti.' On the near side it purports to be a precise explanation ('gene shifts accelerated by the radio-phosphorus'), like the technicalities in traditional sf. On the far side, however, everything is mysterious once more, unscientific, even illogical ('lunar garden'). The movement parallels the way Ballard creates his disastrous new worlds. Each is a logical development from the present, but that logic is devalued in the process of change: 'old categories of thought would be merely an encumbrance.' After explanation, new mystery.

Sf can often seem flawed by an intrinsic incompatibility between the language of science and the language of fiction. The language of science is definitive; its objective is clarity; it must be independent of both experimenter and reader; ideally it would be value-free. However, we know that the language of fiction is associative; it works in many ways simultaneously; the personalities and values of writer and reader are indispensable elements in its expression and interpretation; its most acclaimed passages are rich, subtle, and complex. Ballard is able to reconcile the denotative and connotative principles without obvious effort; many readers speak of him with awe, calling him a poet.[47] His amalgamation of sonorous, emotive words with categorical terms from the sciences is a kind of alchemy. A new reality is generated, in which discrete elements (lunar, garden) can co-exist. Reading these sentences we apprehend a process part analytic, part synthetic.

We can now relate this more specifically back to Surrealism. Ballard's image of mutant kelp recalls paintings by Max Ernst such as *The Eye of Silence* and *Europe after the Rain*. First using a technique such as decalcomania, a haphazard smearing of gouache on a glossy surface, Ernst would then pick out shapes that had been produced accidentally and retouch them, adding figures and sky, until he completed a fantastic landscape. These strange panoramas of alien worlds are highly suitable, as Brian Aldiss pointed out to Penguin Books, for sf cover designs. This is the inspirational side of Surrealism, pure invention based on chance and imagination. On the other side is investigative Surrealism, as seen in René Magritte's *Personal Values* or Giorgio de Chirico's *The Song of Love*: a very different kind of painting, using plain and even crude depictions of familiar objects in surprising situations, distorted in proportion and perspective, to reveal unexpected qualities in them. This kind of painting invents no new worlds but reinterprets this world instead. When Salvador Dali painted pictures like *Burning Giraffe*, filled with wooden crutches and open drawers, he was illustrating his own dreams with specific reference to Freud. The imagery of these paintings is allegorical, predisposing us to examine it analytically. Dali offers his subjective landscapes as a comment on memory and perception, and encourages us to decipher them according to the generalised system of values first tabulated by Freud. This is applied fantasy. Surrealism used psychoanalysis to investigate the latent content of reality – an alliance of creative and analytical procedures.

Ballard took up the task forty years later. His essay 'The Coming of the Unconscious', first printed in *NW*, discusses Surrealism as an artistic school with scientific purposes.[48]

> The images of surrealism are the iconography of inner space.
> Popularly regarded as a lurid manifestation of fantastic art concerned with states of dream and hallucination, surrealism is in fact the first movement, in the words of Odilon Redon, to place 'the logic of the visible at the service of the invisible'. This calculated submission of the impulses and fantasies of our inner lives to the rigours of time and space, to the formal inquisition of the sciences, psychoanalysis pre-eminent among them, produces an alternate reality beyond and above those familiar to either our sight or our senses.

The claim has been made by other critics. In *Surrealism: The Road to the Absolute* Anna Balakian shows that the Surrealists paid close attention to contemporary advances in science.[49] After the Romantic severance of 'feelings' from 'facts', the Surrealists, Balakian says, were the first artists to embrace science wholeheartedly. Lautréamont was influenced by Darwin, Apollinaire was excited by the automobile, Breton (like Ballard) turned from medicine to art when he glimpsed the opening vistas of psychoanalysis. 'Both Saint-Pol-Roux and Apollinaire refer to Einstein, and long for the day when the artist may be able to make breakthroughs in the concept of reality in step with the mathematician's theories.'[50] This reconciliation was made possible by adjustments on both sides. Balakian cites

Einstein and Heisenberg as especially responsible for a re-orientation of thought in physics, displacing the old Newtonian image of a mechanistic, explicable universe, and reaffirming the contingent and unquantifiable.[51] Science, by accepting principles of relativity and uncertainty, had reinstated the imagination, whose exclusion Blake and Wordsworth had apprehended with dread. At the same time the bounty of technology could be revalued as more magical than monstrous. 'The scientist had become not a destroyer of fantasy but a producer of marvels.'[52]

However ingenuous their delight may have been, the Symbolists and Surrealists derived an altogether new impetus from it. Balakian agrees with Ballard that the methods they adopted reproduced, or at least imitated, the 'formal inquisition' of science.[53]

Breton and his colleagues went so far as to establish a Central Bureau of Surrealist Research to experiment with writing and to accept communications relative to their research from outside their ranks. . . .

Surrealism has been the first to break the dichotomy and to communicate the desire to appropriate the data of the modern scientist in order to bring about the necessary revisions of our notion of reality and to produce a drastic transformation of the function of the artist in a scientifically advanced society.

'Breakthroughs in the concept of reality'; 'necessary revisions of our notion of reality', resulting in 'a drastic transformation of the function of the artist' – these are the very claims that Ballard sets forward in *NW*. That science and technology have changed reality itself is cardinal to his theory of fiction. Traditional forms of fiction are obsolete because the world no longer corresponds to the constructions they put upon it. So with the Surrealists, according to Balakian.[54]

While literature had been neglecting imagination, science had learned to make maximum use of it. It had cast aside the known patterns of matter and through ingenuity had created new ones. Science's contribution, in Apollinaire's opinion, was *its ability to give reality a relative meaning* and thus to liberate it from its assumed synonymity with the *natural*. The unnatural could become a reality, as twentieth-century objects, which had no connection with nature, were proving more conclusively every day. The factory worker was all the time creating reality.

Rash assertions like these are apt to repel the more cautious critic. Casting aside known patterns, making maximum use of imagination – we may doubt whether any modern scientist, even Heisenberg, would recognise himself in the Pygmalion image Balakian projects. We could even take these statements as evidence that the Surrealists appreciated science not at all, whatever they believed. The important thing, however, with all the theories I am examining, is not whether they are justifiable but that they were believed, and that art was created in that belief. Artists have never needed to be right, least of all in their opinion of the work of others, or of their own. The significance of the Surrealists' vision is that they worked in the belief that an apocalypse had taken place, both in the intellectual sphere and in daily life. The apocalypse they attributed to science and designed their art accordingly, in hostile opposition to the assumptions of their predecessors and unconvinced contemporaries.

This conviction, of standing at a break in history, after the disaster, in a new and unprecedented reality, is an important factor in Modernism. It becomes more central and urgent as we follow it through to the 'Post-Modernism' of art today, especially since the conviction has become popular, the one common element in all the ideological dissent thrown up in the elaborate confusion of the 1960s. It is also one of the most difficult principles for the well-informed critic to recognise. His sense of history prevents him from seeing it as anything more than a mistake, while its adherents refuse to submit to historical comparisons. Whereas the Modernists tried to shore themselves up with history and tradition, the Post-Modernists, like the hippies, achieve their freedom of creativity by rejecting the claims of the past.

Having practised, so to speak, on imaginary disasters of hurricane, flood, drought, and crystal, Ballard turned to a world in which he believed history and society had been disrupted already. To deal with it he revised and sharpened the techniques he derived from the Surrealists, whom he saw as the first artists to recognise the disruption. With those techniques he could write fiction appropriate for an environment entirely created by factory workers, where the virtual had become actual and nature was in full retreat. The tasks of synthesis and creation had passed out of the hands of artists into those of industrialists and directors of the mass media. Art, Ballard decided, could be reorganised only on the second principle of Surrealism: the critical analysis of reality. 'The function of the writer is no longer the addition of fiction in the world, but rather to seek its abstraction, to direct an enquiry aimed at recovering elements of reality from this debauch of fiction.'[55]

3 A science of fictions

'Right from the start what I wanted to do was write a science fiction book that got away from space-ships, the far future, and all this stuff which I felt was basically rather juvenile, to writing a kind of adult science fiction based upon the present . . . which is more difficult to do than one realizes, because the natural tendency when writing in a basically allegorical mode is to set something at a distance because it makes the separateness of the allegory that much more obvious.'[56]

Ballard was deliberately vague in locating his disaster novels. *The Crystal World*, set in the jungle of Central Africa around a town called Mont Royal, is the most specific of them; but the names of towns, like the names of characters, are indistinct: in *The Drought* he already had a city called Mount Royal, leaving its country and even continent uncertain. Kerans, of course, inhabits a world whose countries have vanished and continents shrunk. Old placenames are of academic importance only. 'Despite the potent magic of the lagoon worlds and the drowned cities, he had never felt any interest in their contents, and never bothered to identify in which of the cities he was stationed.[57] The world has changed and, as usual, Ballard and his central character are more interested in the present than the past. In each book Ballard makes a small attempt at a scientific explanation for the catastrophe, 'isolated', as Aldiss noted, 'so that an uninterested reader can skip that bit.'[58] The period is the later twentieth century, unspecified because the calendar has gone the way of atlases and street maps. Ballard has no wish to distract us with futurity. Artifacts are familiar: the characters are coping with a new world with our own tools, so that their stories are closer to the 'alternative present' than the 'possible future' category.

With 'The Terminal Beach' Ballard came out of the allegorical distance and closed in upon the present. Traven chooses a real and very particular spot to maroon himself. 11.30°N, 162.15°E: Eniwetok, site of H-bomb tests.[59]

Its ruined appearance, and the associations of the island with
the period of the Cold War – what Traven had christened 'The
Pre-Third' – were profoundly depressing, an Auschwitz of the
soul whose mausoleums contained the mass-graves of the still
undead. . . .
     The Pre-Third: the period was characterized in Traven's
mind above all by its moral and psychological inversions, by its
sense of the whole of history, and in particular of the immediate
future – the two decades, 1945–65 – suspended from the
quivering volcano's lip of World War III. Even the death of his
wife and six-year-old son in a motor accident seemed only part
of this immense synthesis of the historical and psychic zero, the
frantic highways where each morning they met their deaths the
advance causeways to the global armageddon.
Dr Osborne the biologist misunderstands Traven's resolve to stay
on the island as martyrdom, but Traven is not on Eniwetok for
purposes of protest or despair.[60]
     'For me the hydrogen bomb was a symbol of absolute *freedom*.
I feel it's given me the right – the obligation, even – to do
anything I want.'
     'That seems strange logic,' Osborne commented. 'Aren't we
at least responsible for our physical selves, if for nothing else?'
     'Not now, I think,' Traven replied. 'After all, in effect we are
men raised from the dead.'
Ballard's location of this story in an unambiguous present, with
verifiable references and co-ordinates, gave a new immediacy to his
work. The catastrophe – the development and use of a thermonuclear weapon – has already happened. A new age began on 6 August
1945. Reality is transformed since man realised his latent dreams of
destruction and perfected the technology to achieve it – not only the
Bomb itself, but the popular and everyday death-machines multiplying on the 'frantic highways' (of which Ballard would have much
more to say later). The age is called 'The Pre-Third': that there will
be a Third World War, nuclear and final, 'the global armageddon',
Traven takes for granted – as if that too had already happened. In
the context set up between these two fixed points – the datable past
and the inescapable future – man has a terrible existential freedom.
Having usurped power over his own existence as a species (the word
'genocide' was first used in 1944), he owes nothing to anyone,
except perhaps to 'the still undead', to act in full consciousness of

and accordance with their certain annihilation. Hence the 'moral and psychological inversions': 'in effect, we are men raised from the dead.'

Faced with Ballard's earlier disasters, sf fans had labelled him a pessimist. His preference for inhuman worlds and dissolving heroes was, they assumed, a depressive attitude. Epithets like 'melancholy' and 'maudlin' were bestowed. This new extremism seemed mere hyperbole, a sensationalism allied to the lugubrious outrage of protest poetry. But protest poets were always revisionaries, demanding that civilisation turn back from the Bomb, employing images of a Third World War as omens, premonitions that must not be allowed to come true. Traven makes it clear that he is not a protester or a martyr. Like all his predecessors in Ballard's fiction, Traven's role is to accept the disaster and acclimatise to the new environment. For him there is no appeal to considerations derived from other conditions, ideal conditions without H-bombs. Like the drowned world, the Pre-Third is another 'radically new environment, with its own internal landscape and logic, where old categories of thought would be merely an encumbrance.' Traven exemplifies his acknowledgment of that by seeking to live on the target zone, in a desolate place of sand and concrete that seems to be an advance model of 'the historical and psychic zero.'

This deliberate suppression of expected emotional response separates Ballard from the protesters, the maudlin and melancholy, setting him out on his own. He perceives clearly man's complicity with this catastrophe of his own making. While it seems a dreadful mistake and fills his conscious mind with horror, it is also the ultimate tool, the end product of his technological drive. Man now has absolute power over his own existence: the power of uncreation. The moral rectitude of the protest poets sometimes seemed curiously at odds with a certain relish for denunciation, as if they enjoyed having a Bomb to vilify. Ballard offers his psychoanalysis: destruction was what man wanted, unconsciously, all along.

Hence Traven's urge to accept it. We have seen how other writers for *NW* were uncertain about the condition of man in his scientifically advanced society. They shared much the same view as Ballard, but their emotional and artistic responses were different. Their images of the sex-robots and the mad astronauts express anxiety over man's self-destructive relationship with his machines. Such images issue out of a profound alienation from the state of civilisation now and to come. The writers may not set up alternative images, of desirable states, but they commonly reject the present, even when they sense it is already too late to do so. Ballard himself had taken up these attitudes in earlier stories whose heroes hated their cities and sought to escape them, usually without success.[61] But in his later fiction he deliberately went beyond that position, declaring acceptance of the present and breaking with the past. A new age, the Pre-Third; a new reality – just as the Surrealists determined in response to the dilemma of scientific advance. Even with the worst possible interpretation of events, Ballard insists: our artifice has become reality, nor are we out of it.

The new reality is twofold. First, it is effectively man's own choice and creation.[62]

I feel that the balance between fiction and reality has changed significantly in the past decade. Increasingly their roles are reversed. We live in a world ruled by fictions of every kind – mass-merchandising, advertising, politics conducted as a branch of advertising, the instant translation of science and technology into popular imagery, the increasing blurring and intermingling of identities within the realm of consumer goods, the pre-empting of any free or original imaginative response to experience by the television screen. We live inside an enormous novel.

The 'enormous novel' of contemporary culture is not traditional in structure or plot. It is a fragmented novel, the work of many authors, individuals as well as corporations, for the characters also have usurped the power of fiction and can realise their own fantasies, imposing them upon one another. There are alternative plots and sub-plots, mutually contradictory but co-existent. The multiplication of options and imperatives, the window displays and neon signs of a city street, threaten the integrity of the personality on the pretext of catering to it as fully as possible. In this respect the 'alternative society' was no different from the established one. The hippies preaching only 'do your own thing' and assuming that utopia would naturally follow, actually hastened their own disintegration. *The Atrocity Exhibition* is Ballard's own critical version of the 'enormous novel'. T–, like Jerry Cornelius, lives and dies many times, under many names.

The second aspect of the new reality is its self-destructiveness. In Ballard's earlier disaster fiction destruction seemed to be the way to resolution. The conformity of identity within society was a chrysalis out of which a soul could burst to wing directly into a larger reality. Ballard would take a society and contribute a disaster in order to stimulate that liberation. In the stories of *The Atrocity Exhibition*, which follow directly from innovations made in 'The Terminal Beach', society has provided its own disaster. First Ballard concentrated on the central symbol, the H-bomb; but, as he noted in that story, the disaster is actually far larger and more diffuse than that. It is an 'immense synthesis of the historical and psychic zero', in which the car crash that killed Traven's wife and son is no accident.

On Eniwetok Traven encounters the corpse of a Japanese man. Naming him Dr Yasuda, he has a hallucinatory conversation with him in which he apologises for trying to kill a fly.[63]

> *Traven*: . . . These ingrained habits, you know, they're not easy to shrug off. Your sister's children in Osaka in '44, the exigencies of war, I hate to plead them. Most known motives are so despicable, one searches the unknown in the hope that . . .

> *Yasuda*: Please, Traven, do not be embarrassed. That fly is lucky to retain its identity for so long. That son you mourn, not to mention my own two nieces and nephew, did they not die each day? Every parent in the world grieves for the lost sons and daughters of their earlier childhoods. . . . Each of us is little more than the meagre residue of the infinite unrealized possibilities of our lives.

The phrases echo observations of R.D. Laing's. 'No one can begin to think, feel or act now except from the starting-point of his or her own alienation,' he wrote. 'Humanity is estranged from its authentic possibilities.'[64] Laing diagnosed 'ontological insecurity'. Social conditioning is a process of reality determination, in which authorities, from the parents on, impose their own grids of perception and behaviour on the subject mind. Often, increasingly often these days, the grids do not mesh with each other, and especially not with the predispositions of the subject. As long as he continues to operate from each grid successfully in its appropriate area, he is labelled sane – though each sane person has, according to this theory, several potentially conflicting personalities. Once he allows them to become confused or cannot cope with the contradictions between them, he is labelled insane. His problem is of the most profound kind, 'ontological', because it is his very sense of reality which is destroyed.

Ballard's peculiar notion of characterisation conforms to this picture, with the important addition that 'reality determination' is not only a personal imposition by those who mould and direct our lives, but an impersonal, commercial one too. Our fantasies are staked out and broadcast by advertisers, media programmers, interior decorators. Our lives diversify ever wider in space and time. We do not require an H-bomb to fragment us; we are all dissolved heroes. Death, the apparent purpose and logical outcome of the fragmentation, offers fixity, an end to change, whereas living merely erodes identity further. Hence our preoccupation with violence and destruction, our demand for more, faster, deadlier cars, our fascinated contemplation of the atrocity newsreels.

Ballard outlined the nature of the catastrophe in his interview with Goddard and Pringle.[65]

Pringle: The disaster 'has happened' in your more recent stories – or that's the implication.

Ballard: Well, it is happening. Even the stories in *The Atrocity Exhibition* are disaster stories of a kind. The book is about the communications explosion of the '60's. From my point of view, the '60's started in 1963 with the assassination of President Kennedy – his death and Vietnam presided over the whole of the '60's. Those two events, transmitted through television and mass communications, overshadowed the whole decade – a sort of institutionalized disaster area.

We live in an area of disasters, which are adapted and institutionalised by our own imaginations. The very artificiality of our environment makes it probable that we are fully responsible, if unconsciously, for the disasters. In his earlier stories Ballard had to suggest how humanity was implicated in natural catastrophes. In *The Atrocity Exhibition* the fingerprints are everywhere: the landscape is man-made. Ransom lived among sand dunes which were the unforeseen but direct result of pollution of the seas. T– lives among sand dunes displayed on advertisement hoardings – actually giant images of the female body, photographed and blown up. The woman chosen to 'model' ourselves, our inner fantasies, blots out the natural horizon and determines the contours of our world: for example, Marilyn Monroe,[66]

'this screen actress who is presented to us in an endless series of advertisements, on a thousand magazine covers, and so on, whose body becomes part of the external landscape of our environment. The immense terraced figure of Marilyn Monroe stretched across a cinema hoarding is as real a portion of our external landscape as any system of mountains or lakes.' This landscape of images with which we surround ourselves indoors and out is a deliberate projection of human desires and beliefs. The urban landscape can and must be decoded. Surrealist technique and a 'condensed' style enabled Ballard to make fiction out of his analysis, a minimal overlay of narrative gestures on a mass of theory.[67]

The Fractured Smile. The hot sunlight lay across the suburban street. From the radio of the car sounded a fading harmonic, the last music of the quasars. Karen Novotny's fractured smile spread across the windshield. Talbot looked up at his own face mediated from the billboard beside the car park. Overhead the glass curtain-walls of the apartment block presided over this first interval of neural calm.

The whole of one 'chapter' of one of the 'condensed novels' collected in *Atrocity*. The fictional form is a thin, transparent veneer over the conceptual content – deliberately reproducing the proportions of 'manifest' to 'latent' content in Freudian dream-analysis, and in Dali's paintings of it. Equally, the embodied thought may not wholly be discovered through the veneer, but it is obvious that it *is* more substantial, whatever it is. As with dreams, and Surrealist paintings, the meaning coalesces imaginatively as more examples are examined.[68]

'I tried to develop – and I think successfully – a tec[h]nique of mine, the so-called condensed novels, where I was able to cross . . . events, at right angles if you like. Like cutting through the stem of a plant to expose the cross-section of its main vessels. So this tec[h]nique was devised to deal with this fragmentation and overlay of reality, through the fragmentation of narrative. Although the plot lines are very strong in these stories.

'And they're all variants. Each of the main stories in that collection describe[s] the same man in the same state of mental crisis, but they treat him, as it were, at different points along a spectrum – as you might compile a scientific dossier about someone, explore various aspects of his make-up.'

Ballard continues the Surrealist tradition of accounting for his work in quasi-scientific terms. How far we accept his explanation depends on whether we take those terms as analogical or as, somehow, literal. Certainly, what we normally identify as the stuff of fiction – the presentation and description of characters in action and interaction – he reduces to the merest schematic function. His characters are illustrative models, like mannequins, or the physiological simplifications in a textbook of biology.[69]

'I once said those condensed novels, as I called them, are like ordinary novels with the unimportant pieces left out. But it's more than that – when you get the important pieces together, really together, not separated by great masses of 'he said, she said' and opening and shutting of doors, 'following morning' and all this stuff – the great tide of forward conventional narration – it achieves critical mass as it were, it begins to ignite and you get *more* things being generated. You're getting crossovers and linkages between unexpected and previously totally unrelated things, events, elements of the narration, ideas that in themselves begin to generate new matter.'

Ballard's scientific manner and jargon are not a ruse to blind us with technicalities, but an attempt to provide modern conceptual analogies for an operation of imagination in fiction. This is a detailed study of the Surrealist juxtaposition.

The unconscious mind seems not to work sequentially in time, but to associate ideas. De Chirico and Magritte, by distorting perspective and size, could detach objects from contexts of history and futurity, and bring together what otherwise would never meet: the umbrella and the sewing machine on the dissection table. Ballard's condensed novels contrive the same kind of illusory revelation: jetsam on the terminal beach after the ebb of the great tide of narrative time. There is no magic aura to them, as there was to his lunar gardens of mutant kelp. The analytical purpose is more pressing, so Ballard's manner is less alchemical, more clinical. Bland repetitions of phrase and label, incident and lapse, a detached tone and characterless syntax, all combine to make these disjointed segments appear to have been permutated by computer from several sets of equivalent variables.[70]

In the postures they assumed, in the contours of thigh and thorax, Travis explored the geometry and volumetric time of the bedroom, and later of the curvilinear dome of the Festival Hall, the jutting balconies of the London Hilton, and lastly of the abandoned weapons range.

In the perspectives of the plaza, the junctions of the underpass and embankment, Talbot at last recognized a modulus that could be multiplied into the landscapes of his consciousness.

In the planes of her body, in the contours of her breasts and thighs, he seemed to mimetize all his dreams and obsessions.

In these equations, the gestures and postures of the young woman, Trabert explored the faulty dimensions of the space capsule, the lost geometry and volumetric time of the dead astronauts.

In the eroded causeways and porous rock towers of this spinal landscape Trabert saw the blistered epithelium of the astronauts, the time-invaded skin of Karen Novotny.

Yet in the contours of his wife's thighs, in the dune-filled eyes of Karen Novotny, he saw the assuaged time of the astronauts, the serene face of the President's widow.

Ballard's familiar pseudo-similes have been replaced by these stark clashes of imagery, with no conventional 'like' or 'as' to comfort the mind. Those conjunctions announce the artificiality of the comparison and remind us of the presence of an all-mediating narrator. Ballard withdraws them so that, he hopes, 'it begins to ignite and you get *more* things being generated'.

Not only is the fragmented method another example of Ballard's fundamental Surrealism, but it also serves a mimetic function, reproducing what he sees as the condition of our environment – 'this fragmentation and overlay of reality', an abundance of fictions whose only connections are in the fantasies out of which they are projected. His insistence that meaning is not to be found on the surface but only inside the coded messages of personal gestures and public display allies him with practitioners of semiology, the science of signs derived by Roland Barthes from the lexical structuralism of Ferdinand de Saussure. Indeed, there are many areas of overlap between Ballard's analyses of popular imagery and those in Barthes' earliest essays.

Barthes turned the instruments of anthropology around to discover the present cultural values of his own race as denoted by their characteristic artifacts and activities. Popular assumptions and identifications intrigued him to investigate *'what-goes-without-saying'*, the nature of contemporary fetish and taboo. All too often he found that values attributed by advertising, the press, or simply by public opinion, once examined, seemed unrealistic, fictional, even mythological, derived not from the object or activity itself but from elsewhere. Unlike Ballard Barthes does not ascribe this to universal unconscious desire, but to ideological and economic deceit, which infiltrates bourgeois propaganda at a subtle and previously undefined level. The meaning of the myth and the virtual identity of the artifact are discovered by concentrating on its reception by the consumer, on 'what-goes-without-saying', its significance in aspects other than the utilitarian. Barthes decodes the popular images of wine, hairstyles, and wrestling; he anticipates Ballard by discussing the face of a film star (Garbo) as a contemporary icon, and discovering both the erotic sensuality and the celestial idealism of automobile design:[71]

In the exhibition halls, the car on show is explored with an intense, amorous studiousness: it is the great tactile phase of discovery, the moment when visual wonder is about to receive the reasoned assault of touch (for touch is the most demystifying of all senses, unlike sight, which is most magical). The bodywork, the lines of union are touched, the upholstery palpated, the seats tried, the doors caressed, the cushions fondled; before the wheel, one pretends to drive with one's whole body. The object here is totally prostituted, appropriated: originating from the heaven of *Metropolis*, the Goddess is in a quarter of an hour mediatized, actualizing through this exorcism the very essence of petit-bourgeois advancement.

Signification makes an object or practice carry a message that may not be integral to it. Writing in France in the fifties Barthes saw a typical Western environment increasingly loaded with messages, in far more mass media than anyone had enumerated before.[72]

The development of publicity, of a national press, of radio, of illustrated news, not to speak of the survival of a myriad rites of communication which rule social appearances makes the development of a semiological science more urgent than ever. In a single day, how many really non-signifying fields do we cross? Very few, sometimes none. Here I am, before the sea; it is true that it bears no message. But on the beach, what material for semiology! Flags, slogans, signals, signboards, clothes, suntan even, which are so many messages to me. Barthes admits that there may be 'a mythology of the mythologist', reflecting his decipherings back as myths he himself is interpolating from an intrusive imagination, but maintains, with Ballard and Heisenberg, that it is no longer sufficient or even useful to polarise scientific objectivity and artistic subjectivity.

All in all, it is surprising to find that Ballard had not read Barthes when he wrote *The Atrocity Exhibition*. Ballard, of course, operates within the tolerances of the 'mythology of the mythologist', since he writes books of fiction, not sociopsychology. He is concerned as much with constructing myths as deconstructing them. The scientific processes in his fiction are used as artistic techniques and directed towards artistic ends. Like Salvador Dali, Ballard seeks to substantiate and elaborate his own obsessions, not rid himself (or us) of them. As Moorcock said,[73] 'Ballard has complete confidence in the validity of his own obsessions and this confidence gives his work an intellectual clarity lacking in any of his rivals within the field and lacking in most of those outside it.' Among the internal references of his fiction Ballard never for a moment allows that the fixations of the protagonist might, after all, be delusions. Just as Kerans, Ransom and Sanders are implicitly right to embrace their own catastrophes instead of fighting back, so T–'s suspicions are justified. It all fits, with the crystalline lucidity of paranoia. In the earlier books, despite the general fragmentation of society, Ballard's characters are all extremely good at understanding each other's covert meanings and motives. Their agreement reinforces the objectivity of the new system presently cohering among the ruins of the old. In *The Atrocity Exhibition* Dr Nathan proves able to identify the subjects of T–'s most fantastic assemblages without any hesitation. This is the ultimate affirmation of the paranoid's fear: to have his psychiatrist believe it too. In *Crash* the narrator, who bears Ballard's own name, is gradually but inevitably drawn into complicity with the murderous erotic fantasies of Vaughan.

This Laingian reversal of delusion and common sense continues through Ballard's later fiction, for which he has reverted to the structures of conventional narrative, if not those of conventional sanity. He still tells stories of 'psychic fulfilment' which by any other standards would be galloping psychosis. In *Crash* Dr Robert Vaughan pursues orgasm, mutilation, and eventually death by participating in a series of carefully contrived car crashes. In *Concrete*

Island Robert Maitland is injured and marooned when his car plunges onto waste ground isolated between three converging motorway routes. He finds he is not alone there and soon his attempts at escape become devices to consolidate his supremacy. In *High-Rise* the inhabitants of a luxury tower block cut themselves off from the outside world and revert to primitive savagery.[74] These three contemporary 'catastrophes' are detailed studies in the latent violence of the urban landscape. They comprise a triptych illustrating the thesis presented in *Atrocity* that modern technology satisfies the irrational urges of the human mind more than the rational purposes for which it was apparently designed.

Writing these stories which propound such unreasonable (and unpleasant) interpretations, Ballard sustains an unyielding irony which is his most devastating effect. It is impossible to accept that he really believes or wants us to believe that car crashes are sexy; yet his immodest proposals, unlike those of traditional satire, do not allow us to make sense of their texts merely by reversing the positive and negative signs. His deviant analysis of contemporary culture is still an analysis, argued most persuasively with a cunning mixture of scientific and rhetorical techniques. The premise, that its violent and disastrous aspects are sufficient indications if not direct products of unconscious, self-destructive impulses in the human mind, is grimly plausible, however wildly he demonstrates it. The conflict between conviction and unacceptability, apparently resolved in Ballard's own thinking and certainly resolved on the page, continues in the reader's mind. Ideally the function of this conflict is to make it impossible for us to make an unequivocal response (positive or negative) to the myths and icons in the stories, which we recognise as the myths and icons of our own urban environment. The assumption that commercial centres determine reality is a common and potent one now that urban conditions are normal for over half the population of the world, no matter how arrogant and even erroneous that assumption might be. As Ballard shows, paranoia makes sense of urban chaos; on the other hand, the sense it makes is completely paranoid. Readers who can cope with the paradox by emulating Ballard's ironic entertainment of unacceptable ideas are thereby forcibly detached from the landscape of signs. This disenchantment is conducive to demystification and enlightenment, and at least a step towards freedom of understanding and choice in the world we seem to have made.

Chapter Eight

The works of Michael Moorcock

1 The multiverse merchant

Michael Moorcock had left school and was editing a magazine, *Tarzan Adventures*, by his seventeenth birthday. He worked for Fleetway Publications for three years, hammering out thousands of words of juvenile fiction every day, then left after a row in which he threw a typewriter out of a window. He played guitar across Europe, climbed mountains in Sweden, and was sent home starving by the British Embassy in France. He wrote political pamphlets for the Liberal Party before deciding they had no policy worth writing about; and he supplied Carnell's *Science Fantasy* with some rather unorthodox, badly written, and very popular stories.

Reviewers and copywriters have glamourised Moorcock's early life. Sf fans relish eccentric biographies, and young readers of the 1960s could identify wayward impulses like their own in his erratic career. His arrival in public was in the nature of an assault, and the arrogance of his guest editorial for *NW*, a year before his surprise accession to the chair, must have offended many older readers. His call for revolution in the science fiction ghetto included derogatory remarks on the state of 'the field' at the time, deploring the lack of 'passion, subtlety, irony, original characterisation, original and good style, a sense of involvement in human affairs, colour, density, depth, and, on the whole, real feeling from the writer'.[1] He affirmed that 'the day of the boy-author writing boys' stories got up to look like grown-ups' stories will soon be over.'

Moorcock's own achievement at that date must have caused many to doubt both his judgment and his promise. Apart from two or three heavily stylised pieces in *NW* and *Science Fiction Adventures*, obviously 'serious' in intention but strained in execution, he was known only for his heroic fantasies, 'The Eternal Champion' and the early Elric stories, published in *Science Fantasy*. To check any one against the list of qualities Moorcock supplied in the guest editorial is to find it deficient in every respect (except perhaps 'colour', which appears in psychedelic profusion). The prose is not so much mannered as formulated, after his earliest models, Edgar Rice Burroughs and Robert E. Howard, and the generations succeeding them in the coterie magazines. It hobbles its heroes, burying their violent actions under a ton of description.[2]

Another catapult sounded and this time a tower full of archers was squarely hit. Masonry erupted outwards and those who still lived fell sickeningly to die in the foam-tipped sea lashing the wall. This time, angered by the deaths of their comrades, Imrryrian archers sent back a stream of slim arrows into the enemy's midst. Reavers howled as red-fletched shafts buried themselves thirstily in flesh.

Nevertheless Moorcock was already demonstrating a larger vocabulary than others, and an interest in the accurate appropriation of technical words. Improvements of style can be seen even within the collection *The Stealer of Souls*, whose first and last stories were written only a year and a half apart. Though his later heroic fantasies are still racy, they become far less awkward, and if they are still ornate, that ornament is well polished and does not burden the reader.[3]

He blocked the thrust of the slim longsword, turned it and chopped with a kind of delicacy at the owner's wrist. Wrist and sword flew into the shadows and the owner staggered back screaming.

More swords now and more cold eyes glittering from the black hoods. Stormbringer sang its peculiar song – half-lament, half-victory shout. Elric's own face was alive with battle-lust and his crimson eyes blazed from his bone-white face as he swung this way and that.

Shouts, curses, the screams of women and the groans of men, steel striking steel, boots on cobbles, the sounds of swords in flesh, of blades scraping bone.

For the most part heroic fantasy, 'sword-and-sorcery' as it is often called, is the most degenerate kind of fantasy fiction. An indiscriminate mix of elements from ancient literature and legend, distilled from an ever more dilute epic tradition, it is imitative, crude, and rarely more than a reiteration of conventions. Predominantly adolescent in appeal, it offers escape to a world where individual will is the most important principle, and no problem is too complicated to be solved with a sword.[4] The purpose of the 'boy-author writing boys' stories' certainly survives in Moorcock's sword-and-sorcery. Elric, 'proud prince of ruins', is a noble outcast adventurer in a corrupt and confusing world. It is not exactly the stuff of wish-fulfilment, but Moorcock was aware of sublimating his own moods through the figure.[5]

> Elric *was* me (the me of 1960–1, anyway) and the mingled qualities of betrayer and betrayed, the bewilderment about life in general, the search for some solution to it all, the expression of this bewilderment in terms of violence, cynicism and the need for revenge, were all characteristics of mine. . . . The story was packed with personal symbols.

Whether or not the form was adequate for what Moorcock wanted to put into it, his new, less virile, more questioning version proved topical, popular and relatively easy for him to write. Later fantasies, especially The History of the Runestaff and The Books of Corum, were produced in the grip of this demand and, though more accomplished, are perhaps less personal and immediate. This was how Moorcock provided the money to keep *NW* going through its continual crises.[6]

> None of the writers was supported by the Arts Council Grant, which David Warburton and subsequently Silvester Stein had put towards printing costs, and I was having to write books to pay them, as well as staff wages, running expenses and so on.

He was forced into recycling his own conventions, spinning out themes and ideas, if his magazine and the work he really believed in were to continue. Few people who know Moorcock only as the prolific fantasist appreciate how hard he worked, or why. His training in the 'fiction factories' of Jet-Ace Logan and Sexton Blake Library enabled him to perform astonishing feats of authorship.[7]

> Most of my fantasy novels and sf novels of the 1965–70 period were written very rapidly to a limited wordage and to a strict self-imposed deadline – 45,000 words on the nail, 3 days per book on the Runestaff books, at 15,000 words per day – they're usually in three sections, even. It maintains plot tensions, by

and large, and probably gives the story an attractively hectic quality, but it doesn't allow you to do all you could with those elements.

Moorcock's reputation still suffers from the fact that so much of his enormous output (fifty books in sixteen years) consists of this commercial trivia. Light, attractive, exotic, even well-written for their genre, his heroic fantasies have sold most and most readers still identify him by them.

There is imaginative substance to them, however. As Moorcock says, 'I decided that I would think up a hero as different as possible from the usual run of S[word] – and – S[orcery] heroes, and use the narrative as a vehicle for my own "serious" ideas.'⁸ The differences between the heroes Moorcock created and 'the usual run' are significant. However naïve, conscious symbolism (rather than unconscious projection) was new: heroes had not formerly suffered an author's own grievances, much less been subject to his frustrations. Their worlds had been predictable, their responses simple, their triumphs inevitable. Moorcock's heroes are not facile juggernauts of self-gratification. They are complex, harrassed, neurotic. Among them only Erekosë and Urlik Skarsol are titans.⁹ Elric is a frail albino, dependent for his vitality on the vampiric broadsword Stormbringer which he is doomed to carry and which, after killing off all his relatives and friends, destroys him. Corum is another slightly built aristocrat, academic and aesthete, forced to take up arms after the massacre of his entire race and his own mutilation by the loss of an eye and a hand. Dorian Hawkmoon, Duke of Köln, begins his saga as a prisoner of war, reduced to a shell.¹⁰

A guard . . . pushed him gently forward. Hawkmoon staggered in spite of the lightness of the pressure, for he had not eaten for almost a week. His brain was at once clouded and abstracted; he was hardly aware of the significance of his circumstances. . . .

The air in the dungeon was fetid, and there was a film of foulness on flagstones and wall. Hawkmoon lay against the wall and then slid gradually to the floor. Whether he fainted or fell asleep, he could not tell, but his eyes closed and oblivion came.

A week before, he had been the Hero of Köln, a champion against the aggressors, a man of grace and sardonic wit, a warrior of skill. Now, as a matter of course, the men of Granbretan had turned him into an animal – an animal with little will to live. A lesser man might have clung grimly to his

humanity, fed from his hatred, schemed escape; but
Hawkmoon, having lost all, wanted nothing. Since we want heroes to suffer as well as act for us, such a scene is
not generically unusual, but Moorcock's insistence on reducing
Hawkmoon so completely before he begins is significant, and comparable with the torments of heroes in other books by Moorcock.
Erekosë, the giant among these invalids, is cursed differently.
Immortal, subject to repeated invocation through time and space to
fight in different bodies the causes of different nations, he is agonised by being able to remember other incarnations. The sequence is
infinite: he is all heroes. He is Urlik, Elric, Corum, and Hawkmoon.
    The Eternal Champion is the central figure and continuing theme
of Moorcock's work. All his books interlock. People and scenes
recur, hypnotically. Occasionally, when their planes intersect, all
the heroes link arms and fight together. It is a useful device to
persuade the reader to keep buying, and the minute attention of the
devoted fan is rewarded by what one critic has called the '*frissons* of
recognition' as familiar characters reappear, translated, disguised,
or anagrammed. But there is a symbolic purpose too, and this is only
the first example of Moorcock's reintegration of 'popular' and
'literary' material. The hero is a representative, not just of a cause or
a people, but of mankind. Eternally reincarnated, he becomes an
aspect of Everyman: life as a campaign, a struggle. Moorcock is the
first sword-and-sorcery writer to build the psychological function of
reading fantasy into the work itself. Enlarged and simplified, the
hero is a symbol of the reader. Hence the stigmata and the sufferings: the hero is as much victim as champion of his struggle.
Moorcock heaps calamity on him, and makes it obtrusively obvious
that the suffering will never end, for there will always be another
battle, another incarnation, another sequel. The hero risks himself
for the cause, but can never win or lose altogether. Risk, unabated,
is the condition of his existence. Nor is it always a meaningful fight.
Moorcock persistently wrenches the hero from his home, his country, his world, his epoch, and even his self, and pitches him into a
foreign battle. Neither Erekosë, Corum, nor Hawkmoon ever gets
the chance to fight on behalf of his own people. Elric leads the
attack on the capital of his own empire.
    Fighting is the principal activity in heroic fantasy, and Moorcock
satisfies that demand. In the story the traditional requirements of
hazard, battle, and escape are supplied, while safe, familiar currents

of emotive attraction and repulsion flow unchecked. Women are beautiful, villains vile, monsters ravening. But the larger issues – 'my "serious" ideas', as Moorcock called them – are new to the form. The conflict Moorcock dramatises is not Good against Evil. Morality is merely a manifestation of a greater dispute: Law against Chaos.[11]

'It is believed by many sorcerers and philosophers that two forces govern the universe – fighting an eternal battle,' Elric replied. 'These two forces are termed Law and Chaos. These are values supposedly set above the qualities men call Good and Evil. The upholders of Chaos state that in such a world as they rule, all things are possible. Opponents of Chaos – those who ally themselves with the forces of Law – say that without Law *nothing* material is possible.

'I, like most sorcerers, stand apart, believing that a balance between the two is the proper state of things.'

This is ironic, of course. No one may 'stand apart' from the eternal battle. The principles are at issue in every move of the human mind, in its own division into rational and irrational faculties. Elric of all people may not abstain: he is beholden to Arioch, a Chaos Lord, for power and protection. And yet he longs for order and the comfort of a reasonable cosmos.[12]

'Does an ultimate God exist – or not? That is what I need to know, Shaarilla, if my life is to have any direction at all. Does Law or Chaos govern our lives? . . . My mind goes out, lying awake at night, searching through the black barrenness of space for something – anything – which will take me to it, warm me, protect me, tell me that there is order in the chaotic tumble of the universe; that it is consistent, this precision of the planets, not simply a brief, bright spark of sanity in an eternity of malevolent anarchy. . . .

'I have weighed the proof, Shaarilla, and believe that anarchy prevails . . .'

Yet is Law so preferable? Law is the condition of Hawkmoon's Kamarg, a happy little feudal enclave under the benevolent monarchy of Count Brass, a sort of armoured Santa Claus. But Law is also the condition of the Dark Empire of Granbretan, in which suppression and slaughter enforce tyrannical edict and a paranoid caste-system prevails. Absolute Chaos is perfect discontinuity, the destruction of identity; but absolute Law is the destruction of individuality, a determined state where spontaneous action is impossible: a plain of fused obsidian, a waste of ice. Which way does human life tend? And which way entropy?

Humanity in all its divergent forms seems to be at the mercy of the Lords of Law and Chaos, but, as in Homeric cosmology, things are no more absolute among the gods. There is frequent mention of a Cosmic Balance – colossal scales of Law and Chaos which swing but always seek equilibrium. The efforts of gods and men are as grains of sand in one pan or the other. The idea seems impartial and reassuring – but there is a Hand holding the Cosmic Balance. Does that determine its vacillations, or is there free will? Elric is a vassal of Chaos, his sword a 'shard of Chaos' itself; yet at the last battle he deserts and fights for Arkyn and the Lords of Law. Is that a bid for freedom, or another chaotic act? In the final book of Corum, *The Sword and the Stallion*, the hero has himself been deified by the tribe who have summoned him out of the past. Yet he understands almost nothing of what is going on, is supervised by two gigantic companions, and achieves little in his own right. His function seems completely determined by legend and expectation: he repeats ritual actions, which produce ritual effects. Then he is suddenly and treacherously murdered.[13]

Around the symbolic figure of the Eternal Champion in his interminable ethical struggle, Moorcock designed a symbolic environment of equal uncertainty: the multiverse. This is his own term for a temporal system derived from the theories of J.B. Dunne which has some standing as a convention in sf, having facilitated plots for many writers from the thirties to the present. Harry Harrison describes it, contrasting it with the more common conception of time like an ever-flowing stream, a single and uni-directional drift:[14]

What if time is more like an ever-branching tree with countless possible futures? If each decision we make affects the future then there must be an infinite number of futures. In the river-of-time concept the future is immutable. If, on the way to work in the morning, we decide to take the bus instead of the tube and are killed in a bus accident, then that death was predestined. But if time is ever-branching then there are two futures – one in which we die in the accident and another in which we live on, having taken the tube. It therefore follows consistently, or at least consistently to a science fiction author's mind, that if there are an infinite set of futures why there must then be an infinite set of pasts as well.

And, Moorcock adds, an infinite set of presents: an infinite set of possible worlds, all the possible results of all the possible outcomes of all decisions and chances. These equivalent universes co-exist, mutually undetectable. One-track time, the 'river' of our own experience, is just one among infinite ramifications, all of which have happened and are true, each in a separate universe. The multiverse is the ultimate paradoxical reconciliation of Law and Chaos. Infinitely divergent time is perfectly logical, allowing for infinite causal developments. On the other hand, since it is infinite, it excludes nothing, and therefore constitutes a chaos of total equivalence.[15]

If the environment is chaotic, infinitely malleable but totally undependable, the onus is on man to provide his own stability. While most other *NW* writers were still discovering the delights and terrors of dismantling the systems of the external world by drugs or other devices and cutting loose in inner space, the three major contributors all agreed that it was the search for a new standpoint that was most important. In *Barefoot in the Head* Aldiss described Colin Charteris's painful, erratic quest for a new philosophy and morality, while Ballard detailed the alienated strategies of T– to invent a cognition appropriate to *The Atrocity Exhibition*. We shall see Moorcock continually reworking the chaotic environment, through the infinite inferno of history in *Breakfast in the Ruins* to the alternative apocalypses of Jerry Cornelius. In his stories of the Dancers at the End of Time Moorcock eventually contrived a utopia where all matter, animate and inanimate, is entirely plastic, obedient to the will.[16] Here the last vestige of heroism consists in identifying something worth wanting. For Jherek Carnelian and Werther de Goethe discomfort is elusive, suffering almost unattainable; yet there remains a certain dignity of self-definition to be won. By confronting Carnelian's infantile innocence with the militant repression of Amelia Underwood the Victorian time-traveller, Moorcock was not attacking his new Eden, only clarifying the necessity for leaving it. This is at the other end of his scale from the sword-and-sorcery. The Eternal Champion is trapped by his unstable, uncaring environment, required to draw his sword but deprived of an adequate reason to do so. Elric's whining demands for authority and order as protection are at odds with his compulsive violence and his cynical pact with chaos. Moorcock would be the first to diagnose the anxiety as adolescent, which is surely why teenagers find these stories so attractive; but the adolescent paradigm is far from irrelevant to the adult reader. By emphasising the symbolic elements of sword-and-sorcery Moorcock was attempting to restore some of its dissipated inheritance from the epic. His confusing, irresponsible, cheap paperback extravaganzas offer at least a cartoon mythology: a vision of the cosmos as the complex interaction of embodied forces, one of which is humanity itself, magnified to heroic proportions yet overwhelmed by the conflict of still larger, incomprehensible powers, with no prospect of a permanent resolution. However, the material of the mythology was primitive, so its correspondence with our own immediate circumstances, our own modern myths, could only be tenuous. As Ballard found with his imaginary disasters, more could be accomplished by bringing the imagery up to date and closer to home.

2 The eternal crucifixion

In 1966 Moorcock published in *NW* a story of his own called 'Behold the Man'.[17] In that form it won the American Nebula Award for the best sf novella of the year. Later he revised and expanded it into a novel of the same title. It is a classic of New Wave sf: physics is thrust into the background and psychology dragged to the fore. The nerves of sex are thrown in patterns on a screen, and problems both material and metaphysical are posed that provoke only unacceptable answers. The progression of the story and the surface appearance of the prose are broken up and scattered. The manner of narration switches between blank innocence and overexposed conscience. In this book Moorcock intensified his investigation of the hero-victim. It is a vivisection, brutal, noisy, and poignant.

Karl Glogauer seems as far from any order of heroism as could be. Hypersensitive son of a Jewish Austrian refugee and an Englishwoman, after their divorce he remains with his mother, alternately smothered and neglected, always lonely. Glogauer is dispossessed of Judaism by an insipid Anglicanism, and suffers more than his share of juvenile sexual trauma. He pours his energies and aspirations into a rapid succession of unsatisfying jobs, enthusiasms and affairs; he wastes his own opportunities with a

lugubrious and masochistic relish. Karl Glogauer is, typically, modern man in search of a soul, and in fact is fascinated by Jung, whose
work promises the possibility of building a whole man out of fragments. So damaged is he, and so exemplary a social casualty, that
Glogauer seems almost a caricature, but Moorcock does not simp-
lify him so much; indeed, there are times when character disappears
and only complexes are left. Glogauer is something more than the
sum of his conditions, but he never discovers what. Repeatedly he
divides things up according to mysticism, then according to
psychology: still he is troubled by an inconvenient remainder.

So far this is the synopsis for a mid-twentieth century novel of
character, grubby, despondent, and altogether ordinary. Glogauer,
however, is given the chance to test a time machine. He sets off for
AD 28, to check on the Crucifixion, hoping to satisfy religious and
rationalist yearnings simultaneously. The machine crashes on
arrival; stranded, he is taken in by John the Baptist and his Essene
community. Glogauer journeys in search of Christ, attracting public
attention by his strange manner and mysterious talk. He finds Mary
and Joseph in Nazareth, and meets Mary's illegitimate son Jesus, a
congenital imbecile dribbling in a corner. Shocked and distracted,
Glogauer stays at a synagogue for a while. He is treated with
reverential caution and people come to stare, believing the madman
may be a prophet.

Glogauer has always wanted to help and heal. He does nothing to
discourage the growth of a cult.[18]

> They followed him now, as he walked away from Nazareth
> towards the Lake of Galilee. He was dressed in the fresh white
> linen robe they had given him and he moved with wonderful
> dignity and grace; a great leader, a great prophet; but though
> they thought he led them, they, in fact, drove him before them.
>
> To those that asked on the way they said, 'He is our messiah.'
> And there were already rumours of many miracles. . . . When
> he saw the sick, he pitied them and tried to do what he could
> because they expected something of him. Many he could do
> nothing for, but others, obviously with easily remediable
> psychosomatic conditions, he could help. They believed in his
> power more strongly than they believed in their sickness. So he
> cured them.

For the first time in his life Glogauer finds happiness and success, by
recreating the life of the Christ he remembers from scripture. Most

of it comes naturally to one with his sense of mysticism and persecu-
tion.[19]
I have done all that I could think of to do. I have worked
miracles, I have preached, I have chosen my disciples. But all
this has been easy, because I have been what the people
demanded. I am their creation.
He acts the part by the book, confident time will obscure his few
lapses, such as requesting a puzzled Judas to call the Roman militia:
'There had been no other way to organize it. He did not think it
would matter. The chroniclers would rearrange it.'[20] And so he is
crucified and dies. Doctors steal his corpse to dissect, looking for
superhuman properties. Disappointed, they dispose of it.

Behold the Man, which has drawn both acclaim and outrage from
readers who profess Christianity, is itself a cross, between a traditional sf puzzle of temporal paradox and a preoccupation of contemporary fiction. The paradox, principally concerned with a traveller to the past, is whether he can 'change history' or whether he has
'always' been there, in his own past, and his actions are therefore
'already' determined and accord with history as he knows it. Time-
travel writers have tailored the fourth dimension to the needs of
their plots: elastic or rigid, a single channel or an ever branching
tree. Contemporary psychological fiction, with its intricate inspection of personality and neurosis, has developed an image of character baffled and damaged by circumstances. Moorcock picked up the
deterministic bias in each of these conventions and brought them
together. Glogauer chooses to become Christ because the messiah
role, complex of saviour and scapegoat, appeals to him. He knows
the part; he could deliberately avoid it, but does not. But in another
sense, he is the victim of his followers, as he claims; he is the puppet
of the people, and at the mercy of his own weaknesses, his urge to
please everybody by imitating what they like and meeting their
needs. 'Trapped. Sinking. Can't be myself. Made into what other
people expect. Is that everyone's fate? Were the great individualists
the products of their friends who wanted a great individualist as a
friend?'[21] Over and above these inner ambiguities is the possibility
that time is rigid, ordered, inflexible; in which case Glogauer is
compelled to become Christ and Christ has always been Glogauer,
rearranged by the chroniclers.

Though *Behold* was a departure from sword-and-sorcery, it
allowed Moorcock to clarify the themes of his heroic fantasies.

Christ, the ultimate hero, is also the ultimate victim, the Lamb brought to the slaughter.[22]

'In fact, it wasn't an interest in Christ that led me to the subject, but an interest in certain kinds of impulse in the human psyche. . . . I thought if I was going to describe a man with a Messiah complex I might as well invoke the Messiah.'

By using the conventions of sf Moorcock was able to recreate the Messiah in the image of modern man. Christ is Glogauer, who is a walking textbook of psychological disasters. His mental agonies, like Elric's, are still very much the large aches of adolescence, but Moorcock shows them in operation, motivating Glogauer's actions and passions. The neuroses of Elric, Corum and Hawkmoon were too rarely demonstrated, too often a matter of authorial assertion, but Glogauer is opened up and exhibited. It has been standard practice since the mid-century for the author to invade the intimacy of his characters. Moorcock assumes the right and wades in. Glogauer is spotlit at moments of exquisite embarrassment and pain; in bed; at prayer; during sex; during masturbation; during domestic rows. Moorcock delves into his unconscious and exposes his private symbolism. The inner monologues of this agonised introvert are even more self-obsessed than his speech.

Translated in time to lead a nation to which he does not belong, Glogauer ostensibly becomes someone else: the continuing tragedy of the Eternal Champion. But it is significant that being Christ represents self-fulfilment for Glogauer. Whether or not AD 28 is the year of his destiny, it certainly suits him.[23]

'Time and identity,' Headington used to say enthusiastically, 'the two great mysteries. Angles, curves, soft and hard perspectives. What do we see? What are we that we see in a particular way? What could we be or have been? All the twists and turns of time. I loathe those ideas that insist on treating time as a dimension of space, describing it in spacial metaphors. No wonder they get nowhere. Time is nothing to do with space – it is to do with the psyche.'

Time and identity: Moorcock's two great themes, perhaps the great themes of all New Wave sf. Sir James Headington, eccentric British inventor of the time machine, is himself a stock figure from traditional sf, but here repudiates traditional policy on time and identity. 'Spacial metaphors' are commonplace. Sf has its time-*travellers*, but we all speak of *stages* and *points* in time. Traditionally chrononauts treat their vehicles just as astronauts do, getting in and being transported to another century. Moorcock has made comedy of this presumption. In some stories Jerry Cornelius's time machine is an old bicycle; his sister Catherine and Una Persson share time-trips in a speedboat. Leafing idly through a copy of *Vogue* in 1933, Una says,[24]

> 'I was thinking of leaving tomorrow.'
> 'So was I. For 1910?'
> 'Or thereabouts.' Una studied an advertisement for riding
> boots. 'I thought 1917. Would that suit you?'
> 'Fine. If you could drop me off in London.'
> 'Of course.'

The parodic tone reminds us of the preferred viewpoint of the new writers. Ballard has blamed sf for 'treating time like a sort of glorified scenic railway.'[25] Time is, they insist, a dimension of inner space. Stranded in the 'wrong' time, Glogauer is more at home among the Essenes than he was among the English.[26]

> He reached the river and bent to wash his face, seeing his
> reflection in the dark water. His hair was long, black and
> matted, his beard covering the whole of his lower face, his eyes
> slightly mad. There was nothing at all to distinguish him from
> any one of the Essenes, save his thoughts. And the thoughts of
> many of the Essenes were strange enough. Were they any
> wilder than his belief that he was a visitor from a future
> century?

Behold the Man is a cross between science fictional and mainstream literary investigations of time and identity, Wells and Anderson meeting Joyce and Proust sideways on. At the intersection Moorcock casually tosses up a startling symbol: the time machine itself. Not a bicycle or a police box, but 'a sphere of milky fluid',[27] it is deliberately and blatantly a mechanical womb. Karl Glogauer is born in AD 28 no less than in AD 1940; nor can he return. The machine that is a precondition of the sf story becomes the womb that is a precondition of the human story.

The book is also a cross between religion and psychology, vertical and horizontal approaches that cut the human figure like the crosshairs of a rifle sight. The title, *Behold the Man*, refers to God incarnate ('Ecce Homo') while drawing attention to the human vessel in all its frailty. At the centre of the grand design of Christianity, spread for 2,000 years across the world, is a solitary man –

134/The works of Michael Moorcock

perhaps only that. Perhaps all the rest is mass hysteria and the multiplication of neuroses just like Glogauer's. Moorcock once said, 'I write about heroes, tragic but still heroes, so I contradict that by leading always to final statements where gods and heroes and grand designs are shown to be pointless.'[28] Its fixated quality makes *Behold* untypical of Moorcock's work, which tends to portray instability, the multiverse, the fluid quality of the heroic fantasies. The hero of this book is pinned down – literally – for our inspection. Glogauer's self-imposed mission in the past is to close down the alternatives, the ramifications of history which could result if the central figure of the grand design were not the Son of God but a slobbering idiot. He undertakes to follow a single path through history – that of the Biblical legend – as closely as possible. As hero, he is completely the creation of time. He submits to the conditions of the past as he never could to those of the present. Glogauer is a pawn of twentieth-century Chaos, national, social, and psychological, who makes a deal with Law and becomes a hero.

In *Breakfast in the Ruins* Moorcock gives him back to Chaos.[29] This book barely glances at *Behold*; it is not so much a sequel as a catalogue of alternative crucifixions. An unpublished prologue explains Glogauer's reappearance.

Imagine that such people exist: those who are, by virtue of magic, a machine, madness, unable to remain for long in one period of time and are consequently shunted here and there through the decades, constantly desiring to settle in one particular age but, by the will of the Gods (or some Higher Science or their Mental Aberration), are allowed no such rest.

Lobkowitz said something that cannot be repeated too often: 'The struggle is endless. The most we can hope for are moments of tranquillity in the midst of the conflict.'

Karl Glogauer, eternal champion (or surrogate) of Man in his search for Harmony and (if the two are not the same) Freedom from Fear, marches on. He is used to being crucified, which is something he has over most of us.

Karl Glogauer has died on the cross, aged about thirty-two. Aged about thirty-two, he is back, resurrected for a new adventure. We find him relaxing in the Famous Roof Garden of Derry and Toms, Moorcock's urban Eden, a place for moments of tranquillity between bouts of acting and suffering in the world below. But Eden has its tempter: an anonymous negro who claims Glogauer's attention and takes him to a hotel where they spend the night playing out perverse rituals of dominance and submission. At first Glogauer is the victim. The black man patronises him, promising him freedom, money, influence, a new life. Glogauer hovers between petulance and acquiescence, disgust and desire. He has a migraine, he falls asleep. On waking he assumes a new confidence and asserts himself. The black man's serenity crumbles. Glogauer had earlier permitted himself to be painted black. Now the dye seems permanent, while the black man is growing paler. His eyes turn blue; he becomes depressed; he loses weight. At last Glogauer, now a grinning, finger-popping blackamoor, bounces out into the new day to buy himself a suit.

This fantasia of exploitation and liberation gives the book its main narrative thread, but between the first and last chapters occupies only small sections of the text. The rest is divided into seventeen time-trips – brief, densely written stories of Glogauer in other incarnations, beginning as a child in 1871 and ending up derelict, at fifty-one, in the ruins of 1990 – and a series of problems under the title 'What Would You Do?'. Based on the weekly 'posers' Moorcock once wrote for the comic *Boys' World*, these do not test quick-wittedness, but present distressing challenges to moral and intellectual preconceptions. No answers are given.[30]

You are a priest, devoutly religious, you are made miserable by the very idea of violence. . . . One morning you are cutting bread in the small hall attached to your church. You hear screams and oaths coming from the church itself. You hurry into the church, the knife still in your hand.

The soldier of the enemy currently occupying your country is in the act of raping a girl of about thirteen. . . . You shout, but the soldier pays no attention. . . .

If you kill the soldier with your knife it will save the young girl from being hurt any further. It might even save her life. . . .

If you merely knock him out – even if that's possible – he will almost certainly take horrible reprisals on you, your church and its congregation. It has happened before, in other towns. Yet you want to save the girl.

What would you do?

The problems range from the nightmarishly improbable to the sordidly familiar. Alongside them the alternative lives and times of Karl Glogauer offer slices from specified historical milieux. The characters and their environments are vividly depicted, stating or implying a continuity ('the struggle is endless') which the posers obscure with their demand for personal and immediate decisions. The stories show contexts for similar moral choices, demonstrating that decisions are not made in isolation.

Morality is often an automatic function of social status. Karl, son of a German ship-broker in Shanghai in 1932, is quite insulated from the street riot, by his culture as well as by the body of the Rolls. No one wants or expects him to involve himself, neither the Japanese police, the Chinese boy they are clubbing, Mrs Glogauer, her impassive chauffeur, nor Karl himself. He feels the smallest nudge of discomfort. As he winds his window up we can either condemn him for not making an idealistic, heroic stand, or feel fatalistically, as the policeman does, that 'such things happen in even the best-run city'.[31] Though corrupt and inhumane, that is the realistic view. To dive from the car might be the kind of glorious futile gesture that romance is made of, but life is run differently. The fate of Karl's brother, a rebel against the Spanish in Havana in 1898, reminds us what always happens to protesters. In that incarnation Karl, aged ten, responded by trotting off to join the rebels too. Aged sixteen, he has grown wiser. Or more callous. Or both.

In *Breakfast* Moorcock brings home the chaos-visions of the heroic fantasies. He confronts us with the infinite productions of time, with our own history as a colonial power, dumping problem after problem squarely in our laps. Meanwhile he projects the example of Karl Glogauer and the wretched choices open to him. His happiness, his 'moments of tranquillity', are the occasional results of compromise with the catastrophe, brutalising himself and others. His career is a moral vortex that sucks him into inevitable, soul-destroying action or flings him out to bob in helpless uncertainty around the edge, neither acting nor refraining. Moorcock reduces his hero-victim to a tiny creature who is damned whichever way he hops, and damned if he doesn't. Tripping through time and identity, Glogauer multiplies his story. He is the Eternal Champion, who is Everyman, who is us. What would we do? *Breakfast* overpowers the reader with a kind of pornography of despair: Moorcock once more exploits his expertise with affective techniques of popular fiction. Yet the writing is anything but crude.

Karl, a black marketeer in Calcutta in 1911, brings a consignment of hemp to a sailor named Marsden in a church: 'One hundred poundsworth, as promised.' Marsden says he has only four pounds ten on him; he snatches the bag and runs off.[32]

Karl sat down in one of the pews. If Marsden really did have four pounds ten, then at least Karl would have lost nothing on the deal. He would return the bag to his friend in Armenian Street and wait until he had a proper customer.

A short while later the young Sikh from Delhi came into the church. He was holding the bag. The Sikh had been staying at the Imperial Indian Hotel and had had trouble paying his bill. The manager of the restaurant had told Karl this and Karl had told the Sikh how he could earn the money to pay for his room. The Sikh evidently did not relish working for Karl but he had no choice. He handed Karl the bag.

'Did he have enough money?' Karl asked.

The Sikh nodded. 'Is that all?'

'Excellent,' Karl told him. 'Where is Marsden now?'

'In the tank. He was probably drunk and fell in there. It happens to sailors, I hear, in Calcutta. He may drown. He may not.'

'Thank you,' said Karl.

He waited for the Sikh to leave and remained in the church for some minutes, watching the mosquitoes dancing in the light from the windows. He was a little disappointed, he had to admit.

Extremely removed from his adjectival fantastic style, this flat, uncommenting tone permits Moorcock a valuable duplicity of effect. He presents a sensational scene unsensationally: carefully withholding and feeding information, he persuades us to interpret for ourselves, bringing our own moral and emotional dispositions to the events. These stories involve us in complexities they leave unstated. The three parties in this little triangular incident allow for any number of sympathies and condemnations, identifications and rejections. Find the criminal. Conversely, find the innocent. This Karl Glogauer is twelve years old. Does that make a difference? Should it? And so on.

Yet while it spins, invisibly, the intricate moral web, the prose also simplifies the scene, laying it calmly and reasonably in the perspective of Karl's own understanding. A Buddhist resignation prevails. 'It happens to sailors, I hear, in Calcutta'; it has happened before, in other towns. Such things happen in even the best-run city.

Karl and the Sikh detach themselves from their own actions and achieve passivity; yet we hear the echoes and know that their disclaimer is an ironic reflection of our own refusals of responsibility. Like Kipling and Forster Moorcock portrays an India of corrupt serenity: a direct challenge to the British reader. A prospective synopsis of *Breakfast* (provisionally titled *The Fear Syndrome*) announced, 'this is a novel about the nature of fear and attempts to show, in an historical perspective, the origins of certain modern ills.' The finished book is perhaps better than the projected one, its subject broader and its method, though still analytical, far from explanatory. The struggle is endless, its origins everywhere and nowhere. The new title is more effective: it indicates survival, the ability to feed amid destruction, the sustenance of life on the morning after the disaster. More ambiguous than the repulsive apocalyptic meals in Ballard (Laing's roast Alsatian in *High-Rise*, for example), it suggests both carrion and cornflakes, man brutalised by catastrophe and elegant despite it – Karl Glogauer's cannibalism in 1990 on the one hand, and on the other Jherek Carnelian's oysters and meringues on a beach of powdered bone at the End of Time.[33]

In his notebook for *The English Assassin* Moorcock made a journal entry.[34]

Progress: NIL.

Am working out broader version of similar theme in 'Fear Syndrome' – but even that's taking time. The effort involved in writing – the depression which is a result of thinking about the themes – makes it all very hard going – and financially barely worthwhile. In a way, this is easier than 'F.S.' in that I can put my heart and soul into it whereas 'F.S.' is merely an opportunity for various moral and intellectual – and sometimes technical – exercises. I've done no real work since January on anything.

Hope to make a run at 'F.S.' and get it over by July 1st. And stop taking on books just because a publisher asks for one. My mistake in the past was to do outlines for books on demand – and then find the outline ridiculous. . . . I'm slowing down so much, these days, it's at once frightening and reassuring.

Though his career is too complicated to divide convincingly into periods, this is a useful point to think of Moorcock 'slowing down', writing less for his market than his muse, concentrating his ideas rather than attenuating them through strings of sequels. The multitude of working drafts for the first chapter of *Breakfast* is evidence of a conscientious stylistic overhaul, a remarkable record of the interaction of inspiration with patience. If *The Jewel in the Skull* was ready in three days, *The Condition of Muzak* took something like eight years from conception. As for the author's sense of dejection and uneconomical effort in writing *Breakfast*, it is true that the themes and techniques of the book make it depressing to read. It is commercially unappetising, and Glogauer is the least attractive of his heroes.

In *Heroes*, her study of the phenomenon, Jenni Calder observes a disruption of heroic tradition in our time. She traces this back to the First World War, when the chivalric image was shot to pieces; soon afterwards heroes began to seem more of an escape than an inspiration. Modern art has tended to avoid the hero, consigning him to the realm of sport, romantic film, rock music and the popular press. 'His most notable twentieth-century function appeared to be to entice us away from reality, rather than to confront all its difficulties. Intellectually, the hero was suspect.'[35] In modern literature two shadow figures emerged: the anti-hero, in whose hunched form the death of the social hero is perfectly expressed, and the angry young man, whose righteousness is born of disillusionment, not idealism, and who resists elevation to heroic status through his passionate concern for the everyday. We no longer agree on what is admirable. 'The true contemporary hero is hard to find. Like society, the hero sometimes appears to be fragmented.'[36]

The highly personal revaluation that Moorcock began by creating Elric turned into a ruthless assault on the hero. The romantic, doomed Champion stood revealed as a fetish by which mankind glorifies its own vicious habits and ducks responsibility. Moorcock chased him down through the anti-hero Glogauer, crucified him, and scattered him in the million petty, dirty struggles of *Breakfast in the Ruins*. Yet the hero-image persisted. People continued to buy heroes and make their own. A direct frontal attack would never dissuade them. So Moorcock turned the image about and used it to dramatise and examine the minds of the people themselves, their need for heroes, and the whole continual catastrophe. Expert at the type by now, he made a popular 'true contemporary hero' – Jerry Cornelius.

3 The fragmented hero

At a symposium on the novel in 1969 Leslie Fiedler (paraphrasing Walt Whitman) urged, 'We must cancel out those long overdue accounts to Greece and Rome. . . . The new mythology must come out of pop songs and comic books.'[37] By that date Michael Moorcock was well into the job.[38]

> Jerry Cornelius began as a version of Elric of Melniboné when, in late 1964, I was casting around for a means of dealing with what I regarded as the 'hot' subject matter of my own time – stuff associated with scientific advance, social change, the mythology of the mid-twentieth century. Since Elric was a 'myth' character I decided to try to write his first stories in twentieth century terms. *The Final Programme* was written, in first draft, in about ten days in January 1965. It began as a kind of rewrite of the first two Elric stories, *The Dreaming City* and *While the Gods Laugh*. . . . I borrowed as much from the Hammett school of thriller fiction as I borrowed from SF and I think I found my own 'voice' as a writer.

The Eternal Champion slipped neatly into his new environment. The modern city seemed no less fantastic than any of the improbable, glittering worlds he had been used to – indeed, from Moorcock's viewpoint it could be seen as a model from which their landscapes had been drawn.[39]

> Jerry . . . got into his Cadillac . . . and drove through the weary streets of London's southernmost suburbs, heading for the important centre: the hot, bubbling core of the city.
>
> He parked the car in the Shaftesbury Avenue garage he used and, stepping light, sallied out into his natural habitat.
>
> It was a world ruled these days by the gun, the guitar, and the needle, sexier than sex, where the good right hand had become the male's primary sexual organ, which was just as well considering the world population had been due to double before the year 2000.
>
> This wasn't the world Jerry had always known, he felt, but he could only vaguely remember a different one, so similar to this that it was immaterial which was which. The dates checked roughly, that was all he cared about, and the mood was much the same.

In the mid-1960s England rode a boom of wealth and optimism.

'Pop' arts and industries peaked while the mass media and the Tourism Board sold images of 'Swinging London', a giant urban playground. Casualness was the fashionable virtue. Sex and drugs and rock and roll formed a powerful combination that masked a threatening vein of violence. The heroes of the young were not out of old moulds. Contradictory ideals were proclaimed. Moorcock, sensing an imaginative liberation in the air, but disapproving of most of the rest, produced Jeremiah Cornelius as an ironic comment.

The Final Programme, which spotlights him in the ascendant, notes his initials and hints at a label: Messiah to the Age of Science. Yet Cornelius does not wholly accept the role. He has abandoned his Nobel prize-winning theses, including 'the unified field theory that he had eventually destroyed, save for the single copy on a shelf somewhere in the Vatican Library.'[40] The coincidence of success and iconoclasm is important. Cornelius possesses with one hand what he throws away with the other: science, religion, money, fame, technology. His image unites the appeals of conformity and anarchy, elevated to an impossibly glamorous height. His life and personality are heterogeneous and unconfined. Moorcock's experience of writing in popular heroic modes, together with his keen feel for the critical temperature of the moment, enabled him to synthesise a perfect hero. Cornelius can go anywhere, do anything; and Moorcock implies that he has been and done most of them already. A reviewer, Neil Spencer, analysed some of the mix.[41]

Cornelius, for the uninitiated, is Moorcock's hero supreme. The son of the unholy union between a brilliant scientist of aristocratic European ancestry and a crass Cockney girl from the seediest streets of London's Ladbroke Grove, Cornelius is an unlikely cross between Mick Jagger, James Bond and Flash Gordon.

He is beautiful, ageless, bisexual, multi-talented, murderous, drug-sodden, an eternal adolescent who is privy to the secrets of time travel and semi-immortality. He is both ruthless and sentimental, equally at home in a squalid crash-pad or the exotic palace of an obscure Indonesian potentate.

This monster was calculated to fascinate the new audience. He embodies the principle of experience without commitment, of living in all directions at once, and his air of success seemed to verify the' young assumption that the world was theirs, to eat now or take away. Cornelius's enigmatic authority, his irreverence for convention, and his casual way with science, society and money, not to mention time and space, make him a paragon of self-determination: though he resembles James Bond or Batman, he serves no law. For much of *The Final Programme* he initiates action of the 'secret agent' kind popular in mid-1960s fiction: he conducts a band of mercenaries into his brother's Normandy château, leads the expedition to discover the secret Newman manuscript, infiltrates a research lab and assassinates Dr Baxter to steal the last vital documents for the Programme itself, and finally earns an absurd apotheosis as one half of a hermaphrodite superbeing. He lives in a private fortress in Holland Park with three very expensive cars, any amount of clothing and hi-fi equipment, and vast stores of food and petrol (none of which he uses much); he flies a helicopter, maintaining fuel caches all across Europe, rents a permanent suite at the Angkor Hilton, and plays a custom-built, jewel-encrusted guitar. And so on, and so on.

But Cornelius is also an innocent, co-opted for the apocalypse by the rapacious Miss Brunner, the Programmer herself, and forced into his messianic role with increasing reluctance. His original response to omens of the world's end had been to retire to his mansion and sit it out. He tells her,[42]

'I thought I'd remain comparatively static while my surroundings were in a state of flux. But I appear to have been caught in the flux. It's just no good making preparations. On the other hand, I don't like being aimless while the world is aimless, and my old aim is gone.'
'What was that?'
'To survive.'

From the first it is made clear that Cornelius's motivations are altogether selfish. He has no more desire to lead or fight than the Eternal Champion ever had. He wants only security, an enclave cushioned from the general catastrophe. He escapes from Miss Brunner's project and hides for a year in bourgeois domestic comfort in Sweden, where such retreats are still possible, but she eventually drags him back. He is forbidden immunity from his environment. Like Elric's and Corum's, his actions repeatedly produce unpleasant reactions. When he attacks the château, wishing to destroy his past and reclaim microfilm of his father's scientific discoveries from his villainous brother Frank, he accidentally kills his sister and only love, Catherine.

He learns from Miss Brunner her trick of stealing souls: feeding directly on the energies of others – an exquisite vampirism which leaves nothing but a pile of clothes. Finally, fully compromised and absorbed into Cornelius Brunner, the hermaphrodite 'all-purpose human being', he leads the entire population of Europe on a pilgrimage into the sea. As well as repeating his previous observations of the dangers of hero-worship, the end of the story shows Moorcock's clear appreciation of the self-destructive trend of the riotous counter-culture. This death-orgasm of insurrection, technology and sex is Cornelius and Miss Brunner's cataclysmic resolution of the creeping decline they detect beneath the apparent exuberance of the decade. Cornelius robs a bank of £2 million with impunity, confident that the rate of inflation is so high that the law can no longer find it worthwhile to protect money. He becomes uncomfortable only when the decay comes closer to home and the crowd in his favourite club turns into a torpid 'pyramid of flesh', the temperature drops, and the music slows down. Mr Crookshank, one of Miss Brunner's team, comments,[43]

'Oh, we are living in an odd kind of limbo, aren't we? . . . Society hovers on the point of collapse, eh? Chaos threatens!'. . .

'Maybe the West has got to the quasar stage – you know, 3C286 or whatever it is.' Miss Brunner spoke rapidly. . . .

'What's that?' . . .

'Quasars are stellar objects,' Jerry said, 'so massive that they've reached the stage of gravitational collapse.' . . .

'The more massive, in terms of population, an area becomes, the more mass it attracts, until the state of gravitational collapse is reached,' Miss Brunner explained.

'Entropy, I think, Mr Crookshank, rather than chaos,' Jerry explained kindly.

The hyperbolic suggestion that the heat-death of the world is imminent is merely a variation on one of the first principles of science fiction. On the other hand, the absurd reduction of a scientific theory and its popularisation as a metaphor is a new and surprising contribution to social fiction – and a process which parodies degradations that Moorcock sees operating in society at large.

When the second Cornelius book, *A Cure for Cancer*, opens, the dislocation of the world is advanced.[44]

Jerry . . . caught up with the newspapers.

It seemed that Israel, having annexed Turkey, Greece and Bulgaria, was putting it about that Rumania and Albania were threatening her security. U.S. President Teddy 'Angel Face' Paolozzi had increased the number of military advisors sent to Europe to three million, They were under the command of General Ulysses Washington Cumberland whose mission was to keep order in Europe and seek out 'certain fifth column elements'. The British parliament, both government and opposition, had been arrested as their jumbo Trident was about to take off for Gibraltar. President Paolozzi had sent a diplomatic note to Israel that read *Stay off our turf, Israel, or else*. A riot in Prague had received universal censure from the European press. 'Uncool' was the *Daily Mirror* verdict. Bubonic plague remained unchecked in Berlin and Lubeck.

Jerry stopped reading. Evidently, there was little news of any relevance.

In some aspects this book is an alternative to *Programme* – for example, there is still a Europe to be dislocated. In others it is a sequel, capturing the change of Zeitgeist as the 1960s gave way to the 1970s. Its picture is less frivolous and youthful; the decadence is more pronounced, the disasters more grim. Superficially farcical, it continually erupts into unpleasantness. Wearing a white silk turban and a panda-skin coat, Cornelius drives his amphibious Rolls Royce beneath the American pirate radio ships blockading the Channel, dodging their depth-charges.

Miss Brunner and Cornelius are separate beings again. She is now a man, commandant of an American concentration camp; he has turned black like Glogauer in *Breakfast*, with white hair and a suit of midnight blue – a photographic negative of his previous appearance. Putting the romantic ideals of escape and heroism behind him, Cornelius now works for an organisation operating a 'transmogrification service'. This helps people discover and maintain their 'real identities' in the conflicting tensions of the dissolution of their times. His principal opponent is the obese Bishop Beesley who, having turned to journalism after the liquidation of the Church, now leads a rival operation to counteract this spread of anarchic individuality and restore some previous form of order.

As we might expect by now, Cornelius's main weapon is an ambiguous and thoroughly doubtful asset. This is his 'black box', which is a key to the multiverse.[45]

'The machine creates a "possibility" field opening gateways into dozens of alternate versions of Earth. . . . The machine makes all things possible because it gives entry into all possible worlds. . . . On the other hand it requires a lot of energy to do this and, even while it is working to offer so much possibility, it is also diffusing everything further – accelerating the rate of Entropy. Beesley wants one world, one truth, one life with a place for everything and everything in its place. Beesley has a tidy mind. In an effort to stop the diffusion . . . he puts the machine into reverse. He slows the rate of entropy right down – therefore slowing the rate of time. . . . My mission is the elimination of time and death and the restoration of identity.'

'But what are you fighting?'

Jerry's swollen lips smiled sadly. 'The human condition – the odds.'

What Cornelius does not mention here is that the black box's power source is DNA. Like Miss Brunner in *Programme* and Elric's sword Stormbringer, it fuels itself by sucking human beings in whole. As Glogauer demonstrated in *Breakfast in the Ruins*, there is no way to secure one's own identity except by exploiting others.

Frank Cornelius, mysteriously resurrected, is now a major under General Cumberland. When Beesley steals the black box and Cumberland carries out his programme of reducing England to order with bombs and napalm, Jerry Cornelius abandons his mission to devote himself to Catherine, kept on ice since he shot her in *Programme*. In a world slowed down by Beesley's interference, he gets back the box, refuels it with the help of Capt. Brunner, and restores his sister to life for a short while. They make love in the snow before she relapses. The book ends with Jerry aware that he is pregnant with their baby.

A Cure for Cancer is a book of extravagant perversity. The complexities and obscurities of the plot are deliberately unclarified; changes of colour and sex, transvestism and incest abound. Moorcock, satirising what he has called 'the general kinkiness of present day thinking and imagery',[46] resorts to extreme techniques. His preliminary 'Note to the reader' warns: 'THIS BOOK HAS AN UNCONVENTIONAL STRUCTURE.' Divided up into numbered sections with baffling titles taken from popular magazines, interrupted and cut with quotations, adverts and reprinted trivia of all kinds, it makes confusing reading –

alternately speedy and laconic, but always impenetrable. In-jokes and opaque innuendo predominate, especially in conversation. Conventionally dialogue is a place where the author can reveal things, but in this book we might as well not be overhearing.

Cornelius, calling himself Aserinsky, visits a library and speaks with a Mr Beale.[47]

'Which book? We have fifty thousand.' Beale's sibilant voice took a long time to reach Jerry.

'The names,' murmured Jerry. . . .

'London, the city of dolorous mist,' hissed Beale. 'The names, Mr Cornelius, yes; the confidential names. You say he's called S?'

'According to Okharna.'

'Nothing else?'

'Something in code about a mouse strangler of Munich, I'm told. But that could be a reference to an anagram of Mephistophilis. . . .'

'Catching, Mr Aserinsky, hmph,' Beale said, as if in reply to a question, and began to cough.

'Not in my book, general. It's oh, oh, five and wild skidoo.'

'Unused – unusual. . . .' Beale began, puzzled, as well he might be.

And so might we. Defending such apparent nonsense is difficult, but in a later note, glossing a similarly cryptic exchange in *The Condition of Muzak*, Moorcock justifies the style somewhat.[48]

The whimsicalities to be found in all the books are, in fact, not random, not mere conceits, but make internal references. That is to say, while I strive for the effect of randomness on one level, the effect is achieved by a tightly controlled system of internal reference, puns, ironies, logic-jumps which no single reader may fairly be expected to follow . . . and should give the effect, among others, of time in a state of flux, men in a state of introverted confusion, close to fugue, and so on. But its internal logic is straightforward: the two characters know exactly what they are talking about. To 'explain' all this, to editorialise, would be to break the mood, break the dramatic tensions, and ruin the effect I was trying to achieve. The apparent obscurity should not confuse the reader because the narrative should be moving so rapidly that he shouldn't care if he doesn't understand every reference.

The device is especially appropriate to *Cancer*, a book wholly bound up with 'introverted confusion' and the private response. Nothing is obvious or even universally true in this world; subjectivity rules a cast whose identities are in varying conditions of overgrowth and decay – the Cancer of the title. The text facetiously imitates the disease. The black box is lost in the 'possibility field' of its own creation. Moorcock's perversity of style is not only an example of the 'kinkiness' but an examination of it too. The image of cancer is the same as Miss Brunner's idea of 'the quasar stage' in *Programme*: overdevelopment resulting in collapse. The modern city is disintegrating into an amorphous assortment of private schemes, private worlds. 'Kinkiness' is the deliberate pursuit of the perverse, the election of private fantasy over normality. Though this produced the richly varied society of the 1960s, Moorcock was already looking through the differences and seeing entropy, tending to an extreme undifferentiated state. Law and Chaos are more subtle than Elric believed, as Cornelius realises in a story by another author, James Sallis. 'The chaos, he knew, was apparent. An illusion. The real problem was over-organisation, entropy, the seeming confusion only the final struggle against its imposition. Fact and metaphysics were, finally, the same thing.'[49] Cornelius promotes a chaos of anarchic individualism in the hope of curing the cancer, but his black box advances the entropic declivity. His career is a clear case of the disease – over-ambition followed by defeat. Reluctantly involved at first, he hopes to save the world. When the world proves already well out of hand, he reduces his objective to the salvation of as many souls as possible. Then he abandons that to concentrate on Catherine.

In the third volume, *The English Assassin*, he is even further in retreat. He spends almost the entire book inert, in a peculiar state of catatonia.[50]

'How long was he down there?'

The biologist shrugged and scratched behind his left ear with his right hand. 'A year? The brain has been flushed. The flesh, however, is surprisingly fresh. Like a baby's, general.' . . .

Jerry Cornelius was all but insensate. His eyes glowed, his lips curled back from his stained teeth, his fingers curved like claws and he still stank of brine and tar. Even after they had cleaned him up . . . he had continued to glare at them silently, like a mad gull.

Washed up, after his prolonged submersion, on the beach at Tintagel, he is salvaged by Una Persson and lugged round from faction to faction, traded for arms or political advantage by the splinter-groups of a disintegrating world. This is the dormant stage of the heroic life-cycle, when personality goes under and everyone is free to attribute whatever meaning they like to the helpless corpse. Cornelius is an absurd Christ-surrogate, a new King Arthur.[51]

'They have a legend, you see, that when you awake peace and beauty will come again to the world.'

'Well, it's very kind of them. I didn't think I was that popular.'

'You wouldn't be, if it wasn't for the fact that for the past decade you've done absolutely nothing. You're the stuff of which hero's [sic] are made, Jerry my boy!'

The English Assassin introduces the rest of the characters in the Cornelius entourage: Major Nye, Prinz Lobkowitz, Una Persson, Sebastian Auchinek, Colonel Pyat, and the indomitable Mrs Cornelius, Jerry's dreadful mother. Boldly but sensitively drawn, they provide the only narrative continuum in a book which moves unperturbed over great flaws of time and space. This is the fruition of the scenic 'technical exercises' in *Breakfast in the Ruins*. The action shifts from meticulously done Victorian and Edwardiana to an alternative 1970s, a future constructed according to the dreams and fears of those reigns. It is sunset for the Empire, a conservative utopia of steam-cars, airships, the Crystal Palace, and the designs of Mucha and Mackintosh. Neither World War has ever happened, but imperialism is being baffled and broken at last by anarchists at home and insurrection in the colonies.[52] Appropriately for Cornelius's condition, Moorcock is more concerned here with the past than the present or future, and with the meaning and the debris of history.[53]

In his speech to the Court of Appeal, shortly before his exile, Prinz Lobkowitz said:

'In our houses, our villages, our towns, our cities, our nations, time passes. Each individual will be involved, directly or indirectly, in some 150 years of history – before birth, during life, and after his death. Part of this experience will be received from parents or other adults, from old men; part will be received from his own life, and his experience will, in time, become part of his children's experience. Thus a generation is 150 years. That is how long we live. . . . Such knowledge is apt to make a man like me feel that it is useless to try to alter the nature of his society.'

Assassin reinforces the tyranny of generational continuity, the pressure of time on identity that *Programme* modishly pretended to escape, and that *Breakfast* reaffirmed. Within this historical determinism the main characters experience temporal alienation, feel trapped or adrift in time. Images of helplessness and infancy recur. Epigraphs and news items record deaths (and miraculous recoveries) of children, and memoirs of how childhood in wartime might affect an adult of the 1960s and 1970s.

Other inserts, a series called 'The Alternative Apocalypse', show Cornelius at large in the midst of the conflict, in guerilla skirmishes at Grasmere, crucified at sea, watching the world end from the ruins of Ladbroke Grove. Each is somehow distanced in effect and atmosphere, mysterious and dreamlike.

There is no similarity between the style of this book and the one before. Where *A Cure for Cancer* is arch, nervous, fragmented, *The English Assassin* is relaxed, studied, even graceful. The description of reality in flux is less hectic, more poignant, and more engaging. The cryptic element of this book is not incomprehensible dialogue but the urge to bridge the gaps between scenes and so modulate the discontinuities into a single, logical narrative. It is impossible, of course; but Moorcock's assured, undemonstrative manner always seems to suggest that one might.

A good example is the career of Sebastian Auchinek. Introduced as an Israeli guerilla in Macedonia receiving a consignment of German arms from Una Persson, he participates in the sack of Athens and then, with Cossack troops, takes Berlin. Later (or is it?) we see him as manager to Una, now a singer in a gaslit Theatre of Varieties – 'one . . . of the newer, better class of music halls.'[54] A patriotic Ode to the Queen is sung (but which Queen?). Una's career progresses. Performing in a 1920s-style musical comedy, she notices 'her old agent, Sebastian Auchinek, in the front stalls. Auchinek was in politics now and writing thousands of articles and pamphlets. His latest production was called "A New Deal for Britain's Jews".'[55] In the interval he is summoned away by police and interrogated in Brixton under suspicion of spying. The constable asks about Macedonia. Suddenly a force of English freedom fighters attack the prison. Auchinek is rescued by a girl with a machine-gun, who looks 'like a young Una Persson'. It is Catherine

Cornelius, an enthusiastic if inept young radical. As they are about to leave she admits,

'The ins and outs of the revolution – if it *is* a revolution – are a bit beyond me. I just work for the cause.'
'But I'm not a revolutionary. I'm a businessman. I think you know more. . . .'
'Honestly, no. . . .'
'Perhaps I should go back? A mistake.' He hesitated beside the car.
'Don't you remember Macedonia?'
'Were you there?'
'You were an idealist. A guerilla.'
'I've always been in show business. All my life. Promotions. Management.'

Awkwardly she drives him away, observing, 'We've still got a long journey ahead of us . . . Modification of species and so on. Perhaps it isn't really a revolution at all.'[56]

When Auchinek makes his last appearance he has 'gone to earth' as an English farmer. He brings the cows home, boils new-laid eggs for his supper, and reads 'novels of rustic life' before going to sleep.[57] His new provincialism, like Cornelius's in *Programme*, proves no protection from the war, the revolution, the catastrophe. That night an unidentified destroyer casually shells the entire area, killing, apparently, all the main characters except Una Persson, Cathy Cornelius, and Jerry, resurrected at the last minute as a seaside pierrot.

There is a sense of development here, but the causation is perfectly obscure. Though it passes through times and places that are discontinuous if not utterly scrambled, there is an apparent continuity in Auchinek's own lifeline. The essential proposition of a time-travel story is a disruption between the traveller's personal, biological ageing and the historical date of his surroundings. Moorcock retains this in his portrayal of 'time in a state of flux', but further complicates it by giving his travellers biographies which seem irrational to us and uncertain to them. Auchinek the show promoter seems not to remember his involvement in Macedonia, but Auchinek the farmer seems to. 'It had been a dream, that period in Macedonia and Greece. A nightmare. He'd done some funny jobs in his life before finding the one which suited him.'[58] His career parodies a certain instability in modern life – there is thematic, almost allegorical significance in its three stages: states of participation, observation, and withdrawal; the promotion of death, illusion and life respectively. Moorcock has often implied symbolic correspondence between revolution and showbiz. But all this is no more than suggested. It is important that there should be no definitive interpretation. Moorcock's subject is uncertainty, ambiguity, the drift of time and identity. Cornelius makes a hero more ambiguous than even Glogauer. He is the spirit of a world which seems to be more than one world, multiversal; and of a time which seems to be all times. Perhaps this is the peculiar achievement of the later twentieth century; perhaps a legacy, the imprint of the 150-year generation; perhaps the eternal cancer of the human condition. Law and Chaos, meaning and intention, shift and may not be fixed. In *Programme* Moorcock was content to set a few paradoxes ticking; in *Cancer* he adopted a manner that was merely evasive; but in *Assassin* and the fourth book, *The Condition of Muzak*, he perfected more subtle techniques that suggest perpetual slow motion between order and chaos, like the falling patterns of a kaleidoscope.[59] The splintered, schizoid prose of *Cancer*, as of so much in *NW* at that date, represents an assault on language, on assumption and perception, necessitated by a radical reinterpretation of reality. Later Moorcock learned to redesign prose instead of exploding it, to manipulate traditions instead of attacking them, and especially to set narrative structure working against the style of narration. The prose of *Assassin* and *Muzak* is lucid and detailed, describes and characterises with conviction and clarity. But the process of the various levels and sequences of plot is dismantled, arranged in symmetrical sections and subsections, grouped under abstract titles. Each section is self-contained, as if we were visiting a story at several intermediate stages. The scenes are separate, brief but clearly lit; what happens in between is shadowed and obscure. Moorcock scatters hints and allusions, so that we infer all manner of possible and impossible things.[60]

Thinking about methods – prefiguring things with *apparently* random remarks, chapter headings etc. This is why, even if readers don't *remember* reading a certain ref. it appears familiar to them when it turns up again. Thus a chapter heading (A) will refer to an event in chapter (G). This creates flow in place of traditional narrative dynamics while at the same time doing something to destroy restrictions of linear narrative – i.e.

'non-linear' is not the same as 'random'. Books – any art – must have shape, but the shape can be very different. . . . It's an attempt to describe and to dramatise my own view of the world – i.e. one which is non-linear. I can see so many possibilities all at once I can't choose one – and would not wish to choose one. I'm not confused by multiplicity – I'm delighted by it.

Not choosing between multiple possibilities is the central problem of *The Condition of Muzak*, last of the tetralogy. Moorcock notes that the books, being 'non-linear', may be read in any order; but *Muzak* reworks much material from the first three, and resembles, to borrow from the author's favourite musical analogies, a final movement, with an intricate Mozartian restatement of themes. Despite the spectre of entropy nothing stops forever in Moorcock's fictional multiverse – everything and everyone is cyclic and recycled – but in *Muzak* the conflict of fantasy and reality seems to reach climax.

The divisions of the novel bear musical titles. 'Introduction' and 'Development' cover an area equivalent to the first three Cornelius books. Direct echoes of scenes, images and incidents show that this is yet another alternative history or set of several. Once again Jerry confronts Frank, visits the fake Le Corbusier château, orders his books burnt, and loses the ebullient innocence of the 1960s as the decade ends, seedily. Painting himself black, he opens his transmogrification clinic in the old convent of the Poor Clares, Notting Hill, and survives the coming of General Cumberland and his military 'advisors'. After a period of indolence with Una Persson in imperial Borneo, entertaining Bishop Beesley and his daughter, Cornelius is removed by airship in a rapidly worsening schizoid fugue. He attends the Reunion Party, a half-time jamboree featuring almost every character Moorcock has ever invented, including an alternative Lenin, Conrad, and two of his own pseudonyms. Cornelius's arrival on the dingy beach of Tintagel suffering from amnesia, his rescue by Major Nye and his introduction to the colonial uprising at Grasmere repeat, as if in a dream, the story of *The English Assassin*; but his inability to win Catherine back and his encounter with his mother and Colonel Pyat in a devastated Brighton invert the sunny end of that book. This time it is Frank, a disaster vampire manipulating the black market, who survives, and Jerry who passes out.

The next division, 'Recapitulation', fancies a compete new political and social history of the twentieth century, one decade to a chapter, culminating in a wistfully glorious vision of a future Britain divided into 72 independent states: Moorcock's own utopia, combining Morris with Dickens and Wells. Again, as the title indicates, Cornelius re-enacts a version of his heroic life, the botched career of a failed Messiah to the Age of Science. Emerging from Empire via war, he wanders innocently through the drizzle of the 1950s into the 1960s, where Miss Brunner conscripts him for her mechanistic schemes. He collapses in the 1970s, burrowing himself a nest of nostalgia in the jungle that was once the Roof Garden of Derry and Toms. Pulled out of this terminal Eden by Major Nye, he spends ten years in coma, emerging just in time to be crowned King of London in the 1980s. The whole city is a funfair, a pleasure-dome at his disposal. At last it seems he can be the hero everyone wants, a figurehead with no responsibilities at all.[61]

'Am I really the King? Or just a play-actor?'

Major Nye shrugged. 'Does it matter? Elfberg or Cornelius. You are their ideal. Wave to them, Your Majesty!'

Una came close, murmuring: 'It's an honorary title, with very little actual power. But the honour really is considerable.'

'But what are my duties?'

'To exist.'

But even this prospect of anarchy triumphant, perfect Chaos as perfect Order, is not satisfying. In the last of these chapters, a Christmas costume party in the 1990s, Moorcock resolves the Commedia Dell' Arte theme with which he has been playing since the end of *Assassin*. Just as the characters in eighteenth-century pantomime would suddenly fling off their costumes and revert to the traditional roles of the Harlequinade – Pantaloon, Scaramouche, Polichinelle, Columbine, Pierrot, and Harlequin himself – so the party-goers, all Cornelius's old friends and enemies, don the garb of familiar figures from English folklore and myth, showing themselves as incarnations of archetypes. Half parodic, half revelatory, this scene substantiates mythological suggestions that Jerry Cornelius has exuded throughout the shape- and scene-shifting pantomime of his lives and times. But what is his role? Harlequin is the hero, but Cornelius, the only one not enjoying the party, is dressed as Pierrot, the loser. A guest, 'Flash' Gordon Gavin, says,[62]

'You'd have been much better as Harlequin, Jerry.' . . .

'I used to be,' Jerry crossed his billowing legs, 'but Harlequin somehow metamorphosed into Pierrot. It happened in France, I think. Don't ask me how. I used to believe I was Captain of my own Fate. Instead I'm just a character in a bloody pantomime.' 'It's not too bloody now, at any rate.' Flash always tried to look on the bright side. 'Everyone's cultivating their own gardens.'. . . 'I'm just pissed off. I've ruined it, as usual. I can go anywhere I like in the city. Do anything I like. . . . But all I want to do is stay at home and make love to Catherine.'. . . 'They say that's the trouble with Utopia. You get bored. While there were big countries to fight, or big corporations, or just very powerful people, it was easier to be an individual.' He sighed artificially. 'Now everyone's an individual, eh, Mr C? It's taken a lot of the fun from life, I'll tell you.'

Cornelius, who first appeared as Harlequin the Trickster, multi-coloured juggler of time and space, wielder of the magic wand, is unmasked as Peirrot, the lachrymose unrequited lover. In 1870 E.C. Brewer described Pierrot as 'a character in French pantomime representing a man in growth and a child in mind and manners'. Taken from the stage by artists and writers such as Willette, Laforgue and Verlaine, Pierrot became a literary figure of Romantic pathos, 'at once', as Enid Welsford says, 'a thwarted idealist and a rake with the heart of a child'.[63]

Ne voilà-t-il pas un étrange drame, mêlé de rire et de terreur? . . . Pierrot qui se promène dans la rue avec sa casaque blanche, son pantalon blanc, son visage enfariné, préoccupé de vagues désirs, n'est-ce pas la symbolisation de l'âme humaine encore innocente et blanche, tourmentée d'aspirations infinies vers les régions supérieures?

The vital, immortal magus, the Eternal Champion, the all-purpose human being, is only a mask, a wishful projection by which Everyman avoids seeing the blank, foolish cipher of his own face. The hero is everyone else's victim, slave of their desires; bereft of that support, he becomes a sorrowful, stumbling creature, unable to realise a desire of his own. Una Persson, the new Harlequin, kindly restores the dying Catherine, whom she also loves, to her helpless brother.

This would make a poignant but happy ending to the adventures of Jerry Cornelius, perhaps a little unsatisfying in its recruitment of a new hero to redeem the outworn one. But these sections, 'Introduction', 'Development' and 'Recapitulation', are musically framed by a 'Prelude' and 'Coda' of more sombre and less pleasant scenes, deliberate debasements and trivialisations of the glories Cornelius has trailed, like a falling firework, from the first spectacular rush of *The Final Programme*. The pun on Pater's famous maxim in the fourth book's title describes both 'tunes': the sentimental cadences of the middle sections in which Cornelius's motley slowly fades to white, and the wry, banal refrain that brackets them. In 'Prelude' and 'Coda' Jerry Cornelius is a feckless kid from a cheap tenement in Blenheim Crescent animated only by Mandrax and dreams of a brilliant future for his amateur rock band. He eventually blows his finest hour, a free concert on waste ground under a motorway flyover, when the ramshackle stage gives way. His guitar smashed, he forsakes rock and roll for trite musical shows and finds fame and fortune in revivals of music hall and Harlequinade, and promoting Rolls Royce's new 'mini-Phantom' on tv.

This is the least heroic and somehow most elementary incarnation yet. The familiar Cornelius characters have counterparts here: Miss Brunner is Cornelius's Draconian old schoolmistress; Frank is a Portobello antique-shark; Sebastian Auchinek is (of course) a musical promoter with his heart in the box-office. Everyone seems, by the family tree his mother provides, to be related to Cornelius and to everyone else in a dreary huddle of incest and adultery that ties together the penurious tribes of Notting Hill and Ladbroke Grove. It is as if all the rest of the Cornelius legend were this boy's selfish and hallucinatory dreams, overblown by the cancer of the age and riddled by impermanence and the withering of the heart's desire. These fantasies are neurotically sensitive to the edge of modernity, the call of nostalgia, and the lure of the future. In them his author gives a complex interpretation of contemporary Western culture as a state of mind. As we have been told, not only by *The Final Programme* but also by the works of Ballard and other inner space writers of *NW*, the public liberation of private fantasy is at once the characteristic advance and catastrophe of this age of science. Technology and the mass media encourage and embody it, but the resultant dispersal and attenuation of human communication produces the devalued reality, the increasing entropy of which these writers speak.

This dialectic of fantasy and reality requires that we take this inferior Cornelius as the real one, not equivalent to the others, if only in the sense of pre-existing them, as the ground for their elaboration. Moorcock seems to want us to, recording in his notebook remarks such as 'It should be noted that the "real" Jerry is far less sophisticated than his "fantasy" counterpart.'[64] This view is expounded by John Clute in his introduction to *The Cornelius Chronicles*:[65]

> [The] basic theme, as I read it, Jerry Cornelius's fundamental obsessive concern through all his various incarnations, is simply the problem of how to acquire and maintain an identity strategically capable of constituting urban life, because identity in the city is a costume drama. . . . Jerry Cornelius is the paradigmatic native of the inner city; his roles constitute a genuine paradigm set of strategies for living there. His inner city is London (but could be New York), his patch is Ladbroke Grove. His real story (I believe) runs from about 1965 to about a decade later, a period during which London has been destroying itself as a place to live, hence the rapacity of his need for safety and solace. It is for this reason that the various masquerades and venues which make up his story read as a series of precariously achieved enclaves. . . .
> There is no enclave secure against time. No style has a permanent lock on the shape of the world. No tune can last, certainly not as played on Jerry's dismal guitar. If you ask whether or not it is possible to maintain homeostasis in a decaying world, the answer is that all art constantly aspires towards the condition of Muzak.[66]

Clute refers to *Soft City*, Jonathan Raban's 'socio-literary study of the meaning of urban life', Raban's record of the impressions and interpretations of one citizen offers a persuasive view of urban life as 'a form of theatre', a richly equipped repository of locations and roles amongst which the individual can and must choose. He attributes this view not to his own sensibilities and predispositions as a critic and novelist, but to the nature of cities themselves, as artificial centralisations of resources, and as densely-populated zones. He takes issue with the traditional principle that the city is a 'domain of reason', the doctrine implicit in, say, a street-map of New York.[67]

> The idea that the city is in essence a rational structure, and that evidence of irrationality is a sign of decadent deviation from its intrinsic cityness is entirely comprehensible; it is even perhaps administratively and psychologically necessary. But it seems

intuitively wrong. . . . The city I live in is one where hobos and loners are thoroughly representative of the place, where superstition thrives, and where people often have to live by reading the signs and surfaces of their environment and interpreting them in terms of private, near-magical codes. . . .
To live in a real city is to live in just as indomitable an environment as any valley full of rocks and stones and trees. Streets, shops, cafes, houses, underground railways, office blocks are not, for most of us, matters of choice and reason merely because someone built them out of bricks and mortar and decided that they would be useful there. The city dweller is constantly coming up against the absolute mysteriousness of other people's reasons. . . . When the needs and reasons for things of 'culture' become sufficiently divorced from our personal needs and wishes, they turn as intractably alien as anything in nature. . . .
And cities, by their nature, *as* nature, grow out of just such processes of separation of ends from means. . . . For most of their inhabitants, cities like New York and London *are* nature, and are as unpredictable, threatening, intermittently beautiful and benign, as a tropical rain forest. That they are in point of fact *constructs* is a mighty and deluding irrelevance. Park's description of the savage mind groping with a universe of unrelated episodes and phenomenal accidents may apply as well in Earl's Court as in the Congo.

This panorama of the city as a complex of thousands of individual schemes and purposes, the whole appearing frantic, inscrutable and random, makes a perfect background to Moorcock's writings. It corresponds, from Miss Brunner's quasar city in *Programme*, through the kinky world of *Cancer*, to the 72 British nations parading in *Muzak*. The city is a multiverse of private Laws appreciable only as a public Chaos. So Jerry Cornelius, the 'paradigmatic native of the inner city', has all the innocence of the 'savage mind', as Major Nye understands.[68]

'The city was his security, with all its horrors. As the jungle is security to the tiger, you might say. . . . A creature like Cornelius takes technology for granted. It is real enough to him for it to possess a genuinely mythological significance. . . . He had all the primitive's respect for Nature, the same tendency to invest it with meaning and identity, only his Nature was the industrial city, his

idea of Paradise was an urban utopia.'
After Barthes and the semiological analysis of totem and taboo in
the urban jungle comes Raban and the discovery of the typical
urban native. Every man tackling the daily ritualised warfare of the
city or venturing into the sinister hinterlands beyond his customary
bus-stop is like the primitive brave, guided only by his private
reading of 'signs and surfaces', his adopted mythology. Jerry Cornelius, spirit of the age, becomes the hero of a thousand legends, but
it is only his innocence and malleability that make them possible.
' "He wasn't his world's Messiah. He wasn't the Golden Trickster.
He was his world's Fool." '[69] The Global Village breeds the Global
Village Idiot.
    This is the primary message of the Cornelius books. They repres-
ent Moorcock's definitive analysis of the hero-victim complex.
Seducing the popular imagination by personifying the most envi-
able powers and attributes in appropriately bold, facetious hyperbole, he penetrates our attention with an intense, uncompromising
scrutiny that deflates the image and disturbs our admiration. Clute
says that, 'After seeming to give Jerry Cornelius to the world as a
pop saviour, he went and took him back.'[70]
    That, at least, is the theory, based on the ideal reading. But there
is a problem. Like Milton, Moorcock suffers from giving all the best
tunes to the devil. Most readers still seem to admire Cornelius
rather than pity him, ignoring the bathos, the ironic images of souls
sucked dry by the English assassin, of ecstatic disciples following
him into the sea. Moorcock's skill at gripping the reader with one
hand while baffling him with the other has undermined his own
authority over his creation, as has his policy of encouraging other
writers, from Norman Spinrad to Brian Aldiss, to borrow Cornelius
for their own stories.[71] Moorcock has given repeated instructions
that Corneliana are not meant to be studied. 'It was never my
intention to write "difficult" books. . . . They don't have to be
"understood" to be enjoyed. If they give you a good feeling, that's
enough.'[72] On top of this, by discarding all the traditional fixities of
narrative (time, place, causation, character development) from the
works, he has turned over to us a large part of the responsibility for
their interpretation. The reader must be forgiven if he misses the
point that, in this dissolution of reality and fantasy, the unhappy
adolescent Cornelius is yet supposed to be somehow more real than
his other selves. Not everyone can achieve the balanced appraisal of

M. John Harrison, who wrote in response to *The Condition of Muzak*: 'Rather than a bitter revelation of reality, a cancellation of the daydream, we have an alternative. Life is offered as a substitute for the fantasy, which was never offered as a substitute for life.'[73] In a time of much reprinting, Moorcock is still thought of as the man who wrote all those Eternal Champion books. Those casually acquainted with him can see Cornelius only as the most glamorous and outrageous of a line of improbable heroes. Like Cornelius the physicist manqué, Moorcock may never be free of the task of destroying his own early writings. Yet for the critic to rescue him from 'mere' popularity and the acclaim of uncomprehending fans would be equally misjudged. The work that Moorcock has chosen to do, denying any barrier between the popular and the literary, is a precarious one, particularly – ironically – vulnerable to the devolutions of time.

Chapter Nine

Angst and angströms
stylistic practice

> English, which had become the French of the last century, then
> a kind of mirror-image Mandarin – sparse and subtle in its
> rhythms but yielding great resonance, a quality first noted by
> mid-century mystery writers and exploited by certain American
> poets – was now atrophying, dying in upon itself. Words
> tumbled readily off the tongue, too readily, in brief economical
> strings like a kind of verbal semaphore, and increasingly had
> relevance only to themselves – poets, Jerry knew from personal
> experience, were having a hard time of it. . . . What was the
> precise relationship of language to society, of spoken to written
> language?[1]

Jerry Cornelius has a remarkable facility for elegant, abbreviated,
and inscrutable speech. He discards the scientific treatises and
books of poetry he once wrote. His question begs itself: whatever
the relationship between man and his words, it can no longer be
described as precise.

The sophistications of the Modernist writers typically included a
nervous awareness of the intricacies and paradoxes of their
medium. Eliot describes writing as 'a raid on the inarticulate/With
shabby equipment always deteriorating.'[2] Lawrence decries 'the
evil-smelling old Logos'.[3] By elevating wordplay to art, Joyce
dramatised the flexibility and opulence of language, but also its
inconsistency and deceptiveness. Eliot, Lawrence and Joyce dealt
with the sense of instability by referring back to myths which they
asserted were cyclic and eternal, and could redeem the deteriora-
tion and corruption of society and of language. Contemporary
theories identify myth as just another assortment of words, which

have no intrinsic meaning. Language is detached from reality, the two even set in opposition: language is made up of words, reality is not.

Working with the devalued word, the successors of Eliot, Lawrence and Joyce have not become more arbitrary but more earnest. Unable to claim that they are mirroring or building up reality with words, many of them have found a new purpose in dismantling myths. They try to show how words do not give access to reality but actually obscure and camouflage it (though they have only words with which to do the job). William Burroughs, whose works parade a horrified fixation with language, has said, 'Words . . . are used by vested interests as a control machine to manipulate humanity.'[4] His fantasies on the theme recur, showing that these 'vested interests' are not just established corporations and conspiracies, but also private, unconscious blocks in the individual mind.[5]

Word is an organism . . . a separate organism attached to your nervous system on an air line of words. . . . From symbiosis to parasitism is a short step. The word is now a virus. The flu virus may once have been a healthy lung cell. It is now a parasitic organism that invades and damages the lungs. The word may once have been a healthy neural cell. It is now a parasitic organism that invades and damages the central nervous system. Modern man has lost the option of silence. Try halting your sub-vocal speech. Try to achieve even ten seconds of inner silence. You will encounter a resisting organism that *forces you to talk*. That organism is the word. . . .
The realization that something as familiar to you as the movement of your intestines the sound of your breathing the beating of your heart is also alien and hostile does make one feel a bit insecure at first.

To attack the alien invader Burroughs bombards and overturns the verbal system. He bends and breaks the rules of sentence composition, which are the mechanics of the 'control machine'. As one critic says, '*Naked Lunch* gives us a world beneath or beyond syntax and all that that implies.'[6]

Burroughs, with his devoted attention to his own paranoia, might be expected to be abnormal in this as in other respects, but at the opposite extreme of contemporary writing Alain Robbe-Grillet, by his own design the least fantastic of novelists, is no less paranoid about secret conspiracies of syntax and semantics. He denounces previous narrative conventions for their deceptive and reactionary implications.[7]

All the technical elements of the narrative – the systematic use of the past definite tense and of the third person, the unconditional adoption of chronological development, linear plots, a regular graph of the emotions, the way each episode tended towards an end, etc. – everything aimed at imposing the image of a stable universe, coherent, continuous, univocal, and wholly decipherable.

Which universe, Robbe-Grillet maintains, is entirely fictional, a narrative convention in itself, perpetuated for the ease of novelists in flagrant disregard for the chaos of experience.

B.S. Johnson, who agrees that 'chaos is the most likely explanation', recognises mournfully that even writing as conscientious as Robbe-Grillet's cannot hope to deal properly with the flux; writing also flows.[8]

No sooner is a style or technique established than the reasons for its adoption have vanished or become irrelevant. . . . I feel myself fortunate sometimes that I can laugh at the joke that just as I was beginning to think I knew something about how to write a novel it is no longer of any use to me in attempting the next one.

Cornelius's sense of atrophy prevails. Each writer declares a sharp break with the past, discrediting previous assumptions of narrative and replacing them with less confident ones that will make writing more difficult from now on. It has generally been a characteristic of all arts that they pass through cycles of revolution and redefinition of design, each revolutionary intending to start a new tradition with the consent and co-operation of his contemporaries; each new tradition has been established in the name of 'realism'. These latest rejections of literary history all isolate the modern writer, giving him only negative principles for his new beginning. He is forbidden to appeal to 'real life' any more; the only reality words convey is their own. Whatever his strategy, it will be surprising and perhaps suspicious if many other writers agree to cope with their atrophying task in the same way.

The critics have noticed this divergence of creative purpose. The title of David Lodge's book *The Novelist at the Crossroads* is an apt image: the writer now stands at a point of choice between equivalent routes. (In fact the image is probably outdated, an insufficiently complex model – 'The Novelist at Spaghetti Junction' might be better.) Lodge comments,[9]

> We seem, indeed, to be living through a period of unprecedented cultural pluralism which allows, in all the arts, an astonishing variety of styles to flourish simultaneously. Though they are in many cases radically opposed on aesthetic and epistemological grounds, no one style has managed to become dominant. . . . We should not be surprised that many contemporary writers manifest symptoms of extreme insecurity, nervous self-consciousness and even at times a kind of schizophrenia.

Pluralism in style presupposes pluralism in influence: each writer reorganises his ancestors to suit himself, borrowing and adapting as he likes, without regard for classical precepts. This is even more noticeable when the disintegration effect spreads out to reach the critics. Wayne C. Booth, publishing his *Rhetoric of Fiction* in 1961, was entering into a scene of growing critical confusion with an attempt to clarify the operations of style.[10]

> It may be that every critic has in his system somewhere, recognized or not, at least one or two constants which he requires of all literature. But what is different about the modern period is the widespread abandonment of the notion of peculiar literary kinds, each with its unique demands that may modify the general standards . . . the loss of distinctions between levels of style suited to different literary kinds. . . .
>
> Unassisted by established critical traditions, faced with chaotic diversity among the things called novels, critics of fiction have been driven to invent an order of some kind, even at the expense of being dogmatic. 'Great traditions' of innumerable shapes and sizes, based on widely divergent universal qualities, have in consequence been discovered and abandoned with appalling rapidity. *The* novel began, we are told, with Cervantes, with Defoe, with Fielding, with Richardson, with Jane Austen – or was it with Homer? It was killed by Joyce, by Proust, by the rise of symbolism, by the loss of respect for – or was it the excessive absorption with? – hard facts. No, no, it still lives, but only in the work of. . . . Thus, on and on.

Observing that uncertainty and disagreement divide writers and critics to an unprecedented extent, we may not perhaps conclude anything about the state of the language itself, as Jerry Cornelius wanted to. Dethroned from the umpire's chair of the omniscient narrator, contemporary authors have to find new ways to re-establish confidence with their readers. They are at liberty to attribute the failure of that narrative tradition to a major fault in communication, as Burroughs, Robbe-Grillet, and Johnson all do, saying that language is parasitic, deceitful, unstable. Critics may encourage them, diagnosing a breakdown in history that results in 'cultural pluralism' and even chaos. These assertions may be fanciful, but the linguists are making them too.[11]

It needs but half an eye to see in these latter days that science, the Grand Revelator of modern Western culture, has reached, without having intended to, a frontier. . . . The frontier was foreseen in principle very long ago, and given a name that has descended to our day clouded with myth. That name is Babel.
. . .

What we call 'scientific thought' is a specialization of the western Indo-European type of language, which has developed not only a set of different dialectics, but actually a set of different dialects. THESE DIALECTS ARE NOW BECOMING MUTUALLY UNINTELLIGIBLE. The term 'space', for instance, does not and CANNOT mean the same thing to a psychologist as to a physicist.

The new Babel is not only a literary conceit. It is interesting that Benjamin Lee Whorf construes dialectal divergence as a hindrance to the progress of science – just as Johnson spoke of stylistic obsolescence as a break in the continuity of literature. The two statements are exactly parallel. More interesting, and perhaps the most convincing point in the argument, is that what the writers and critics call simply 'chaos', disorganisation, Whorf analyses as the effect of over-organisation, as Cornelius did in Sallis's 'The Anxiety in the Eyes of the Cricket'. The disintegration of language into 'dialects' is the result of specialisation. One science: one dialect, says Whorf. One novel, even one chapter: one style, demands Johnson.

Pressing their way out of the alley of genre sf, the *NW* writers came directly to the crossroads of this Babel. Just as they rejected the attitudes and assumptions of their predecessors as outdated and untenable, so they renounced their stylistic inheritance. It was in any case rather meagre. Sf fans and the editors who direct them may be the most demanding of consumers of popular fiction, but they have never been too particular about style. For the professional pulp writers of the 1930s science fiction was only one variation of the formula for adventure stories from which they were also constructing the cowboy and detective magazines their companies published. The term 'space opera', the intergalactic melodrama of sf, is directly analogous to the western's 'horse opera'. Scorning this indiscriminate commercialism, John W. Campbell and his team set up the enduring principle that sf is different from all other fictional modes. It is 'a Literature of Ideas'. What they meant by this was that each sf story should be erected to support an abstract proposition of a scientific kind, clearly discernible from the story, which was to be the mainspring of the plot and the reason for the story's existence. The fictional elements were considered secondary, as if somehow detachable: the shell and albumen surrounding an intellectual yolk. As such, the egg-white had to be appetising, preferably exciting, but was held in less esteem than the golden 'Ideas' it contained. Editors and fans commonly referred to stories as 'yarns', a rather deprecatory term expressing an attitude of slightly superior indulgence. Yarns were jolly, colourful, and dramatic; and imperturbably naïve. ' "We're competing with a machine intelligence." "The cunning swine!" ' expostulated Cromwell.[12]

Faced with readers who believed that, compared with 'Ideas', poverty of style was unimportant, Moorcock's first duty to fiction was to shift the balance. In a typical editorial of 1966 he rallied them.[13]

Writing standards are being raised, plots become more sophisticated, characters more convincing. There are fewer new real ideas in the world than there are notions – but it is how we dramatise them that is important. To get them across we must reject many of the conventional trappings of the past and writers must look to themselves rather than their predecessors for the ways in which they will present their stories.

Shorn of their capital letter and the special consideration reserved for them by the fans, the 'ideas' of sf come comfortably into perspective. In this appeal Moorcock was bowing to the traditional critical discrimination between 'form' and 'content'. Whether the writer's content is a 'new real idea' or a mere 'notion', he says, it is the form he gives it that counts. As usual the message is to 'reject many of the conventional trappings of the past' and produce new forms, independently devised. The new writers, isolated from the past, must depend not on adherence to a group or school, but on their personal resources: 'writers must look to themselves'.

The history of sf necessitated Moorcock's emphasis on style as an area for development, and as one thing the new writer had to pay attention to if he were to express an individual vision instead of a conventional one. Inevitably, perhaps, the attempt to find new styles, like the attempts to treat the subject of sex, misdirected many readers. Both friends and enemies assumed that since Moorcock was publishing more and more fiction written in bizarre styles, anything written in a bizarre style counted as 'New Wave' sf. More than any other factor, this misunderstanding has prolonged the underestimation of Moorcock's intentions and achievements. The elevation of style over content, and especially of individual whim over convention, was the principle of much of the change that characterised the 1960s. It was also the principle that made so many of the products of the decade ephemeral and insubstantial, and now gives them their antiquated feel. Isaac Asimov referred to the new writing as 'froth'; many others also believe it was shallow, affected and effectless. Moreover, it was style as an issue which made the radical difference between the British 'New Wave' and the American 'New Wave' that immediately followed. There was no counterpart to *NW* in America, so interested writers had to inspect the original to find out what was going on. Generalising from what they read there, they quickly identified a 'New Wave' formula, described here by Christopher Priest.[14]

> The writing would be obscure to one degree or another. There
> would be experiments with the actual prose: with grammar,
> with viewpoint, with typography. There would be reference to
> all sorts of eclectic sources: philosophy, rock music, newspaper
> articles, medicine, politics, automobile specifications, etc. There
> would be a 'down-beat' or tragic resolution to many stories, if
> any resolution at all. There would frequently be explicit
> descriptions of sexual activity, and obscenities were freely used.
> This is an analysis of published work, not an approach to
> understanding the process behind it, but never mind. Because
> the *type* of writing could be labelled, New Wave, in the
> American sense, became an idiom.

American writers responded to only part of the British challenge.

Instead of 'looking to themselves' they took *NW* as a model to be emulated. Creating outlets for the writers, American editors took up only part of Moorcock's complex and thoroughgoing initiative. Judith Merril, continuing her series of annual *Best S-F* volumes, became more and more eclectic in pursuit of what she identified as the speculative factor in fiction. Few British writers recognised the picture of the movement she attempted in her anthology *England Swings SF*.[15] Damon Knight's series of original anthologies, *Orbit*, begun in 1966, showed him to be concerned principally with stylistic innovation, while for *Dangerous Visions*, published the following year, Harlan Ellison took the line that subversion was all-important and invited only stories whose subjects offended against 'taboos' imposed by conservative editors. Though these responses generated powerful and important changes within the sf genre itself, as Priest sees it they 'missed the point'.[16]

The purpose of the New Wave, if indeed it can be said to have a purpose, was to release writers and readers from the preconceptions of the pulp magazine idiom. The American argument was about a *product*: a 'type' of story with an invented label. The *process*, which Moorcock and others had been encouraging writers to explore, was to find an individual approach to writing speculative fiction.

With many American writers resident in London in the late 1960s, while British writers were contributing to *Orbit* and *Dangerous Visions*, to contrast the British initiative and the American response so starkly is of course oversimplification, but too many readers and commentators assume that there was no transatlantic difference at all, especially when treating the 'New Wave' as indiscriminate 'froth', an unnecessary digression in the history of sf, manifested as an effusion of psychedelic prose. Moorcock's principles could not govern every story in his magazine. In the excitement and uncertainty of the period, with many people influencing the selection of material, a monthly deadline to meet, originality at a premium, and conventionality to be avoided, *NW* gave space to many things that now seem merely extravagant or involuted. In any case, the principles were anarchic, so it was impossible (and undesirable) to lay down firm editorial criteria. There had to be variety. A single issue of *NW* might include barbed satire from John Sladek, Brian Aldiss in genial mood, and some deviant speculation of J.G. Ballard's.[17] In between were featured the creations of an extraordinary number of contributors, in a great diversity of styles. In hindsight we can see that some of these styles were genuine attempts, however awkward, to get at revolutionary implications of the subject matter, while others, especially American ones, were excursions into mannerism, surface novelties with perfectly conventional interiors.[18]

Quick, a world in 300 words or less! Picture this. . . .

One land mass, really, containing three black and brackish looking seas; grey plains and yellow plains and skies the colour of dry sand; shallow forests with trees like mushrooms which have been swabbed with iodine; no mountains, just hills brown, yellow, white, lavender; green birds with wings like parachutes, bills like sickles, feathers like oak leaves, an inside-out umbrella behind; six very distant moons, like spots before the eyes in daytime, snowflakes at night, drops of blood at dusk and dawn; grass like mustard in the moister valleys; mists like white fire on windless mornings, albino serpents when the air's astir; radiating chasms, like fractures in frosted windowpanes; hidden caverns, like chains of dark bubbles; seventeen known dangerous predators, ranging from one to six metres in length, excessively furred and fanged; sudden hailstorms, like hurled hammerheads from a clear sky; an icecap like a blue beret at either flattened pole; nervous bipeds a metre and a half in height, short on cerebrum, which wander the shallow forests and prey upon the giant caterpillar's larva, as well as the giant caterpillar, the green bird, the blind burrower, and the offal-eating murk-beast; seventeen mighty rivers; clouds like pregnant purple cows, which quickly cross the land to lie-in beyond the visible east; stands of windblasted stones like frozen music; night like soot, to obscure the lesser stars; valleys which flow like the torsos of women or instruments of music; perpetual frost in places of shadow; sounds in the morning like the cracking of ice, the trembling of tin, the snapping of steel strands.

Roger Zelazny is obviously not trying for any profound impression here, so perhaps it is irrelevant to remark how whimsical and insubstantial all this is. Nevertheless, he is seeking to arrest and fill our attention, evoking an entire alien world with an energetic, all-embracing sensibility that is missing from the punctilious factualism of so many science fiction writers. He promotes a confusion that would outrage their rationality, and seems more 'artistic' for daring to do so: Ray Bradbury under the influence of Dylan Thomas. But in writing like this everything is geared to the first impression. Zelazny's similes and associations persuade by distraction rather than concentration, leaving a trail of broken images, unfocused and so not retained. If he seems extremely imaginative, it is only because he works his imagination to extremes. Beneath the high poetic tone we may detect an old science fiction arrogance, the heady simplifications of the armchair author dreaming only on the largest scale, vaulting lightyears and epochs. Instead of granting his planet the greatest possible authenticity, he reduces it to a feat of style: 'a world in 300 words or less!' Its inhabitants, 'excessively furred and fanged' or 'short on cerebrum', he measures by human standards, with colonial fastidiousness. In fact most of the imagery Zelazny has chosen for his similes diminishes the phenomena it describes to a safe and domestic size: trees become mushrooms, polar icecaps become berets, six moons are only snowflakes or spots before the eyes.

The presentation of the whole description as one elongated sentence (without verb) seems casual, but soon starts to resemble an itemised catalogue, as if '300 words or less' were the rubric on a report form to be filled in. The implication of that limit is scientific, abstract rather than imaginative: data can be condensed for increased accuracy; experience cannot. There is a powerful contradiction between these constrictions and the liberal overflow of Zelazny's expression. The two could be integrated to show us the ambiguity of our response to an alien landscape, but the author seems not to realise the contradiction. In his assumption of literary freedom he is actually still bound by old habits of mind.

This is early Zelazny, and he has done better. To be fair we must compare it with another minor story in a style only partly developed. Sam Wolf's 'Eyeball' had been published four months earlier. To judge from this, his only contribution to *NW*, Wolf was another young writer, less resourceful than Zelazny but more acute. The event his story relates is bizarre: the narrator's left eye has been occupied by a miniaturised Martian spaceship – literally 'in orbit'.[19]

Enemy within.

Examine the situation as if it were a paragraph in a future history book. A being of superior knowledge in some galactic research academy perusing the primitive era.

In his own language the creature inside a mobile thought pod: At a point in the light wave flow dated by era-three primitives as the one thousand nine hundred and sixties A.D. this hominoid, an occupant of planet Alpha 762 in the offshore galaxy, realized that he had become the involuntary host of a hostile spaceship from a nearby planet.

The invaders using their simple knowledge of matter densification and sub atomic particles had transformed their spacecraft into one of the hominoid's two sight organs . . . maintaining its complete appearance and substance. There was little loss of operational function for the hominoid except for some irritation. . . .

At that pretended distance the awareness is objectified and becomes a curious phenomenon. . . . But put it into now language and the terrifying statement snatches away equilibrium. How is it possible that on a calm Saturday afternoon with the sun shining, with ordinariness everywhere, I realize and am afraid?

Let the tiny muscles snap the sliver of flesh across the right eyeball. Street and people, tired, stupid, gaping at nowhere faces, and crumbling grit of slum stone. Steel boxes on wheels, barrel-shaped slugs with artificial teeth hanging inside the slop mouth push squalling prams. Shrivelled up things in trousers sucking pipes. . . . Scraps of newspaper flopping out life in the gutter. Large black letters saying nothing – ten thousand foreigners dead in some earthquake, a princess turns up for tea a big photograph of her smiling. . . .

Vortex of panic thought. Am I the only one? . . . Impossible to tell others.

A double style for a double vision. The first, the 'future history book', limits the experience to data, in just the way I referred to earlier. The simplifications and institutional arrogance of this report style demonstrate the inequality between the human victim and the supposed alien academic. The narrator, in this language, is an 'era-three primitive' and a 'hominoid': the technical terms negate his individuality and substitute a general classification by species. The academic, from his perch of historical and intellectual superiority, can look down even on the inconceivable Martians, whose unlikely docking manoeuvre, accomplished by technology beyond human comprehension, he calls 'simple'. The device of postulating advanced civilisations to whom humanity is still primitive has long been established as a technique in sf. The remote and elevated viewpoint provides a forced objectivity and provokes (in the ideal reader) a cosmic humility. 'At that pretended distance the awareness is objectified and becomes a curious phenomenon. . . . But put it into now language and the terrifying statement snatches away equilibrium.' Wolf's second style, 'now language', is the spontaneous utterance of unconsidered emotion, the opposite of scientific report. This outpouring is comparable to the whimsical overflow of Zelazny's description, though different emotions are engaged. As we might expect, considering the cellular invasion theme (and the placing of Wolf's story in *NW*), the shadow of William Burroughs falls darkly here. The writing, simultaneously overcharged and weary, breaks syntax and opts for adjectives and participles rather than articles and verbs: gaping, crumbling, squalling, sucking. Grotesquerie is maximised, the outlines of flesh and stone blurred and distorted in the service of horror and despair, as in the tormented canvases of Edvard Munch.

Both these styles reify mankind, into laboratory specimens or 'shrivelled up things in trousers'. Both are crude and overdone; each would be virtually unreadable alone: but together they mark the inhuman poles of a hysterical world in which the narrator is trapped. He is caught between intense subjectivity and laconic objectivity. Each language conveys an attitude, coherent but extreme, like the warring voices in the mind of the schizophrenic. Wolf's narrator observes and exploits the schizophrenia, and comments on it: 'Vortex of panic thought. Am I the only one? . . . Impossible to tell others.' 'Now language', the emotional, subjective style, is of course as intrusive as the future academic's analysis, since it represents the outlook of the Martian spies. Each voice is therefore alien to the human host, to his own attitudes before being invaded, and to the attitudes of other humans. Without benefit of his horrible interpreters they see nothing extraordinary in themselves. The narrator, aware of that, cannot communicate with them. Is it society or himself that is maladjusted? Can he blame the Martians, or is he actually schizophrenic? 'Eyeball' is Kafka for the 1960s, cruder but more immediate. Wolf has adopted the assumptions and materials of traditional sf and elaborated their metaphorical potential. By not committing himself to one style, or even to the two styles he decides to use, he keeps the metaphors open and uses the ambiguity he has created. 'How is it possible that on a calm Saturday afternoon with the sun shining, with ordinariness everywhere, I realize and am afraid?' That is one of the major questions animating modern literature. Wolf's narrator poses it in a kind of science fiction that makes no escape into fantasy, without leaving the planet, or even the city streets where *NW* was written, sold, and read – in fact, without leaving his own head, or, by implication, the reader's either.

While the variety of stylistic approaches and departures in *NW* hinders generalisation, Wolf's 'mixed style' with its dissociations of consciousness is perhaps most characteristic of the magazine. The adoption of several voices is an attractive device for writers wishing to experiment, as it was for Joyce and Eliot, and one especially suited to the *NW* vision of a fluid, ambiguous, and infinitely complex world. As well as aiming for new styles, perhaps the dialects of the future, the new sf writer could mix existing styles, raid specialist vocabularies, and pit their versions and values against each other, as Wolf does. Wolf and Zelazny both show the effect of contrasting vocabularies, one in polarisation and the other in multiplicity. Both make deliberate strains on the flexibility of syntax. Other writers go further, cutting real or imaginary quotations, headlines and advertisements into their texts. Some chop up a narrative into little sections, under numbers or cryptic titles. The sentence gets twisted and broken; the resources of typography are plundered.[20] The technical emphasis is on alternative ways of producing and using fiction, but the aesthetic purpose is not merely to air fantasy or parade cleverness, but to push the reader's intellect and imagination beyond habitual categories. By now it need hardly be added that dislocation of words can dramatise disintegration of culture. These spontaneous, autonomous styles are used because, as Johnson observes, they seem the most appropriate, if not the only possibilities left.

A mixed, degenerated style is often presented as the expression of a typical character, who apprehends the chaos, whose facility for dissociation is high. Wolf's narrator, uncertain whether to locate his madness in or outside himself, is typical. The wise fool, championed by a disconnected generation who could share his understanding through LSD, thinks and speaks in many voices. In the new sf he embodies the disintegrating perspective.

One of the first was David Rome's retarded schizophrenic, narrator of 'There's a Starman in Ward 7'. He wakes one morning to find the Starman in the next bed.[21]

The Starman sat up slowly and said JESUS GOD WHERE AM I?

> Jesus God, mother of all
> Rolled me in porridge
> And let me fall

The Starman was skinny, and he wore pyjama TOP and no BOTTOM. They don't give you pants if they find out you – the bed.

WHAT IS THE NAME OF THIS PLACE asked the Starman.

'Ward 7,' I told him. Then I said he was lucky they put him here. 8 is the one to scream about. JESUS (love him!) 8888 is the place I get scared about. . . . I won't ever go there though, they don't put little kids in 8. I hope.

8

8

8

The Starman didn't even look happy about being in 7. . . .

When I asked PETER about the Starman he said he'd heard he was a quack head-doctor. He said his real name was Charlie Nebraska and he came from somewhere out west.

The Starman got to talking to himself today. He's over a hundred years old and he left Alpha Centauri four years ago.

. . .

888

888

!!!

!!! theStarmanisgoingto try. Not just me!! He's going to cure EVERYBODY!!!

This style, with its jumble of speech and thought, gabble and giggle and nursery rhyme, permits many observations and oblique references without central definition. It characterises a schizoid mentality, while promoting a profound uncertainty of the kind the new writers required, an ontological insecurity. Contradiction thrives. The Starman states that he is an extraterrestrial alien over

100 years old. The judgment of the authorities is that he is 'a quack head-doctor' called Charlie Nebraska, now in need of head-doctoring himself. The irrational narrator sees no need to arbitrate, no incongruity in allotting different values to the same thing at one time: a plausible symptom of mental illness. The reader may resolve the contradictions how he likes; the narrator does not. The Starman's 'quack' cure begins to work, and the narrator discovers that he is not a 'little kid' at all, but a middle-aged man. The inmates stage an uprising, led by the Starman who promises them freedom and escape to Alpha Centauri, but it fails. The rebels are incarcerated more firmly in Ward 8. They do not know where the Starman is.

In *The Rhetoric of Fiction* Booth claims, with reference to *The Sound and the Fury*,[22]

> There are some characters who are not fully qualified to narrate or 'reflect' a story (Faulkner can use the idiot for *part* of his novel only because the other three parts exist to set off and clarify the idiot's jumble).

The distance between that assertion and Rome's story is a good measure of the dissent of the new sf writers. Behind Booth's partial disqualification of Benjy lies a disregard for the abnormal mentality per se: it is unclear, a jumble, and so restricted in value for the normal mind. Many writers now disagree, finding in the literary depiction of madness a release from restrictions. Behind their apparent infatuation with idiots lies a dissatisfaction with normality (what Rome calls 'ordinariness'), and a belief that the language of the abnormal may be of immense value in criticising it. This belief is fortified by Laing's conclusion that such a criticism is already a deliberate purpose of some schizophrenics in their deformations of language. Chief Bromden, narrator of Ken Kesey's *One Flew Over the Cuckoo's Nest*, fulfils exactly this role of critic, invalidating not so much Booth's statement as the social principles that prompted it.[23]

The workings of the dissociated mind can best be presented in disorganised form. Rome's erratic style, with its jumps of reference, lineation, typography, and punctuation, is a device to counteract the single-value interpretation with which we uphold normality. Is the Starman *really* Charlie Nebraska? The author refuses to say. The ambiguities of his narrative, emphasised by its formal eccentricity, reveal the limitations of that habitual discriminatory approach.

which, institutionalised in the mental hospital, says that a 'quack' cannot cure anybody, but a real doctor can. The story seems to show that the opposite is true.

After the Starman, whom Bowie also wrote about,[24] troops a whole harlequinade of the naturally or chemically crazed: Aldiss's Colin Charteris, Moorcock's Karl Glogauer, Ballard's T–, and others employed by James Sallis, Michael Butterworth, Graham Charnock, Thomas M. Disch, and M. John Harrison. Their patchwork perceptions and jumbled expressions refract the common light of day, adding colours at the cost of a little confusion. These stories no more encourage the use of hallucinogens than they encourage schizophrenia; they re-enact the hallucinogenic effect in terms of literary technique.[25]

> The Edwardian facades of the street were crusted white: snow on lintels, ledges and roofs contrasted hard with dark vertical surfaces, turning the view Cubist. Visibility was down to twenty yards. It was bitterly cold.
>
> Arm was alone in a white acid fantasy. The world was soft and anechoic, enclosed in a 4,000 cubic yard hemisphere. *Was this the Big White Sleep*.

A variety of attitudes and 'dialects' are apparent even in this snippet: scientific, artistic, literary, sub-literary, professional, conversational. While speech and writing of any degree of education commonly borrows words and phrases from several frames of reference, it will usually modulate them into something more even, less splintered than this, which calls attention to its own heterogeneity.

Since it unsettles habitual responses, writers may disorganise words for many and even contradictory purposes. Burroughs attacks his own text with scissors to prevent our reassembling it into the categorised shapes of habit. The text itself is entropic and must leave no organised impression in the mind. Another writer may amass many 'dialects', mixing and crossing categories, to 'turn the view Cubist' and give a holistic illusion of reality as multifaceted, with as many aspects as there are conceivable observers. This principle operates in the description by Zelazny quoted earlier. One writer may intend a literary depiction of a disorganised world, like Ballard devising 'non- linear narrative' because he believes we no longer live 'in linear terms': he permits his fiction to join the decay. Another may incorporate the social and mental disorganisation in the hope of counteracting it, like Aldiss allowing Charteris to trip out and then, so to speak, trip back in again. A disorganised style may be an example of decadence, or, as an artistic response to decadence, a restitution of some kind of order, within the structure of the work of art.[26] The distinction depends as much upon the tolerance of the reader as the integrity of the writer. Finally, techniques of disorganising prose must contain at least a residual order, to communicate anything. They rapidly become new methods of organisation, as B.S. Johnson warned.

The most successful writers are those who realise the ambiguities they are creating and expose them in the fiction, as Wolf does, or Moorcock, or Brian Vickers, another of the new writers inspired and published by *NW*. In his 'Area Complex' civilisation has destroyed itself in some (unnamed) catastrophe. Davy, a young mutant, lives with other survivors in a derelict city. His is another dissociated consciousness, out on the fringe of the new tribalism, and he is preoccupied with a frustrated semi-awareness of the old, abandoned values. Unlike his companions he will pick up a pre-disaster book and flip through it. He is, fitfully, an artist too. In Prof. Hubert Kusick's *Dynamics of the Anti-Society* he reads:[27]

'In the terminal period of degeneration in such a culture a distinctive frenzy of directionless creativity characteristically occurs, resulting in a prolific mish-mash of half-formed ideas and unassimilated emotions rather than a fulfilling crystallization of them; virtually a repository for all the psychological torments of failure.' Well that made me burn until i saw how funny it was, frustrated old biddies like Kusicky saying how awful it's going to be without hope. It's fun, that's all, and so's writing.

Prof. Kusick obviously used to read *NW*. The degenerated style is a repository of failure – or, as Davy (who uses it) says, a resurgence of freedom and fun. Davy had certainly read Ballard, for he quotes from 'The Voices of Time', rejecting its stately withdrawal as too passive a response to the end of the universe.[28] Davy's way is more creative and impulsive, though not without 'half-formed ideas' and 'torments of failure'.

Paul, in Vickers's 'The Coded Sun Game', shows similar reactions.[29] Blinking in the California sunlight as he leaves hospital after some (unnamed) breakdown, he finds himself in a synthetic environment made up of style and image, without any reference to an underlying reality.[30]

Of this he was sure: his present 'existence' was false, almost entirely the construct of other people's imagery. His own percepts and behavioural patterns, which did nothing but sustain this distorted phenotype, were manipulated by the instruments of delusion – or, worse, these things *were* the instruments of delusion. They were so all-pervasive and indispensable, however, that it was necessary to work on their terms at this stage, to contrive them into self-destructive oppositions, and so release his subjugated self. He needed consciously to know, explore and exploit the true potentialities of his genotype. Something – existence itself – was lying to him. He felt mutilated. So he had to make the world's illusions annihilate themselves. It did not seem important that, to be effective, any action in that direction would be drastic in a personal sense, or that ultimate relativity might just be the beginning of total dissociation. It *was* important to be free to roam the causeways of valid memory, to get down (Paul grinned cynically) to the real nitty-gritty. His head would fix the universe with its own images. So he typed three words. This first phase attack commenced:

Confusion of media

The abstract convolution of Paul's thoughts here expresses his self-preoccupied detachment from his physical situation. Elsewhere, confidently subsumed in Vickers's stylistic mix, we can detect the influences of William Burroughs, Brian Aldiss, Samuel Delany, and especially J.G. Ballard. Like *The Drowned World*, 'The Coded Sun Game' posits an integrated, ecological reality which it has been the main business of human civilisation to subvert and deny. Like Kerans, Paul hears the call of the biosphere in the primal pulse of the sun and wishes to reverse evolution and swim back down to a protozoic Nirvana.[31]

> Reverse the recapitulation/Down through the micro- onto- and
> phylo-geneses of perception / Down through the mammals,
> reptiles, amphibians, fish, the metazoa / Down through the
> whole bloody lot, back to the proto-scene, the chemical origins /
> Back to where it was all turned on /// Let's get off the Hook ///

He tries to drown himself in a swimming pool but fails, attracted back to life by the body of Michelle as she swims by above him. Without a Ballardian global catastrophe to promote the reversal he longs for, he has to attack the images that surround him.[32]

I've read books, seen films, watched television, listened to the radio, heard music, looked at paintings, listened at doors, been places, been taught, been talked to, been talked at . . . All bits. F/r/a/g/m/e/n/t/s. The media confuse me, so I

Confuse the media

"There certainly seems to be a resurgence of sun-worship, partic ency to reverse the anthropomorphic nomenclature of geographical WONDERFUL!!! *"Clive, he thinks he lives in an ersatz univers a* s camera sense; the only action in the whole eight bloody hours surfing cult, for instance . . ." WHAT? God only knows / NOW, NOW), Sell (Cell), Hair (Heir), Sun (Son), Sole (Soul), Genes (Jean

Studies of optical phenomena – eg: The Ames Room, The Ponzo Illusion, the Hering Illusion, the Muller-Lyer Figure, MacKay's Ray Figure, rotating trapezoids, various 'impossible objects'; indicate that the processes of the shifts in person from first to third, the changes in tense, the absolute conviction of his own sanity in a lunatic world, together with a few recurrent fixities amidst a welter of inconsistency, are typical of the

Vickers exploits the dissociated style to the full. First, it operates as an 'anti-style', disorientating our habits of reading and thinking to produce its own connections. Second, it represents the internal language of a clinically deranged personality, superficially chaotic, but clustered around 'a few recurrent fixities'. Third, it expresses Paul in action as a contemporary and more desperate Surrealist, confusing the media and attacking dialectal specialisation in the hope of liberating a larger, more unified entity, to 'explore and exploit the true potentialities of his genotype'. The style is anarchic and destructive, attacking the form and vandalising the meaning of the media Paul finds all around him; but it is also cumulative, synthetic, since it is from these fragments that the reader assembles his image of Paul and the meaning of his story. The debris of Paul's semantic environment – what he reads, hears, overhears – reveal Paul himself to us, reflected and refracted. Vickers breaks up his style not only to allow contrasting and incompatible views to co-exist, as Wolf and Rome did, but also to excite interaction between them, precipitating compatible and corresponding elements too. He uses a large number of puns, setting up short-circuits between separate dialects. Where Whorf saw disagreement between psychologist and physicist over the meaning of the word 'space' as a failure of communication, Vickers suggests that that ambiguity may signal communication at another level. He lists points of correspondence: 'Sell (Cell), Hair (Heir), Sun (Son),' and so on. 'The Hook' is the snare that catches the fish, and the addict's dependence on supply. As Paul goes into another epileptic ecstasy at noon, he feels himself merging with the sun, 'Angst and Angströms . . . among the faculæ and flocculi.'[33] This is gimmickry, but in earnest.

Vickers's puns, like Aldiss's in *Barefoot in the Head*, suggest possibilities of fixity in the chaos, tracing co-ordinates from hippy slang to biology, psychology and physics, inside to outside. Yet their very capriciousness makes them untrustworthy: the essence of pun is semantic uncertainty, so that at the same time as the fix is offered, the flux is reaffirmed. The pun is a linguistic identity crisis. Vickers's style simultaneously presses for and prohibits a unified reading, as, in other ways, Moorcock's Cornelius stories do. The appearance of the prose dramatises Paul's insanity and encourages us to expect an incoherent, indecipherable vision; but followed through, Paul has his own coherence and logic, like Ballard's terminal men, socially unrecognised but existentially authentic. He forces with brutal pragmatism his last exit from Babel, the artificial environment of California with all its codes. Vickers allows us to make whatever response we like, letting us into Paul's delusion without insisting we accept it as truth. He even cuts sections of psychoanalytical notes into his text, reinforcing the socially authorised interpretation of Paul as a psychotic, inaccessible across a conceptual and linguistic gulf of his own making; but the story is our access to him.

Disruption is not really enough without the suggestion of some kind of order, lost or not quite achieved. It is the tension between the dialects, between order and chaos, communication and confusion, which is the highest power of a dissociated style.

Chapter Ten
A higher albedo
stylistic theory

In February 1969 *NW* featured an article by James Sallis: 'Orthographies', the first part of a survey of contemporary fiction (the concluding second part was never published). Sallis quotes A. Alvarez:[1]

> Certainly, for the past forty years or more, the history of the arts could be written in terms of the continual and continually accelerating change from one style to another. The machinery of communications and publicity is now so efficient that we go through styles in the arts as quickly as we go through socks; so quickly, indeed, that there seem no longer any real styles at all. Instead, there are fashions, idiosyncrasies, group mannerisms and obsessions. But all these are different from genuine style, which in the past has always been an expression of a certain fundamental coherence, an agreement about the ways random experience can be made sense of. . . . Style in short, is bound up with belief of one kind or another.
>
> Clearly, any modern artist starts from premises more dispersed, empirical and ad-libbed than that.

Sallis comments, 'Our recognition of the absence of absolutes (metaphysical, social, personal), then, has led to the impossibility of any aesthetic absolute.'[2]

Once again there is dancing at the end of time. To the modernist critic, an explosion in the gallery of style means ruin and barbarism; to the New Wave writer it signals only a liberation from the classicism of genre sf, with its 'Golden Age' and prescriptive 'unities', and from the larger conservatism that excludes sf from literature. Alvarez glumly sees the 'genuine style' of the past replaced by 'fashions, idiosyncrasies, group mannerisms and obsessions'. In the terms he chooses these things are trivial and shallow: it is for the artist to redeem and elevate them to the status of style by imbuing them with a 'fundamental coherence' of ideology. As we saw in the last chapter, the *NW* writer prefers to affirm their transience and incoherence, deliberately leaving them *un*bound in the belief that incoherence is the most significant feature of contemporary experience and requires expression in fiction. That is what Moorcock has done with fashions and group mannerisms, and Ballard with idiosyncrasies and obsessions. The exploded gallery has become an exhibition of entropy.

Alvarez and Sallis tacitly concur in perpetuating the traditional critical fallacy: that there is 'style' distinct from 'content' and it is possible to produce literature that has one but not the other. Since Wittgenstein and Chomsky (to say nothing of McLuhan) it has become ever more apparent that the distinction *is* fallacious, that to change the manner is to change the matter. There have been those among the new sf writers who have brought that understanding to bear upon their own work, to repudiate the dualistic theory of a 'Literature of Ideas'. Samuel R. Delany's essay 'About Five Thousand One Hundred and Seventy Five Words' rejects any assumption that sf can be defined by a special form or content, and instead distinguishes the properties of the mode in the tenses of its relation to known or presumable history (these events have not happened, might have happened, might happen if we don't watch out, etc.). Delany considers, 'Is there such a thing as verbal information apart from the words used to inform?' and, stressing the literal meaning of 'in-form', decides that, 'put in opposition to "style", there is no such thing as "content". . . . Content is the illusion myriad stylistic factors create when viewed at a certain distance.'[3] 'About Five Thousand One Hundred and Seventy Five Words' is the earliest and least technical of Delany's essays in structuralism, discarding the notion of 'content' altogether to discuss words as signs completely empty of meaning. By being organised systematically words acquire the power to refer outside those systems. The assembly of the structuralist school has been the most interesting and important recent development in sf criticism.[4] Delany and its other exponents claim that structuralism and semiology are not only important but actually obligatory modes for criticising sf. They are reinstating the old distinction between sf and 'mundane fiction' that *NW* attacked so strenuously, but from a different ideological premise: namely, that the imaginary constructions of sf function as criticisms of the real world, and therefore the sf writer is consciously or unconsciously engaged in a structuralist task. Sf is a special structuralist case of literature. The danger of this is perhaps that, to the uncommitted reader, these critics sometimes seem to be co-opting sf for the structuralist cause, using it to support their own worldview rather than to tell us anything about the fiction itself. Sf becomes merely a special case of structuralism.

The structuralist critique of sf has largely been elaborated since the period when James Sallis, M. John Harrison and others were defining (or rather refusing to define) the critical policy of *NW*, but the *NW* writers themselves were already opposed to the terms of structural analysis. Delany's seminal collection of critical essays, *The Jewel-Hinged Jaw*, may have taken its title from Thomas Disch's *Camp Concentration* as serialised in *NW*, but it received an insulting and dismissive review from Moorcock in one of the last issues of the magazine.[5] *NW* authors resolutely maintain the dissociation of style from content, not only when writing casually, like Moorcock with his 'ideas' or 'notions' and the 'trappings' in which to 'dramatise them', but also in the course of intense inquisitions like 'Orthographies'. Sallis is not trying to fool anyone when he renames the ancient pair 'substance' and 'surface'. 'Substance, I take to be the combination of themes, ideas, the complexity of relationships and associations at every level; surface, as the smooth tissue covering it.'[6] Far from proclaiming their indissoluble unity, Sallis goes beyond Alvarez in affirming the disconnection of contemporary styles from all things fundamental and coherent, and taking away their traditional function of making sense of random experience. This dissociation, he says, is the essence of a new kind of fiction, which he had first identified in a review for *NW* the previous year.[7]

It is the manner of expression . . . which gives the particular, and I think unmistakable, tone to this fiction; whereas most contemporary fiction aims for penetration, this new fiction aims for immediacy. Hence, there may be great underlying significance . . . but this will remain basically subliminal. The story *surface* becomes the important thing, and it fills itself with puns, extravagant imagery, energy and movement, exuberant invention and throwaway ideas. The abstract concerns are there, but they exist *beneath* the story surface – occasionally drifting to the surface, but only to be immediately taken back in

a sudden shift of orientation – and functioning chiefly by
resonance and overtone. . . . The surface disruptions conceal –
in fact, *contain* – an underlying order.
In 'Orthographies' his conviction is stronger.[8]
Several current writers are working, it appears, to produce a kind
of structural periphrasis, in which substance and style are
carefully *kept* dichotomous and but rarely allowed to intersect.
. . . Substance is kept neatly tucked away underneath, like a
subterranean cataract, and the whole emphasis is on – rather,
appears to be on – the creation of a smooth, haptic surface. . . .
The new fiction is a fiction of misdirection: it points one way and
happens another.

Sallis could not be ignorant of the weight of opinion set against
the dichotomy of style and content; indeed, the erudition of
'Orthographies' is alarming. His persistence in referring to and even
exaggerating the distinction can only indicate a change of conditions
that has made it newly applicable. 'Current writers', he claims, 'are
working to produce' the 'structural periphrasis'; content and style
are '*carefully kept* dichotomous and but *rarely allowed* to intersect.'
The only justification for trotting out the fallacy again is that it
reflects some actual design in the intentions of the authors, and so is
less fallacious than it was.

'Orthographies' is a particle analysis, a dense mass of information
humming with references and allusions. Sallis distinguishes and
contrasts the minutiæ of contemporary movements, counter-
movements, quasi-movements, and gestures anticipating movements until the scintillation of the dots merely blinds us to whatever
picture they compose, if any. The critical consciousness inflates
anxiously by multiple fission until the article floats off into the void,
never to be finished. But it is not only the critic who has this
problem: Sallis makes it plain that it besets the author too.

In his classic essay 'Tradition and the Individual Talent' T.S. Eliot
celebrated the 'historical consciousness' of artists.[9] The writer,
benefiting from the twentieth century's meticulous preservation
and reproduction of its own and previous arts, is presumed to
possess an all-encompassing familiarity with his ancestors and contemporaries. He is aware of their community around him, pressing
in upon him as he writes. His contribution must take theirs into
account. Sallis agrees that this clairvoyance operates, but feels how
burdensome it has become: 'the contemporary writer of fiction,

then, is technically an old man from his first writing.'[10]
What has happened is that between Eliot and Sallis the amount of
art and information available has increased geometrically. Everything may have been said already. The new writer is 'technically an
old man' because he is aware of the enormity of the tradition, and
also of its decline. The solo voice is drowned in the perpetuated
clamour of history; the author has no authority any more.[11]
He begins with a set of assumptions quite different from those
of his predecessors. He knows by way of Wittgenstein that all
important things are unsayable; that his propositions are
meaningless. . . . According to Godard he is supposed to 'put
the difficulties somewhere else from where they were before'.
Paralysed by both the quantity and the nature of his knowledge, he
is yet 'wanting to write and, if possible, advance the novel'.[12] (Hence
Burroughs and Robbe-Grillet, and the numbers of those who follow
them.) The hyperconsciousness of the new writer, over-informed,
over-sensitised, gives rise to all the effects we have observed: the
desperate search for a viewpoint outside orthodoxy, no matter how
extreme; the elevation of mental dissociation to a heroic virtue; the
relentless ambiguity that avoids choosing among conflicting values;
the restless shuffling of styles; in fact all Lodge's 'symptoms of . . .
insecurity, nervous self-consciousness and . . . schizophrenia'.[13]
Tradition has collapsed on the head of the individual talent. The
intention Sallis describes, to concentrate on 'surface' and keep
'substance . . . tucked away underneath', is the adoption of a fundamentally ironic attitude. The new writer must say less than he
means, because he knows more than he can say. When his poise
falters he will sometimes exude a real fear of that Coleridgean
'subterranean cataract'.

This makes sense of Sallis's peculiar view that while substance is
complex and many levelled, and surface just a 'tissue covering it', it
is surface that now receives all the attention. No one style is adequate; there is too much at stake for such a restriction of possibilities.
There is no 'certain fundamental coherence', in Alvarez's phrase,
and experience appraised in this light is too random to be 'made
sense of'. 'Chaos', as B.S. Johnson says, 'is the most likely explanation.'

Surface, style, the choice and deployment of words, signs, and
spaces: it would seem that this is the only aspect of writing which
remains under authorial control. This is the level, therefore, where

the experiments are made. Sallis talks of surface as delicate and malleable, quoting with approval Lawrence Durrell's metaphor of 'the circulatory system and the skin', and, with even more, Boris Vian's statement that he projects his subject matter onto 'an irregularly tilting, and consequently distorting, plane of reference.' The author can make a smooth, polished surface, as Moorcock does in his stories of the Dancers at the End of Time, or break it up into colourless little bits, as Ballard does in *The Atrocity Exhibition*: the enormity of his 'substantive' themes and ideas is not disguised. Indeed, it could be that fragmentation and misdirection actually enhance deep meaning, allowing the reader more imaginative entry into the text. Hence the repeated injunctions against *study*, in Moorcock's statements about his Cornelius stories, or this from Langdon Jones about his sequence 'The Eye of the Lens':[14]

> The stories . . . should merely be read, and not searched for symbolism. It is almost literally impossible for the reader to pick up all the references and quotes that occur in the stories, but this does not matter. The trilogy is intended to work through juxtaposition of many different images, and should succeed through resonance rather than explicit statement.

Jones refers us to Ehrenzweig's *The Hidden Order of Art*, which also interested Sallis and other *NW* writers.[15]

> According to Anton Ehrenszweig [sic] the most important aspect of any work of art is in the unconscious pattern that runs through it. If this structure is not communicated, then the painting, or story, or piece of music is not a success. Thus the surface flow of the work may be greatly disrupted with no adverse effect on the degree of communication, which may in fact be greatly increased.

Ehrenzweig's book, subtitled 'A Study in the Psychology of Artistic Imagination', advances a theory which, beneath its compulsory new jargon and scrupulously unorthodox procedure, seems to consist of a restatement of the classic psychoanalytic distinction between conscious and unconscious. He asserts that it is on the unconscious level that the great work of artistic creation is first done and then appreciated. Conscious superstructures of aesthetic appeal, classical modality, and compositional logic are immaterial unless they arise from and guide us, the spectators, down to this substratum. 'To feel the submerged depth coherence,' Ehrenzweig says,[16]

> we must, almost with an effort, abandon the conscious need for

logic, order and sequence. Then the superficial fragmentation will not be felt and will be replaced by a feeling of inner necessity far more potent . . ., a more profound continuity. We are far too intolerant of superficial fragmentation. A modicum of surface fragmentation is always needed in order to bring into action the usually starved low-level sensibilities.

The argument is closely analogous to Freudian dream-analysis and Surrealist theory, in which disruption of the rational, conscious 'surface' also allows deeper penetration, by the analyst or artist, into 'inner necessity'. Ehrenzweig diagnoses an 'ego rhythm' of dissociation, descent, and re-emergence in all art, but observes, of painting in particular,[17]

In modern art the ego rhythm is somewhat onesided. The surface gestalt lies in ruins, splintered and unfocusable, the undifferentiated matrix of all art lies exposed, and forces the spectator to remain in the oceanic state of the empty stare when all differentiation is suspended. The pictorial space advances and engulfs him in a multi-dimensional unity where inside and outside merge. . . . It would be misleading to call this near-mystic experience of modern art in any way pathological; what is anomalous is the disruption of the ego rhythm on its way back to a more differentiated state. The elusive pictorial space is a conscious signal of an unconscious coherence and integration which redeems the fragmentation of the surface gestalt.

Though this is not 'in any way pathological' he also detects 'the definite schizoid tinge of modern art, which explains the occasionally extreme dissociation of the surface and depth functions.'[18]

Alvarez sees fragmentation of the surface as evidence of the lack of 'certain fundamental coherence', while Ehrenzweig asserts that fragmentation is 'a conscious signal of an unconscious coherence and integration.' There can be no proof either way. Writers who fear being thought pathological and destructive for contriving dissociations in their fiction can declare some creative, integrated intention, as Burroughs and Ballard have done, with or without the rather confusing assistance of Ehrenzweig. Others, perhaps more wisely, build the ambiguity of chaos and order into their work and make it part of the meaning, as Moorcock and Vickers have, not presuming anything about the operation of the work or the psychology of the reader.

This feeling that the imaginative, intellectual, and moral meaning of a work of art can and must look after itself, whatever happens on the surface, is a serious desertion of 'content' for 'style', no matter how important content is still said to be. The feeling is symptomatic of the condition as Sallis, perhaps unintentionally, presents it: a hypertrophy of consciousness. We are too aware. The information explosion permits too many views from too many points. All the issues with which an artist might deal have been overexposed. Previous art overshadows originality, while making it more urgent. Probably no young writer reading 'Orthographies' had read half of what Sallis describes as his heritage. No individual talent can ever be acquainted with the whole tradition. But now he cannot escape glimpsing how ungraspably huge it all is; nor can he expect to be forgiven by critics or public for failing to acknowledge that hugeness. Outdated themes and outworn modes are grounds for dismissal. Obsolescence has spread to art, and if the model is not altogether new it must at least appear in a new style. Moorcock, devising Jerry Cornelius as a heroic legend for modern times, rewrote a couple of Elric stories with a new sophisticated obliqueness. The public and private problems of order and chaos have not changed, only our awareness of them, and our ways of forestalling them.

Moorcock has said that in the early 1960s popular arts like rock music, cartooning and sf looked all the more inviting to a frustrated artist because of their general unselfconsciousness. Naïve and often retarded assumptions offered all scope for development. Unlike literature and painting, these arts had a paucity of tradition to be reckoned with, and retained a prospect of innocence where a newcomer could go with confidence, but the newcomers had to urge the growth of more conscious and critical thought if anything were to be developed at all. Moorcock's *NW* editorials call repeatedly not for the eager innocents who had supported the magazine until then, but for those prepared to extend their bookshelves to unprecedented lengths. In 'Onward, Ever Onward' he specifically puts away 'Heinlein, Blish, Asimov, van Vogt', and dashes out for the latest Penguin Europeans: 'Kafka, Camus, Sartre, Borges, Wyndham Lewis, Cocteau'[19] – a sure syllabus to ravage the innocent and overload his social, moral, and intellectual sensibilities. The progressiveness that Moorcock urges is a race for modernity and away from history: 'writers must look to themselves rather than their predecessors'. In the modern, overintimate age, understanding can be taken for granted. The themes and problems are obvious, omnipresent; their definition and development by other writers has been noted and absorbed. The new writer must leave all that on one side and concentrate on surface style, distinguishing his work from others and displaying an attitude of superiority to his own understanding. All important things are unsayable; but how neatly and wittily he can allude to them without committing himself to a single attitude and forfeiting his poise! The notion of 'hipness', gaining currency in the 1960s out of jazz and junkie slang of the 1950s, is an important one here. It combines shrewdness with panache, an unblinking awareness of what is happening with the ability to stay aloof from the devastating consequences of that awareness. Irony is a virtue; dexterity with different masks and voices is recommended; being informed is obligatory and may be taken for granted.

Notions and exhortations of this kind create the hyperconscious writer, with his characteristic high regard for subjectivity, his talent for misdirection, his love of ambiguity, and his reliance upon mixed and dissociated styles. His subjects are too large and complex to be reduced to words; he regards words with intense suspicion. Sophisticated before maturity, with his powers and confidence weakened, he is 'technically an old man from his first writing.' The hyperconscious writer, however, demands a hyperconscious reader. Moorcock, Jones, and Sallis, with their assertions that their own fiction does not require study and understanding but will work automatically, unconsciously, go some way to overruling that demand and making their work accessible to the less 'hip', but the condition remains. Not everyone who reads it will make the unconscious response on which the writer depends. Those who follow 'a fiction of misdirection' may miss the 'great underlying significance' altogether, in which case the fiction may well appear trivial, flippant, and as irritating as a private joke. Moorcock refused to publish *NW* as a coterie 'little magazine', even when it was the obvious solution to its economic problems. Popularity was vital. *NW* had to try to cultivate readers up to the level of its writers. As it continued, it seemed to assume that this process would accelerate spontaneously. The first excerpts from *The Final Programme* and *The Atrocity Exhibition* were presented gently if enthusiastically, with introductions by the author or editor. Later, as the incidence of obscure and oblique fictions increased, the willingness to explain them, as if to a new reader, decreased. As contributors became more confident in their experiments they became more confident in their audience too. The carefully edited debates about sex and sf, Old Guard and New Wave, disappeared from the correspondence columns; then the correspondence columns disappeared.

The eventual disappearance of the whole magazine might appear to indicate the failure of the enterprise. The success of *NW* in communicating its new vision was hampered by its assumption that everybody knew what it was on about, or that if they didn't it didn't matter. More damaging was its aim not just to improve or enlarge traditional sf, but to replace it altogether. This would have been ambitious if the new writers were talking only in terms of the genre, a small section of the publishing industry whose limits were pre-set, but their determination to abolish genre sf and subsume its functions within a larger and more exacting kind of fiction made the ambition a vain one. Though the sf boom of the 1960s and 1970s is now well over, the readers of sf today are more numerous and less single-minded than the older generations of fandom, who knew that their chosen fiction needed the heat of their bodies to keep it alive. To this extent Moorcock's policy of intelligent and literate fiction in a popular context has achieved a success measurable in audience ratings, but that audience stubbornly remains less discriminating than he intended. The idealist, reactionary fantasies of Tolkien, which for Moorcock represent imaginative fiction at its most corrupt, still exercise a paternal influence on the market at least as potent as Moorcock's subversion.

Whether or not ideal readers have ever constituted more than a small proportion of its audience, a distinctive contemporary fiction has been created according to the policy. It is a fiction which exhibits an alarming intensity of thought despite a casual, detached manner; it cultivates irony, permitting a high degree of authorial subjectivity while undermining the tradition of the writer's authority; it mistrusts absolute and single responses, seeming arbitrary, speculative and oblique in appearance and operation. At the same time it is animated by the general apprehension that all these haphazard, elusive qualities are the proper methods for dealing with a reality which appears too complex for any individual raid to seize much of it at all. The fiction exists in loosened relations to its maker, its spectator, and its environment. Whatever its label, it is derived from the genre of science fiction not only in its grasp of the precipitousness of modernity but also in the pitch and enterprise of its imagination. It illuminates our enslavement to the idea of the future and to our own technology. It sub-divides reality and adds provisional worlds, each flickering unsteadily, whose reflected light does not always draw our attention back to the source we know to be there.

Chapter Eleven

No more, with feeling
entropy and contemporary fiction

'There's the second law of thermodynamics, things degenerating
from their most complex to their most simple. The fat man in
the double-knit suit sitting watching television and becoming
pear-shaped. The submissive form in the contoured chair.
That's de-evolution. It's what everybody just knows on a gut
level.

'The conditions that people find themselves living in are more
similar than different; the hairdos keep changing but the facts
remain the same.'[1]

The Laws of Thermodynamics state that, while the energy in any
closed system remains constant, its heat spontaneously decreases as
the energy becomes more and more dissipated and unavailable for
work. Entropy is a measure of disorganisation; the entropy of a
closed system increases. Coining the term in 1865, Rudolf Clausius
said that the entropy of the universe tends to a maximum. If it is a
closed system, the universe must eventually suffer a heat-death, and
reach a state in which its energy is the same at every point – the end
of heat and light, form, matter, motion, and time.

Within this great decline the claims of life, a very specialised
condition of matter, seem very small. As Norbert Wiener puts it:[2]

To those of us who are aware of the extremely limited range of
physical conditions under which the chemical reactions
necessary to life as we know it can take place, it is a foregone
conclusion that the lucky accident which permits the
continuation of life in any form on this earth . . . is bound to
come to a complete and disastrous end.

Nevertheless, ever since its introduction men have strained to identify with the principle of irreversible entropy. Rudolf Arnheim observes:[3]

> When it began to enter the public consciousness a century or so ago, it suggested an apocalyptic vision of the course of events on earth. The Second Law [of Thermodynamics] stated that . . . the energy in the universe . . . was subject to more and more dissipation and degradation. These terms had a distinctly negative ring. They were congenial to a pessimistic mood of the times. . . . The sober formulations of Clausius, Kelvin, and Boltzmann were suited to become a cosmic memento mori, pointing to the underlying cause of the gradual decay of all things physical and mental.

The last century has seen the decline of Western faith in an afterlife beyond physical existence, while the influence of Eastern thought with cyclic cosmologies has not been strong enough to provide a substitute. Entropy offers extremely appropriate imagery for modern speculations about the end. Life and the universe will lapse, we feel, into formless inertia. We have, however, passed beyond the 'pessimistic mood' of the *fin de siècle*. Most people would not contemplate entropy with terror or despair. The novels of Kurt Vonnegut illustrate the more popular feeling that man and the universe are no more or less meaningful for being absolutely finite. We already anticipate the end; it colours our expression a good deal. Leslie Fiedler suggested that science fiction came to the fore in the 1960s because of its concern with myths popular at the time: the disruption of history and the end of man. We saw how the millennial aspirations of Leary and the hippies represented a last flowering of faith in a benign apocalypse. The old order would be swept away for the New Jerusalem to be founded – not the End, but Childhood's End. Dissociating themselves from that utopian use of sf, the writers of *NW* predicted the mood of the 1970s more accurately, concerning themselves with images of finality, with entropy.[4]

> 'Mountains erode. Organisms wither, drop and decay.
> Physically, we are eating ourselves. Spiritually, we are disintegrating. Psychologically, we are being gnawed from within. Everything is collapsing.'

In his erudite and fascinating book *The Sense of an Ending* Frank Kermode discusses the End and the preoccupation with it in our time. He admits the 'apocalyptic tenor of much radical thinking about the arts in our century,' but demurs.[5]

Now I also believe that there is a powerful eschatological element in modern thought and that it is reflected in the arts . . . but I don't find it easy to see the uniqueness of our situation. . . . It seems doubtful that our crisis, our relation to the future and to the past, is one of the important differences between us and our predecessors. Many of them felt as we do. If the evidence looks good to us, so it did to them. . . . There is nothing at all distinguishing about eschatological anxiety; it was, one gathers, a feature of Mesopotamian culture, and it is now a characteristic, often somewhat reach-me-down in appearance, of what Mr Lionel Trilling calls the 'adversary culture' or sub-culture in our society.

He refutes Fiedler's claim for 'the uniqueness of our situation' by burying it in the evidence that 'one gathers' about apocalyptic apprehensions from innumerable historical sources.[6] Expecting the End has been a recurrent if not continual habit of human societies; so much so that 'clerkly scepticism' and 'disconfirmation of predictions' have become integral parts of the pattern. Kermode's argument thus contains its own justification. As a clerkly comment on contemporary eschatology it will make enlightening reading in the twenty-first century (I hope); as a study of his own epoch it is devalued by Kermode's insistence that this is not the End and that we are no different from the Mesopotamians and everyone else in between. His literalness obscures the operation of the myth he is discussing. John Barth's essay 'The Literature of Exhaustion' is more illuminating. The values he endorses are precisely the humanist ones that Kermode urges – order, continuity, respect for tradition and form – but he accepts without fumbling one major proposition of apocalyptic radical artistic thought: the 'death of the novel'. 'It may well be that the novel's time as a major art form is up,' he concedes, but remarks,[7]

Whether historically the novel expires or persists seems immaterial to me; if enough writers and critics *feel* apocalyptical about it, their feeling becomes a considerable cultural fact, like the feeling that Western civilization, or the world, is going to end rather soon.

This is, Barth notes, 'an age of ultimacies and "final solutions" – at least, *felt* ultimacies, in everything from weaponry to theology, the celebrated dehumanization of society, and the history of the novel.'[8] The writers he admires are those who do not ignore 'felt ultimacies' or attempt to smother the feeling; nor will he praise those who simply describe it. Ultimacies, as Kermode says, have over-shadowed the artistic imagination in every period. The great artist is the one who 'confronts an intellectual dead end and employs it against itself to accomplish new human work.'[9] Barth's contemporary example is Jorge Luis Borges.[10]

> *Labyrinths* and *Ficciones* . . . illustrate in a simple way the difference between the *fact* of aesthetic ultimacies and their artistic *use*. What it comes to is that an artist doesn't merely exemplify an ultimacy; he employs it.

How far the *NW* writers were succumbing to entropy or making it work for them is a matter for the judgment of each reader. I would emphasise the extraordinary vigour with which they undertook to remake science fiction from first principles, and the intensity and personal power of *Report on Probability A, The Atrocity Exhibition*, and *The English Assassin*, to mention only three novels in which the vision of entropy predominates. My title, 'The Entropy Exhibition', refers to the central paradox of the *NW* group: the conviction that form is degenerating and energy dissipating, asserted with remarkable formal resourcefulness and an energy of expression so compelling we may well call it exhibitionist.[11]

> 'The end of the world. Let me tell you about the end of the world. It happened fifty years ago. Maybe a hundred. And since then it's been lovely. I mean it. Nobody tries to bother you. You can relax. You know what? I *like* the end of the world.'

Moorcock and his associates all drive boldly out of the extreme province of traditional sf into the very middle of the ruins of the modern novel, to deliver fictions that confront the felt ultimacies of verbal and cultural catastrophe and cope strategically with them. 'By "exhaustion",' says Barth, 'I don't mean anything so tired as the subject of physical, moral, or intellectual decadence, only the used-upness of certain forms or exhaustion of certain possibilities – by no means necessarily a great cause for despair.'[12] Hence the delight with which, as Aldiss says, 'Platt and Moorcock and Ballard . . . welcomed catastrophe'[13] – as the source, paradoxically, for a new creativity. 'I *like* the end of the world,' says Disch's Lottie Hanson. Hence the exhibitionism of entropy. Each of my three major authors responded differently to the challenge. The success of the confrontation has enabled each to go beyond 'exhaustion', as Barth suggests we might, to resume some of the traditional forms and possibilities of narrative. Significantly, neither *The Malacia Tapestry*, *High-Rise* nor *The Condition of Muzak* can be easily categorised. Each is neither wholly in nor out of the broad 'field' of sf, or even the vague compass of the 'New Wave'. They come under that most awkward of provisional labels, 'Post-Modernism', as written by people who approached it through sf rather than any other way, and that is as closely as we may define them.

> The law of entropy continues to make for a bothersome
> discrepancy in the humanities and helps to maintain the
> artificial separation from the natural sciences.[14]

Though Arnheim's essay on entropy and modern art does not mention it, for a reconciliation of art and science we should obviously look to science fiction. While the *NW* writers were working to reattach sf to the mainstream of modern literature, other writers without apprenticeships in sf were approaching from the other direction, adopting and adapting the resources of the genre to the peculiar needs of the time. Robert Scholes's study *The Fabulators* suggests some guidelines for seeing this trend as part of a larger international movement in contemporary fiction,[15] but from the viewpoint of the student of sf the phenomenon appears to be principally American. English writers who have made use of sf seem to be isolated, individual figures: William Golding, Anthony Burgess, Doris Lessing, Angela Carter. Americans doing the same thing almost constitute a school or movement of their own. Perhaps in the country of Wells, Lewis, Huxley and Orwell it was felt that the gap was not wide enough to require bridging, while in the country of Gernsback and Campbell and E.E. 'Doc' Smith, the sub-literary and indeed anti-literary excesses of the pulps turned sf into something altogether alien that other writers have to make an effort to reclaim.

Numerous American authors make reference to entropy. In *City of Words* Tony Tanner devotes a chapter to their use of the terms as a literary metaphor.[16] Here he says, 'Among the writers who use the actual word in their work are Norman Mailer, Saul Bellow, John Updike, John Barth, Walker Percy, Stanley Elkin, Donald Barthelme.'[17] He deals separately with two others who have made greatest use of the concept. The first is William Burroughs.

> Without using the word, Burroughs shows in his work a world in
> the throes of entropy (with human regressing to animal, thence

to vegetable, then to mineral, and everything finally ending in a stagnant lake of mud or a vast rubbish heap). The battering urgency of Burroughs's narrative voice characterises the messenger of the end of the world. 'These are the conditions of total emergency.' 'Listen to my last words anywhere.' 'Minutes to go,' he says again and again. Like a medieval preacher he prophesies apocalyptic destruction ('nova') as the inevitable outcome of the uncontrolled disorder of our times. One symptom of chaos is the formal regression Tanner identifies. Burroughs describes it as 'the renunciation of life itself, a *falling* towards inorganic, inflexible machine, towards dead matter.'[18] The simplification of organisation is accelerated by a conspiracy, the Nova Mob, which encourages the dissipation of energy through various drains and addictions. 'The Planet drifts to random insect doom. . . . Thermodynamics has won at a crawl. . . . Orgone balked at the post. . . . Christ bled. . . . Time ran out.'[19]

The second author Tanner discusses not only mentions the word 'entropy' but uses it as the title for a short story: Thomas Pynchon. He also provides abundant imagery of reification. The title of his novel *V*. refers to (among other things and people) a mysterious *femme fatale* who, if she exists at all, seems to have bought immortality to spread her evil through the whole twentieth century at the price of being replaced, bit by bit, with bizarre mechanical devices, like the Tin Man in *The Wizard of Oz*. Benny Profane, night watchman in a research lab, has imaginary conversations with a dummy, a 'synthetic human' for use in radiation tests. 'What are you?' he asks. 'Nearly what you are,' it says. 'None of you have very far to go.'[20] In *The Crying of Lot 49* Pynchon considers another example of entropy, in the cybernetic sense as the measure of energy lost in any mechanical process.[21] In search of one secret conspiracy, Oedipa Maas uncovers another, known acronymically as WASTE. Its members are hobos, derelicts, and the poor, 'a secret organization of the "nameless" everywhere. All machines use energy, and the members of WASTE constitute the wasted energy of the American social machine.'[22] Pynchon's short story 'Entropy' tackles the Second Law of Thermodynamics more directly. Callisto, a middle-aged intellectual, 'found in entropy or the measure of disorganization for a closed system an adequate metaphor to apply to certain phenomena in his own world.'[23] Depressed by 'American "consumerism" ' and its tendency 'from differentiation to sameness', he retreats into the ecological closed system of his 'hothouse' apartment, staring anxiously at the thermometer, which has been registering 37 degrees for three days. Has the heat-death already happened? Meanwhile, the noise from Meatball Mulligan's apartment downstairs reaches 'a sustained, ungodly crescendo'. Meatball discusses information theory, watches a band play silent, deconstructed jazz, and tries 'to keep his lease-breaking party from deteriorating into total chaos.'

The raucous hyperboles of Burroughs and the self-parodic elusiveness of Pynchon may devalue the criticisms implied in their applications of entropy to modern life. Treated in this absurdist way, entropy supplies 'an adequate metaphor' merely. Of no more substance than a Metaphysical conceit, it is effective only as an intellectual novelty, altogether reduced from the cosmic scope of its scientific application. Tanner says, 'It is my impression that the term, taken from its context of the second law of thermodynamics, is used now with a looseness which any scientist would deplore.'[24] Some writers certainly seem to treat it as a fashionable catchword with little or no other value.[25] Fans of hard science fiction view its appearance with suspicion. Robert Scholes and Eric S. Rabkin administer a sharp rebuke, in their survey of 'The Sciences of Science Fiction', to 'careless science fiction writers' who write of the entropy of systems which are not closed, as if sf were the public information service of MIT.[26] This is Zoline's vision of the heat-death of the universe:[27]

Sarah Boyle pours out a Coke from the refrigerator and lights a cigarette. The coldness and sweetness of the thick brown liquid make her throat ache and her teeth sting briefly, sweet juice of my youth, her eyes glass with the carbonation, she thinks of the Heat Death of the Universe. A logarithmic of those late summer days, endless as the Irish serpent twisting through jewelled manuscripts for ever, tail in mouth, the heat pressing, bloating, doing violence. The Los Angeles sky becomes so filled and bleached with detritus that it loses all colour and silvers like a mirror, reflecting back the fricasséeing earth. Everything becoming warmer and warmer, each particle of matter becoming more agitated, more excited until the bonds shatter, the glues fail, the deodorants lose their seals. She imagines the whole of New York City melting like a Dali into a great chocolate mass, a great soup, the Great Soup of New York.

In the absence of Academic legislation, the only limits to an author's latitude in converting science to metaphor are determined, presumably, by how far the figure conveys the meaning intended. But there is an ambiguity evident in how scientists use the word entropy in their popular writings, so perhaps Tanner, Scholes and Rabkin are being unnecessarily defensive. Norbert Wiener, the mathematician who invented cybernetics, may be responsible for introducing entropy to the general reader, as Tanner suggests. In *The Human Use of Human Beings* Wiener states:[28]

> But while the universe as a whole, if indeed there is a whole
> universe, tends to run down, there are local enclaves whose
> direction seems opposed to that of the universe at large and in
> which there is a limited and temporary tendency for
> organization to increase. Life finds its home in some of those
> enclaves.

Life, though not a closed system, shows that there are counter-entropic forces in the universe too. Life tends 'to persist, to multiply, and to organize'; 'we ourselves constitute . . . an island of decreasing entropy.'[29] For Wiener's application of theories of probability and organisation to human society and the mechanics of its operation, this principle is fundamental. But Claude Lévi-Strauss, whose anthropological work follows on from Wiener's principles, sees human life differently. The role of humanity in the cosmic scheme,[30]

> far from according man an independent position, or his
> endeavours – even if doomed to failure – being opposed to
> universal decline, he himself appears as perhaps the most
> effective agent working towards the disintegration of the
> original order of things and hurrying on powerfully organized
> matter towards ever greater inertia, an inertia which will one
> day be final. From the time when he first began to breathe and
> eat, up to the invention of atomic and thermonuclear devices,
> by way of the discovery of fire – and except when he has been
> engaged in self-reproduction – what else has man done except
> blithely break down billions of structures and reduce them to a
> state in which they are no longer capable of integration?

Mankind does not increase entropy only with his more destructive inventions, Lévi-Strauss notes, but also with his creative ones, such as urbanisation and agriculture.

Civilization, taken as a whole, can be described as an extraordinarily complex mechanism, which we might be tempted to see as offering an opportunity of survival for the human world, if its function were not to produce what physicists call entropy, that is inertia.

Seen by Wiener, human history is a little eddy against the flow of universal decline; seen by Lévi-Strauss, it is the swiftest current of the main stream. It all depends on how you identify organisation. Lévi-Strauss reveals another paradox in the rule of entropy. Any machine functions with less than perfect efficiency. This is just as true, Wiener pointed out, of a system of human communications – hence the formulation of information theory. But perfect communication, were there such a thing, would increase entropy too, by reducing differences and stabilising energy. Lévi-Strauss observes:[31]

Every verbal exchange, every line printed, establishes communication between people, thus creating an evenness of level, where before there was an information gap and consequently a greater degree of organization.

Rudolf Arnheim's painstaking analysis clarifies the ambiguity. An increase in entropy, as described by Wiener, is a move 'from a state of organization and differentiation . . . to a state of chaos and sameness.'[32] But, says Arnheim, 'chaos' is not 'sameness'. In the homogeneous state, which is the end of entropy, there is perfect equilibrium, a highly orderly condition, and most unlike chaos, which is differentiated, unpredictable, and disorderly. The fault is not in the theory, Arnheim explains, but in the linear model by which we habitually express it. Entropy is not a force that acts upon matter; it is a measurement of disorganisation, which tends to increase spontaneously. There is more than one effect responsible for the increase. Two different tendencies may both fairly be called entropic. One is what Arnheim calls 'tension reduction', 'a striving toward simplicity'. Energy transfer follows the line of least resistance. Land erodes; water seeks its own level. Freed of restraints, forces and temperatures interact to achieve equilibrium. This tendency is orderly, resulting in uniformity and equal distribution of energy. The other tendency, also an effect of the interference of innumerable patterns of forces, consists in 'the fortuitous destruction of patterns that are unlikely to be rebuilt by mere chance', As Arnheim points out, 'Not every increase of entropy comes about by ordering: an explosion, blowing a structure to bits, rarely increases orderliness.'[33]

Arnheim's explanation widens our concept of entropy and goes a long way towards justifying the 'looseness' Tanner senses in literary uses of the term. Arnheim identifies the entropic element in what otherwise seem to be two separate trends in modern art: the minimalist (Piet Mondrian's 'pictures' of rectangular divisions of the canvas) and the aleatory (John Cage's 'music' incorporating chance events and the random sounds of the environment). One increases order, one decreases it. Both contrive a dissipation, harmonic or explosive, of the traditional tensions inside and outside the work: both demonstrate entropy. So, in literature, we can appreciate that the writer may employ very different techniques to express an entropic vision. Burroughs's prose, cut up, folded in, and thoroughly disorganized, dramatizes linguistic disorder. Robbe-Grillet's prose, erased, reduced, bleached of adjectival and symbolic colour, exploits linguist contingency. Both demonstrate entropy. So, within the pages of *NW*, do *Barefoot in the Head* and *Report on Probability A*. Writers may also concentrate on very different themes and subjects. Burroughs is preoccupied with chaos, the creation and aggravation of 'as many insoluble conflicts as possible' by the Nova Mob.[34] Pynchon emphasises sameness, mass production and 'consumerism', the blurring of distinction between human and machine. The concept of entropy contains its own latitude, and it seems that novelists are covering rather than exceeding it. Charles B. Harris observes:[35]

As Pynchon sees him, man – like his universe – undergoes continuous decay. He is destroyed on the one hand by all the accidents and natural disasters that flesh is heir to . . . as well as by a repetition of wars, crises, and riots. On the other hand, the conforming sameness of modern organization man reflects symptomatically the state of de-differentiation Pynchon believes is becoming increasingly characteristic of our universe.

Ihab Hassan asserts the same thing of Burroughs: 'The apocalypse can be icy (whole planets approaching the Absolute Zero) or explosive (the refrain is always, "Minutes to go").'[36]

Between them Burroughs and Pynchon bracket the English literary movement that centred on *NW*. Moorcock's first issue contained Ballard's article 'Myth-Maker of the 20th Century' in praise of William Burroughs.[37] His last full issue in magazine format included Philip José Farmer's parody 'The Jungle Rot Kid on the Nod' ('If William Burroughs instead of Edgar Rice Burroughs had written the Tarzan novels . . .'), while Barrington Bayley's 'The Four-Color Problem' is a much more accurate imitation.[38] Thomas Pynchon's 'Entropy' appeared in an issue of *NW* for 1969, its first and only publication in Britain.[39] In the critical perspective Arnheim helps us establish, the arrangement of the entropy exhibition in *NW* seems properly complex rather than merely loose. Ballard's hero-victim T– pursues his quietus down to the 'psychic zero' of the terminal beach, or in the orgasmic explosions of crashing cars. Moorcock's Cornelius responds to the catastrophe with violence, 'randomization' and inertia by turns, but cannot free himself from his role in the 'romance of entropy'. The distinctive themes of *NW* writers – ontological insecurity, alienation, the hidden and hostile dimensions of media and machines, the disintegration of objectivity into subjective worlds of inner space, the dangerously exhilarating multiplication of 'possibilities' – are all primary concerns of their times, though they came to them rather in advance of popular assent. The concept of entropy, a degeneration inevitable from either overorganisation or chaos, is the centre of this imaginative cluster; hence the frequency with which the writers return to the term, and its fashionability, even for those who use it least scientifically. It is critically obtuse to reprehend them as Scholes and Rabkin do for misquoting thermodynamics, or as Kermode does for jumping to a conclusion. Literalness can cramp metaphor. In any case, Norbert Wiener had spoken of social entropy and Sigmund Freud of psychological entropy long before.[40] Sarah Boyle and Lottie Hanson do not violate scientific speculation, whatever it does to them.[41]

'And anyhow the world *doesn't* end. Even though it may try to. even though you wish to hell it would – it can't. There's always some poor jerk who thinks he needs something he hasn't got, and there goes five years, ten years, getting it. And then it'll be something else. It's another day and you're still waiting for the world to end. . . . The icebox is empty and you have to think who haven't you borrowed any money from and the room smells and you get up just in time to see the most terrific sunset. So it wasn't the end of the world after all, it's just another day.'

In the end, now that entropy has overtaken the magazine itself, what has all the creative energy of *NW* accomplished? [42]

> We think that we were to some extent successful. (Moorcock, 1971)
> I think we achieved an enormous amount. (Moorcock, 1972)
> To this day I don't know if *New Worlds* achieved anything which would not have happened anyway. (Moorcock, 1978)

Moorcock's irresolution reflects not so much an uncertainty over the quality of the fiction published in *NW* as the ambivalence with which it has been received in the literary world at large: adopted but unacknowledged. *NW* was not an isolated phenomenon, despite the efforts of marketing monopolies and some of the mandarins of sf to make it one. One of the strongest imperatives of Moorcock's editorial policy, continually stated and everywhere demonstrated, was to bring sf back into the arena of contemporary fiction, first by incorporating into sf the characteristic themes and techniques of fictional innovators from Joyce and Beckett to Burroughs and Borges, and then by investing the sf writer's inheritance of images and approaches into a fiction whose primary and most urgent concern was not remote space or the distant future, but the condition of the present. In an editorial of 1971, Moorcock seems weary enough to be on the verge of recanting.

> The bulk of so-called New Wave science fiction has no more claim to be worthy of serious attention than the bulk of so-called Old Wave sf. . . . Reasonable sf readers accept the fact that sf, as such, can never by its nature offer the richer, more profound pleasures of the best novels.

But he goes on immediately:[43]

> But it is equally obvious that in its concern for discovering new techniques, new subject matter and so on, sf may well have made the greatest contribution to the development of the novel in the 20th century, just as the Gothic contributed in the 19th century.
>
> Sf is a genre form. Like all genre forms it has certain restrictions which we have spent some years exploring. At present we seem close to discovering the limits of those restrictions.

The restrictions of sf for the *NW* writers were the habits and conventions it had acquired as a commercial genre artificially separated from the fictional mainstream: its stereotypes, its plot formulae, its uninvestigated assumptions. Moorcock saw it as their task to redesign what they could, and jettison the rest; thereafter, they were open to all literary influences and free to experiment as they chose. Needless to say, Moorcock was not an isolated phenomenon either. His beliefs and proposals were firmly seconded, not only by *NW* critics such as James Sallis, John Clute, and M. John Harrison, but also by other editors – Charles Platt, Langdon Jones, Judith Merril, Harlan Ellison, Robert Silverberg, Damon Knight, Norman Spinrad – who brought forward a host more writers. While the fiction they produced did generate its own conventions and even clichés, and sometimes took on an arrogant, cliquish tone, it was far more remarkable for its individuality, spontaneity and unpredictable diversity. Rapidly breaking out from the confines of traditional sf and fandom, the new writers roamed at large through the modern world. 'New Worlds is not a science fiction magazine,' announced Charles Platt in a 1969 editorial. 'We are not even a short story magazine in the usual sense. The only key to what we are is our contents.'[44] British New Wave sf is one more example, or rather many more examples, of the anarchic and ill-defined movement that critics have tried to label 'absurdist', 'comic-apocalyptic', 'Post-Modernist' or even 'Post-Contemporary' fiction, 'surfiction', and 'fabulation'. Those critics have concentrated on American fiction. They maintain that British authors, 'in their conservative way, are still inclined to believe in reality as traditionally conceived'. Confronted with a prime example of English Post-Modernism, they can only say that 'some modern English fiction is getting more like American fiction'.[45] This self-supporting argument is a logical short-circuit, and jumps a gap in their reading. The imaginary deficiency of British examples is plentifully supplied by the writers of *NW*. Their absence from the innumerable surveys of contemporary fiction that should consider them is a major reason for the existence of this book.

Aldiss and Ballard and Moorcock are not without honour. They are popular with readers and other writers; they are given attentive reviews; two of them were nominated for the Booker Prize in 1981, while the third sat on the panel of judges.

If they have scarcely attracted equal attention from academics and literary critics it cannot be entirely due to critical deafness and prejudice. An interviewer asked Moorcock in 1972 what he thought the failures of *NW* had been.[46]

We claimed too much for what we were doing in the early days and are only now beginning to see the results. We never licked the distribution problem – until it was too late – and so never reached as many readers as we might have done. We failed completely to convince the majority of fans that we felt writers like Heinlein were short-changing them with bad writing and simple-minded notions. We failed to improve the standard of writing in SF, which, in the main, remains abominable. . . . We've certainly failed to convince the majority of U.S. publishers concerning the merits of typical NEW WORLDS fiction for they plainly prefer to publish the sensationalistic and poorly-conceived SF they have always published. . . . We've failed, perhaps, to produce a large market for the kind of fiction we like best, but we have produced a large enough one to make publishing that fiction a viable proposition (which it wasn't, even five years ago). And, by and large, we've failed to get across to most SF fans the seriousness of our intentions, the purpose of our intentions.

Temporarily divided and disturbed by the New Wave, sf has settled back down and shut its doors again – though it is unable, and largely unwilling, to cut itself off from all literary scrutiny in the way it had before Lewis, Amis and Crispin took notice. Genre sf survives, boosted by the cinema, as a large sector of the popular fiction market catering for the tastes of readers not in the least concerned with serious intentions and literary movements. Many of its popular writers show clear evidence of the influence of Ballard or Aldiss; some were connected with later versions of *NW*. Much recent sf – the later novels of Frederik Pohl, for example – has been decidedly more considerable, deeper in characterisation and what Aldiss called 'respect for human software'. It has steered away from the rationalised optimism of the Campbell era, in which the only problems recognised were the ones that would be solved in the course of the story, and the only solutions technical ones. Nor is it at all recalcitrant about sex now, especially with the arrival of feminist writers. But except for the writers' workshops in America, whose labourers are mainly interested in stylistic virtuosity, sf has not backed up the advances of the 1960s; nor has anyone led a concerted revolt against the New Wave as Moorcock did against the Old Guard. Many writers who showed promise in *NW* have not published (or perhaps have not been able to publish) anything which fulfils it: Terry Pratchett, Brian Vickers, Graham Charnock, Pamela Zoline, Sam Wolf. . . . Even with the growth of sf criticism *NW* and the fiction that came out of it have not received adequate attention. Moorcock is at least partly right when he says that this is because of the inflexibility of marketing and critical categories. Sf publishers and distributors, seeing the difference of *NW* sf from what they usually sold, grew nervous and would not promote it, while 'mainstream' fiction publishers would often not look at something that had emerged from a science fiction magazine. Too many readers of every kind have responded in the same way. It has taken much too long for Ballard and Moorcock to achieve the recognition they have.

The critical neglect of *NW* must also be due to a peculiar problem of definition. Such was the anarchy and openness of the British New Wave that, from certain angles, it was completely invisible. This is the reason that there is so much uncertainty and disagreement over the label itself, unsatisfactory as it is, among its old adherents as well as inveterate opponents. Moorcock made it plain in another interview.[47]

> B[urns]: I've a feeling though, that this Movement, whatever it is, will have collapsed long before we get round to resuscitating it.
>
> M[oorcock]: Assuming it is a Movement. It might well be mere literary extremism, which will shift back into and reinvigorate the traditional novel. But we need to talk of Movements in order to get moving, to get any kind of dynamic. We need to think, 'We're eight blokes here, eight musketeers.'
>
> B: But it's false, isn't it?
>
> M: Yes, finally it comes down to individual writers. Movements always break up very fast. The *New Worlds* group soon broke up (quite amicably) into individual writers, each getting on with his own work.

As the unified front the name suggests, the New Wave never really existed. The confidence and determination of the early musketeer manifestos by Moorcock and Ballard tend to distract the reader from the divergence and indeed incompatibility of aims and intentions. Other than external pressure, there was nothing to keep the *NW* group together, no cohesion among these fiercely individual writers, who had little in common but their dissatisfactions. A better model than a Wave would be an explosion, starting at a definable centre and dissipating swiftly in all directions. Its moment was brief, its disintegration swift and total, but its echoes reverberate everywhere, and we still wait for another boom that can silence them.

Notes

1 The cybernetic cuckoos: science fiction and the popular imagination in the 1960s

1 John Wyndham, *The Midwich Cuckoos* (London: Michael Joseph, 1957), p. 226.
2 Arthur C. Clarke, *Childhood's End* (London: Sidgwick & Jackson, 1954), p. 207.
3 Leslie Fiedler, 'The New Mutants', in his *Collected Essays* (New York: Stein & Day, 1971), vol. II, pp. 379–400.
4 Ibid., p. 382.
5 Ibid., pp. 381–2.
6 Mick Farren, *Watch Out Kids* (London: Open Gate, 1972), p. [10].
7 Jerry Rubin, *Do It!: Scenarios of the Revolution* (New York: Simon & Schuster, 1970), pp. 17–19 (author's italics).
8 Farren, op. cit., p. [21].
9 Richard Neville, *Playpower* (London: Cape, 1970), p. 144 (author's italics).
10 Rubin, op. cit., p. 100.
11 Timothy Leary, *The Politics of Ecstasy* (London: MacGibbon & Kee, 1970), p. 141.
12 Ibid., p. 135.
13 Ibid., p. 183.
14 R.D. Laing, *The Facts of Life* (London: Allen Lane, 1976), p. 20.
15 Norbert Wiener, *The Human Use of Human Beings: Cybernetics and Society*, 2nd edn (London: Eyre & Spottiswoode, 1954), p. 185 (author's italics).
16 David Bowie, 'Oh You Pretty Things', *Hunky Dory*, RCA, SF8244, 1971.
17 Bowie, *The Rise and Fall of Ziggy Stardust and the Spiders from Mars*, RCA, SF8287, 1972.

18 Neville, op. cit., p. 67.
19 Fiedler, 'Cross the Border – Close the Gap', *Collected Essays*, II, pp. 473–4.
20 Thomas M. Disch *et al.*, 'The Lessons of the Future', *New Worlds* (hereafter *NW*), no. 173 (July 1967), pp. 2–3 (authors' italics).
21 See, for example, Norman Spinrad, 'No Direction Home', *New Worlds Quarterly* (hereafter *NWQ*), no. 2 (September 1971), pp. 32–49.
22 See, for example, Charles Platt, 'Fun Palace, Not a Freakout', *NW*, no. 180 (March 1968), pp. 31–41.

2 The 'field' and the 'wave': the history of *New Worlds*

1 *The New SF: An Original Anthology of Modern Speculative Fiction*, ed., Langdon Jones (London: Hutchinson, 1969).
2 Michael Moorcock, Preface, ibid., p. 7.
3 Hilary Baily, 'Some Corner of a Funny Field', *Foundation: The Review of Science Fiction*, no. 13 (May 1978), pp. 78–83.
4 Moorcock, 'New Worlds: A Personal History', *Foundation*, no. 15 (January 1979), pp. 5–18.
5 E.J. Carnell, letter to Brian Aldiss, 25 February 1964.
6 Moorcock, 'New Worlds – Jerry Cornelius', *Sojan* (Manchester: Savoy, 1977), p. 144.
7 Moorcock, editorial: 'A New Literature for the Space Age', *NW*, no. 142 (May–June 1964), pp. 2–3 (author's italics).
8 J.G. Ballard, 'Myth Maker of the 20th Century', *NW*, no. 142 (May–June 1964), pp. 121–7.
9 Carnell, letter to Aldiss, 19 October 1964.
10 Aldiss, letter to Lee Harding, 22 February 1967.
11 Aldiss, letter to Harry Harrison, 26 February 1967.
12 Moorcock, 'A Personal History', op. cit., pp. 13–14.
13 14 November 1973.
14 Moorcock, Introduction, *NWQ*, no. 7 (autumn 1974), p. 9. Hilary Bailey, a writer and critic, was Moorcock's wife at the time.
15 Moorcock, Letter to Charlie Brown, 29 February 1976.
16 *Frendz* (23 June 1971).
17 Moorcock, 'A Personal History', op. cit., p. 11.

3 Love among the mannequins: sex and science fiction

1 Langdon Jones, 'I Remember, Anita', *NW*, no. 144 (Sep-

tember–October 1964), pp. 69–80.
2 Ibid., p. 76.
3 Louis Van Gastel, letter to the editor, *NW*, no. 146, (January 1965), pp. 125–6 (author's italics).
4 Harry Harrison, *Great Balls of Fire!* (London: Pierrot, 1977).
5 Harrison, 'We are Sitting on our . . .', *SF Horizons*, no. 1 (1964), pp. 39–42 (author's italics).
6 *Amazing Stories*, no. 19 [June 1953]; all references are to the English edition, reprinted from the American originals.
7 'Maddened by the lure of her lovely body, he became the . . . OUTLAW IN THE SKY, by Guy Archette.' *Amazing*, no. 22 [December 1953].
8 'The Mad Monster of Mogo', *Amazing*, no. 19 [June 1953], pp. 8–55.
9 Frank Kelly Freas, *Frank Kelly Freas: The Art of Science Fiction* (Norfolk, VA: Donning, 1977), p. 36.
10 Paul Ash, 'Big Sword', *Astounding Science-Fiction*, 15, no. 1 (January 1959), p. 73; all references are to the English edition reprinted from the American originals.
11 Harrison, letter to Brian Aldiss, 15 January 1968.
12 Randall Garrett, 'A Spaceship Named McGuire', *Analog*, 17, no. 11 (November 1961), pp. 4–35.
13 Garrett, 'The Queen Bee', *Astounding*, 15, no. 3 (March 1959), pp. 48–72.
14 Christopher Anvil, 'Mating Problems', *Astounding*, 16, no. 1 (March 1960), pp. 26–37.
15 Walter Bupp, 'Card Trick', *Analog*, 17, no. 5 (May 1961), pp. 70–93. 'Walter Bupp' was a pseudonym for Garrett, who was quite able to contribute all the fiction for an issue of the magazine, under various pseudonyms.
16 A. Bertram Chandler, 'The Outsiders', *Astounding*, 15, no. 1 (January 1960), pp. 52–76.
17 Lester del Rey, 'Superstition', *Astounding*, 11, no. 1 (January 1955), pp. 78–108.
18 Garrett, '. . . And Check the Oil', *Astounding*, 15, no. 1 (January 1959), pp. 94–116.
19 E.K. Jarvis, 'You Can't Escape from Mars!' *Amazing*, no. 4 [December 1950], p. 8.
20 Charles V. de Vet, 'The Unexpected Weapon', *Amazing*, no. 4 [December 1950], p. 50.
21 Clinton Ames, 'Victims of the Vortex', *Amazing*, no. 21 [October 1953], pp. 8–39, 98.
22 Guy Archette, 'Outlaw in the Sky', *Amazing*, no. 22 [December 1953], p. 30.

23 Dallas Ross, 'You Might Say Virginia Dared!', *Amazing*, no. 4 [December 1950], p. 77.

24 P.F. Costello, 'The Squares from Space', *Amazing*, no. 4 [December 1950], pp. 78–92.

25 de Vet, op. cit., p. 55.

26 Aldiss, *The Shape of Further Things: Speculations on Change* (London: Faber, 1970), p. 62.

27 See, for example, Joanna Russ, 'The Image of Women in Science Fiction', *Vertex*, vol. 1, no. 6 (February 1974), pp. 53–7; Pamela Sargent, 'Introduction: Women and Science Fiction', *Women of Wonder: Science Fiction Stories by Women about Women*, ed. P. Sargent (New York: Vintage, 1975), pp. 11–51; Samuel R. Delany, 'To Read *The Dispossessed*', in his *The Jewel-Hinged Jaw: Notes on the Language of Science Fiction* (Elizabethtown, NY: Dragon Press, 1977), pp. 239–308; Douglas Hill, Introduction, *The Shape of Sex to Come*, ed. D. Hill (London: Pan, 1978), pp. 7–11.

28 E. French Biscoe, letter to the editor, *NW*, no. 148 (March 1965), pp. 124–5.

29 Biscoe credits the analogy to Amis, but seems more likely to have taken it from Edmund Crispin: see his Introduction to *Best SF Three* (London: Faber, 1958), p. 12.

30 Moorcock, Guest Editorial, *NW*, no. 129 (April 1963), pp. 2–3, 123–7.

31 Richard A. Poole, letter to the editor, *NW*, no. 165 (August 1966), p. 154.

32 Joseph Green, 'Tunnel of Love', *NW*, no. 146 [January 1965], pp. 61–80; and 'Dance of the Cats', *NW*, no. 157 (December 1965), pp. 68–93; John Baxter, 'The God Killers', *NW*, nos 163–4 (June–July 1966).

33 Green, 'The God Killers', *NW*, no. 164 (July 1966), p. 114.

34 Hilary Bailey, 'The Fall of Frenchy Steiner', *NW*, no. 143 (July–August 1964), pp. 2–36.

35 David Harvey, 'Jake in the Forest', *NW*, no. 155 (October 1965), pp. 77–94.

36 Michael Butterworth, 'Girl', *NW*, no. 162 (May 1966), pp. 113–18.

37 American automobile advertisement reproduced in Charles Platt, 'Fun Palace, Not a Freakout', *NW*, no. 180 (March 1968), pp. 31–41.

38 Granville Hawkins, 'Playback', *NW*, no. 191 (June 1969), pp. 21–3.

39 Norman Spinrad, 'Bug Jack Barron', pt 3, *NW*, no. 180 (March 1968), p. 29 (author's italics).

40 John Landau, 'Does Sex have a Future?', *NW*, no. 199 (March 1970), pp. 9–11.

41 Ian Watson, 'The Sex Machine', ibid., pp. 2–4.

42 J.G. Ballard, 'Use Your Vagina', review of *How to Achieve Sexual Ecstasy*, by Stephan Gregory, *NW*, no. 191 (June 1969), pp. 58–60.

43 Ballard, 'A Neural Interval', *NW*, no. 185 (December 1968), back cover.

44 Ballard, 'The Summer Cannibals', *NW*, no. 186 (January 1969), pp. 19–23.

45 Ballard, *The Atrocity Exhibition* (London: Cape, 1970), pp. 23–4.

46 'Sim One', *NW*, no. 186 (January 1969), pp. 29–31.

47 D.M. Thomas, 'X', *NW*, no. 193 (August 1969), pp. 7–10; Tom Godwin, 'The Cold Equations', *Astounding*, 11, no. 1 (January 1955), pp. 48–66.

48 R.D. Laing, 'The Ghost of the Weed Garden: a study of a chronic schizophrenic', *The Divided Self: A Study of Sanity and Madness* (London: Tavistock, 1960), pp. 195–225.

49 Thomas has written another version of 'The Cold Equations' in which the sexes are tellingly reversed: 'Limbo', *Penguin Modern Poets*, 11 (Harmondsworth: Penguin, 1968), p. 106.

4 Pulling out of the space race: anti-space fiction

1 J.G. Ballard, 'Which Way to Inner Space?', *NW*, no. 118 (May 1962), pp. 2–3, 116–18.

2 *Farewell, Fantastic Venus!: A History of the Planet Venus in Fact and Fiction*, ed. Brian Aldiss and Harry Harrison (London: Macdonald, 1968).

3 Brian Aldiss, *Billion Year Spree: The History of Science Fiction* (London: Weidenfeld & Nicolson, 1973), pp. 285–317.

4 Ursula K. Le Guin, 'Science Fiction and Mrs. Brown', *Science Fiction at Large*, ed., Peter Nicholls (London: Gollancz, 1976), p. 20.

5 Ralph Nicholas, 'Clean Slate', *NW*, no. 162 (May 1966), pp. 119–24.

6 Charles Platt, 'The Hard Stuff', review of *The Promise of Space*, by Arthur C. Clarke, *NW*, no. 187 (February 1969), p. 62.

7 Aldiss, *Billion Year Spree*, op. cit., p. 286; cf. a discussion between Aldiss, Kingsley Amis, and C.S. Lewis in 1962, transcribed as 'Unreal Estates' in Lewis, *Of Other Worlds: Essays and Stories*, ed., Walter Hooper, (London: Bles, 1966), pp. 86–96.

8 John Sladek, 'The Poets of Millgrove, Iowa', *NW*, no. 168 [November 1966], pp. 82–8 (author's asterisks).

9 Kenneth Harker, 'Cog', *NW*, no. 161 (April 1966), pp. 57–78.

10 Donald K. Slayton, Alan B. Shepard and L. Gordon Cooper, 'Introduction to Space Flight', pt II, *Man in Inner and Outer Space: Selected Lectures on the U.S. Manned Moon Landing Programme, the Sun, and*

Our Own Planet, ed., S.T. Butler and H. Messel (Sydney University Press, 1969), pp. 393–472.

11 Terry Pratchett, 'Night Dweller', *NW*, no. 156 (November 1965), pp. 83–8.

12 Michael Butterworth, 'Concentrate 1', *NW*, no. 174 (August 1967), pp. 57–8.

13 Gordon Walters, 'No Guarantee', *NW*, no. 161 (April 1966), pp. 25–39.

14 Butterworth, 'Concentrate 3', *NW*, no. 197 (January 1970), p. 1.

15 Moorcock, *The Black Corridor* (London: Mayflower, 1969); *The Final Programme* (London: Allison & Busby, 1969).

16 Ballard, 'You and Me and the Continuum', *SF Impulse*, no. 1 (March 1966), pp. 53–60; 'Journey Across a Crater', *NW*, no. 198 (February 1970), pp. 2–5; 'The Death Module', *NW*, no. 173 (July 1967), pp. 21–4.

17 Barry N. Malzberg, *The Falling Astronauts* (New York: Ace, 1971); *Beyond Apollo* (New York: Random House, 1972).

18 David Bowie, 'Space Oddity', Phillips, BF 1801, 1969; re-issued on *Space Oddity*, RCA, LSP 4813, 1972.

5 Footholds in the head: inner space fiction

1 J.G. Ballard, 'Which Way to Inner Space?', *NW*, no. 118 (May 1962), pp. 2–3, 116–18 (author's italics).

2 See, for example, *Man in Inner and Outer Space: Selected Lectures on the U.S. Manned Moon Landing Programme, the Sun, and Our Own Planet*, eds, S.T. Butler and H. Messel (Sydney University Press 1969), pp. 393–472.

3 J.B. Priestley, 'They Come from Inner Space', *New Statesman and Nation*, 16 (1953), pp. 712, 714; collected in Priestley, *Thoughts in the Wilderness* (London: Heinemann, 1957), pp. 20–6.

4 Ballard, 'Which Way . . .?', op. cit., p. 3.

5 C.G. Jung, Foreword to Miguel Serrano, *The Visits of the Queen of Sheba* (Bombay: Asia Publishing House, 1960), pp. v–vi.

6 Gordon Walters, 'No Guarantee', *NW*, no. 161 (April 1966), pp. 25–39.

7 Michael Moorcock, 'The Golden Barge', *NW*, no. 155 (October 1965), pp. 36–51, published pseudonymously; David Harvey, 'Jake in the Forest', ibid., pp. 77–94; Norman Brown, 'House of Dust', *NW*, no. 161 (April 1966), pp. 40–7; Michael Butterworth, 'Girl', *NW*, no. 162 (May 1966), pp. 113–18; Reg Moore, 'High in Sierra', *NW*, no. 199 (March 1970), p. 15.

8   Brian Aldiss, 'The Source', *NW*, no. 153 (August 1965), pp. 61–74.
9   David Stacton, *Kaliyuga* (London: Faber, 1965).
10 Norbert Wiener, *The Human Use of Human Beings: Cybernetics and Society*, 2nd edn (London: Eyre & Spottiswoode, 1954) pp. 11–12.
11 Moorcock, Editorial, *NW*, no. 151 (June 1965), pp. 2–3, 46.
12 Ballard, 'The Coming of the Unconscious', *NW*, no. 164 (July 1966), pp. 141–5.
13 This unexpected legacy of Hollywood to the literary imagination is shared by many other writers: see Tony Tanner, *City of Words: American Fiction 1950–1970* (London: Cape, 1971), pp. 87, 131.
14 William Burroughs, *The Ticket that Exploded* (London: Calder & Boyars, revised edn, 1968), pp. 150–1 (author's italics).
15 See also Aldiss, *The Shape of Further Things: Speculations on Change* (London: Faber, 1970), p. 52.
16 E.C. Tubb, 'New Experience', *NW*, no. 144 (September–October 1964), pp. 107–18.
17 Similar is Clifford Simak's *Out of their Minds* (New York: Putnam, 1970), in which Earth is threatened with war from the 'Land of Imagination', where all the beings ever invented by man in folklore, fiction and dream have physical existence. After a promising start, in which this otherworld appears numinous and menacing, shifting vertiginously in distance and distinguishability from the mundane, Simak sends in his hero as an agent of Reason, and the Land of Imagination collapses, simply from its author's inability to credit it with the reality he had pretended to grant it at first. Revealingly enough, he presents it not only as a realm of trivia populated by cartoon characters, but also as one of evil, ruled by the Devil.
18 Butterworth, '6B 4C DD1 22', *NW*, no. 198 (February 1970), pp. 13–19.
19 Chris Lockesley, 'Travel to the Sun with Coda Tours', *NW*, no. 195 (November 1969), pp. 26–7.
20 Spinrad, 'Bug Jack Barron', pt 3, *NW*, no. 180 (March 1968), pp. 28–30, 42–56 (author's italics).
21 Pamela Zoline, 'The Heat-Death of the Universe', *NW*, no. 173 (July 1967), pp. 32–9.
22 Aldiss, Foreword to 'Heat-Death', in *The Mirror of Infinity: A Critics' Anthology of Science Fiction*, ed. Robert Silverberg (New York: Harper and Row, 1970), pp. 287–92.
23 Zoline, op. cit., p. 36.
24 Doris Lessing, *Briefing for a Descent into Hell* (London: Cape, 1971).
25 Katherine Maclean, 'The Other', *NW*, no. 164 (July 1966), pp. 30–3.
26 D.M. Thomas, 'Mr. Black's Poems of Innocence', *NW*, no. 188 (March 1969), pp. 28–35.

27 Thomas M. Disch, 'The Squirrel Cage', *NW*, no. 167 (October 1966),
    pp. 56–71 (author's italics).
28 Disch, op. cit., p. 71.
29 Langdon Jones, 'The Time Machine', *Orbit*, ed., Damon Knight, vol. 5
    (New York: Putnam, 1969), pp. 89–113. This story was intended to
    appear in *NW*, no. 174 (August 1967), but was suppressed by the
    printer because of its detailed description of sexual intercourse.
30 Disch, 'Camp Concentration', pt 2, *NW*, no. 174 (August 1967), p. 19
    (author's italics).
31 Frieda Fordham, *An Introduction to Jung's Psychology* (Harmond-
    sworth, Middx: Penguin, revised edn 1966), pp. 77–8.
32 R.D. Laing, *The Politics of Experience* and *The Bird of Paradise*
    (Harmondsworth, Middx: Penguin, 1967), p. 11.
33 Ibid., p. 11.
34 Ibid., p. 50.
35 See cover, *NW*, no. 182 (July 1968), and ch. 5 of M. John Harrison,
    The Committed Men (London: Hutchinson, 1971).
36 Laing, op. cit., pp. 108, 49, and 46 (author's italics).
37 Laing, op. cit., p. 108.
38 Ibid., pp. 139–56.

6 The works of Brian W. Aldiss

1 Brian W. Aldiss, letter to Judith Merril, 3 October 1966. All notes in
   this chapter refer to works by Aldiss, unless otherwise stated.
2 *Report on Probability A* (London: Faber, 1968); a partial version
   appeared in *NW*, no. 171 (March 1967). *Barefoot in the Head: A
   European Fantasia* (London: Faber, 1969); parts appeared irregularly
   in *NW*, nos 174–86 (August 1967–January 1969).
3 *Greybeard* (New York: Harcourt, Brace & World, 1964); *Earthworks*
   (London: Faber, 1965); *Frankenstein Unbound* (London: Cape,
   1973); *The Eighty-minute Hour: A Space Opera* (Garden City, NY:
   Doubleday, 1974).
4 *The Shape of Further Things: Speculations on Change* (London:
   Faber, 1970); letter to Charles Platt, 8 May 1966.
5 Letter to Donald Malcolm, 7 February 1967.
6 Letter to Harry Harrison, 23 September 1967 (author's italics).
7 Letter to Ugo Malaguti, 15 June 1967.
8 *Billion Year Spree: the History of Science Fiction* (London: Weidenfeld & Nicolson, 1973).
9 *Non-Stop* (London: Faber & Faber, 1958).
10 Robert A. Heinlein, 'Universe' and 'Common Sense': first published

in *Astounding* (American edition), May and October 1941, these stories make up *Orphans of the Sky* (London: Gollancz, 1963).

11 *Greybeard*, op. cit., pp. 195–6.

12 M. John Harrison, 'The Ash Circus', *NW*, no. 189 (April 1969), pp. 18–19.

13 Poul Anderson, 'The Creation of Imaginary Worlds', in *Science Fiction, Today and Tomorrow: A Discursive Symposium*, ed., Reginald Bretnor (New York: Harper & Row, 1974), p. 255.

14 M.H. Abrams, *The Mirror and the Lamp: Romantic Theory and the Critical Tradition* (New York: Oxford University Press, 1953).

15 *The Dark Light Years* (London: Faber, 1964), p. 66 (author's aposiopesis).

16 Ibid., pp. 168–70.

17 Ibid., p. 188.

18 This observation I owe to Tom Shippey, who commented, 'Telepathy's fine – thought has nothing to do with language, so that's all right.'

19 Foreword to Pamela Zoline, 'The Heat-Death of the Universe', *The Mirror of Infinity: A Critics' Anthology of Science Fiction*, ed., Robert Silverberg (New York: Harper & Row, 1970), pp. 287–92.

20 *Further Things*, op. cit., p. 88.

21 'The Girl and the Robot with Flowers', *NW*, no. 154 (September 1965), pp. 5–11; collected in *The Saliva Tree and Other Strange Growths* (London: Faber, 1966), pp. 226–32.

22 *An Age* (London: Faber, 1967; retitled *Cryptozoic!*, Garden City, NY: Doubleday, 1968 and London: Sphere, 1973), p. 41. Parts of this novel appeared serially in *NW*, nos. 176–8 (October–December 1967).

23 *Bow Down to Nul* (New York: Ace, 1960; retitled *The Interpreter*, London: Digit, 1961), p. 1.

24 *Barefoot*, op. cit., p. 58.

25 Ibid., p. 258.

26 *Frankenstein Unbound* (London: Cape, 1973).

27 *Non-Stop*, op. cit., pp. 35–6.

28 Philip K. Dick, *Martian Time-Slip* (New York: Ballantine, 1964); Fred Hoyle, *October the First is Too Late* (London: Heinemann, 1966).

29 Letter to the author, 10 September 1977.

30 Letter to Pamela Bulmer, 24 December 1969.

31 'Incentive', *NW*, no. 78 (December 1958), pp. 83–97; revised and collected in *The Canopy of Time* (London: Faber, 1959), pp. 100–18.

32 'Just Passing Through', *SF Impulse*, no. 12 (February 1967), pp. 17–29; revised and collected in *Barefoot*, pp. 13–33.

33 Letter to the author, 10 September 1977.

34 'Amen and Out', *The Comic Inferno* (London: New English Library, 1973), pp. 94–108; 'Who Can Replace a Man?', *The Canopy of Time*, pp. 39–50.
35 'Old Hundredth', *The Airs of Earth* (London: Faber, 1963), pp. 242–56.
36 *Greybeard*, op. cit., p. 206.
37 *Further Things*, op. cit., p. 109.
38 *Report*, op. cit., p. 109 (italicised in original).
39 Suddenly I've seen the mirage of The SF Novel, and am prepared to try and cross deserts of writing to reach it. I feel very much the influence of Europe, and would like to produce something that might not be thought of too badly in Milan, Vienna, and Paris. My latest novel . . . 'The Dark Light Years' has benefitted from a close study of the French anti-novel as written by Mrs [sic] Robbe-Grillet and Michel Butor. In fact, I wrote my own anti-novel, 'Figures in a Garden', before embarking on 'Dark Light Years'. MS. note, perhaps a fragment of a letter, c. January 1964. 'Figures in a Garden' (elsewhere 'Garden with Figures') was the first version of *Report*, without watchers in other dimensions or references to 'The Hireling Shepherd', written in 1962 but unpublished.
40 *Report*, op. cit., p. 162 (italicised in original).
41 Another is featured on the calendar which hangs in the kitchen of the 'waiting man': *Barefoot*, op. cit., p. 46.
42 *Report*, op. cit., p. 112.
43 *Report*, op. cit., pp. 67–8.
44 *Barefoot*, op. cit., p. 244.
45 Ibid., p. 40.
46 Ibid., p. 46.
47 Ibid., p. 38 (author's italics).
48 Ibid., p. 43.
49 Ibid., p. 148.
50 Ibid., pp. 153, 189–90.
51 Ibid., p. 189.
52 Ibid., p. 260.
53 Ibid., p. 257.
54 Ibid., p. 260.

7 The works of J.G. Ballard

1 J.G. Ballard, 'The Day of Forever', *The Day of Forever* (London: Panther, 1967), p. 9. All notes in this chapter refer to works by Ballard, unless otherwise stated.
2 Harold L. Berger writes generally of sf catastrophes in *Science Fiction*

and the New Dark Age (Bowling Green, OH: B.G. University Popular Press, 1976), pp. 147–198. Brian Aldiss discusses the English 'cosy catastrophe' in *Billion Year Spree*, pp. 292–6, and Charles Platt's fantasia 'The Disaster Story', *NW*, no. 160 (March 1966), pp. 86–9, identifies its appeal: 'So long as I am left free and unharmed in an emptied world, I don't mind what my disaster is.'

3   *The Wind from Nowhere* (New York: Berkley, 1962). Carnell serialised an earlier version under the title 'Storm-Wind' in *NW*, nos 110–11 (September–October 1961).

4   *The Drowned World* (New York: Berkley, 1962). Carnell published a shorter version under the same title in *Science Fiction Adventures*, no. 24 (January 1962).

5   *Drowned*, op. cit., p. 43.

6   Ibid., p. 14.

7   Ibid., p. 45.

8   *The Drought* (New York: Berkley, 1964, as *The Burning World*; London: Cape, 1965). Moorcock published an extract, 'Dune Limbo', in *NW*, no. 148 (March 1965).

9   *Drought*, op. cit., p. 252.

10   *The Crystal World* (London: Cape, 1966). Moorcock serialised an earlier version in his first issues of *NW*, nos 142–3 (May–August 1964), under the title 'Equinox'.

11   *Crystal*, p. 92.

12   Ibid., p. 218.

13   James Cawthorn, 'I Love You, Semantics', *NW*, no. 164 (August 1966), pp. 144–9.

14   Interview with Peter Linnett, *Corridor*, no. 5 (1974), pp. 4–7.

15   *The Disaster Area* (London: Cape, 1967).

16   'The Gioconda of the Twilight Noon', *The Terminal Beach* (London: Gollancz, 1964), pp. 192–201.

17   'The Delta at Sunset', *Terminal*, op. cit., pp. 117–33.

18   *Drowned*, op. cit., p. 115 (author's ellipsis).

19   *Drought*, op. cit., p. 15.

20   'The Cage of Sand', *The Four-Dimensional Nightmare* (London: Gollancz, 1963), pp. 134–57.

21   'The Delta . . .', *Terminal*, op. cit., p. 129.

22   *Drowned*, op. cit., pp. 157–8.

23   *Crystal*, op. cit., p. 150.

24   'The Delta . . .', *Terminal*, op. cit., pp. 121, 125.

25   'The Gioconda . . .', *Terminal*, op. cit., p. 195 (author's ellipsis).

26   Quoted by Martin Hayman, 'Future Perfect – the Crystalline World of J.G. Ballard', *Street Life*, no. 8 (7 February 1976), pp. 16–17.

27   *Concrete Island* (London: Cape, 1974).

28 *The Atrocity Exhibition* (London: Cape, 1970). Seven of the fifteen 'condensed novels' that make up this book were first published in *NW* between nos 161 and 186 (April 1966 – January 1969).

29 'The Impossible Man', *Disaster Area*, op. cit., pp. 183–206.

30 'The Waiting Grounds', *Forever*, op. cit., pp. 53–82; 'The Thousand Dreams of Stellavista', *Vermilion Sands* (New York: Berkley, 1971; London: Cape, 1973), pp. 185–208; 'The Cage of Sand', *4-D Nightmare*, op. cit., pp. 134–57; 'The Terminal Beach', *Terminal*, op cit., pp. 134–55.

31 *Drought*, op. cit., pp. 37, 117.

32 'Low-Flying Aircraft', *Low-Flying Aircraft and Other Stories* (London: Cape, 1976), pp. 88–107.

33 'The New Science Fiction', transcript of a conversation with George MacBeth, *The New SF: An Original Anthology of Modern Speculative Fiction*, ed., Langdon Jones (London: Hutchinson, 1969), pp. 46–54.

34 *Drought*, op. cit., p. 117.

35 'Venus Smiles', *Vermillion*, op. cit., p. 114.

36 *Crystal*, op. cit., p. 36.

37 Ibid., p. 78.

38 *Atrocity*, op. cit., p. 63.

39 *Drought*, op. cit., p. 77.

40 Ibid., p. 103.

41 Ibid., p. 83.

42 'My Dream of Flying to Wake Island', *Low-Flying*, op. cit., p. 124.

43 'The Delta . . .', *Terminal*, op. cit., p. 117.

44 Ibid., p. 121.

45 'Journey Across a Crater', *NW*, no. 198 (February 1970), pp. 3–4.

46 'Deep End', *NW*, no. 106 (May 1961), pp. 111–22; revised and collected in *Terminal*, pp. 156–68.

47 'Ballard does not only communicate by factual exploration, but also the inventiveness of his language. In this he is a poet, and should be read as such.' J.S. Torr, Letter to the Editor, *NW*, no. 141 (April 1964), pp. 126–7.

48 'The Coming of the Unconscious', presented as a review of two books on Surrealism, *NW*, no. 164 (July 1966), pp. 141–5; collected in *The Overloaded Man* (London: Panther, 1967), pp. 140–5.

49 Anna Balakian, *Surrealism: The Road to the Absolute* (revised edn, London: Allen & Unwin, 1972).

50 Ibid., p. 89.

51 See 'The World Transformed', ibid., pp. 245–50.

52 Ibid., p. 85.

53 Ibid., pp. 144, 248.

54 Ibid., p. 84 (author's italics).

55 Interview with Robert Louit, *Magazine Littéraire*, no. 87 (April 1974); translation by Peter Nicholls included in Ballard, 'Some Words about *Crash!*', *Foundation: The Review of Science Fiction*, no. 9 (November 1975), pp. 44–54.

56 Interview with the Editors, *J.G. Ballard: The First Twenty Years*, ed., James Goddard and David Pringle (Hayes, Middx: Bran's Head, 1976) pp. 8–35.

57 *Drowned*, op. cit., p. 20.

58 Aldiss, 'The Wounded Land', *First 20 Years*, op. cit., pp. 38–48.

59 'The Terminal Beach', *Terminal*, op. cit., pp. 134–55. An earlier version appeared in *NW*, no. 140 (March 1964), pp. 4–24.

60 Ibid., p. 147 (author's italics).

61 See 'Build-up', *NW*, no. 55 (January 1957), rpt. in *Disaster Area*, pp. 33–57, as 'Concentration City'; 'Billennium', *NW*, no. 112 (November 1961), rpt. in *Terminal*, op. cit., pp. 175–91; 'The Watch-Towers', *Science Fantasy*, no. 53 (June–July 1962), rpt. in *4–D Nightmare*, op. cit., pp. 157–84; and 'The Subliminal Man', *NW*, no. 126 (January 1963), rpt. in *Disaster Area*, op. cit., pp. 58–80.

62 Ballard, Introduction to *Crash*: this was not included in the original English edition (London: Cape, 1973), but written to be translated for the French edition (Paris: Calmann–Lévy, 1974). Peter Nicholls published Ballard's original in 'Some Words About *Crash!*', *Foundation*, no. 9 (November 1975), pp. 44–54.

63 'Terminal Beach', op. cit., p. 153.

64 R.D. Laing, *The Politics of Experience* and *The Bird of Paradise* (Harmondsworth, Middx: Penguin, 1967), p. 11.

65 Interview, *First 20 Years*, op. cit., p. 26. America's national obsessions have mythologised the assasination of Kennedy. Ballard is not the only new sf writer to make use of the myth: see also Ian Watson, 'The Tarot Pack Megadeath', *NW*, no. 200 (April 1970), pp. 18–19; D.M. Thomas, 'Computer 70: Dreams and Lovepoems', ibid., p. 24; Barry Malzberg, *The Destruction of The Temple* (New York: Pocket, 1974); and especially Robert Shea and Robert Anton Wilson, *Illuminatus!* (New York: Dell, 1975). A character in Arthur Penn's film *Night Moves* (Warner Bros, 1975) explains that 'Where were you when Kennedy got shot?' is the one question every American can answer.

66 Interview, *The New SF*, op. cit., p. 50.

67 *Atrocity*, op. cit., p. 37.

68 Interview, *Corridor*, p. 6.

69 Interview, *First 20 Years*, op. cit., pp. 29–30.

70 *Atrocity*, op. cit., pp. 14, 29, 64 (twice), 65 and 69. Compare, for example Christopher Evans and Jackie Wilson, 'Machine Gun Cities', *Ambit*, no. 60 (Winter 1974), pp. 5–8, and no. 61 (Spring 1975), pp. 19–22.

71 Roland Barthes, 'The New Citroën', *Mythologies*, sel. and tr., Annette Lavers, (London: Cape, 1972), p. 90.
72 Barthes, 'Myth Today', ibid., p. 112n.
73 Moorcock, 'No Short-Cuts', review of *The Terminal Beach*, *NW*, no. 144 (September–October 1964), pp. 119–20.
74 *High-Rise* (London: Cape, 1975).

8 The works of Michael Moorcock

1 Moorcock, Guest Editorial, *NW*, no. 129 (April 1963), pp. 2–3, 123–7. All notes in this chapter refer to works by Moorcock, unless otherwise stated.
2 'The Dreaming City', *The Stealer of Souls* (London: Spearman, 1963), pp. 9–39. An earlier version was published in *Science Fantasy* (hereafter *Scifan*), no. 47 (June–July 1961).
3 *The Sleeping Sorceress* (London: New English Library, 1971), pp. 75–6.
4 See Samuel R. Delany, *The Jewel-Hinged Jaw: Notes on the Language of Science Fiction* (Elizabethtown, NY: Dragon Press, 1977), pp. 216–23.
5 'The Secret Life of Elric of Melniboné', *Sojan* (Manchester: Savoy, 1977), pp. 123–30 (author's italics).
6 'New Worlds: A Personal History', *Foundation: The Review of Science Fiction*, no. 15 (January 1979), p. 14.
7 Letter to Dennis Henley, 5 July 1976.
8 'Secret Life of Elric', op. cit., p. 124.
9 *The Eternal Champion* (New York: Dell, 1970): an earlier version was published in *SciFan*, no. 53 (June-July 1962). *Phoenix in Obsidian* (London: Mayflower, 1970).
10 *The Jewel in the Skull* (New York: Lancer, 1967), pp. 48–9.
11 'While the Gods Laugh', *Stealer*, op. cit., pp. 40–72 (author's italics). An earlier version was published in *SciFan*, no. 49 (October–November 1961).
12 'Gods Laugh', op. cit., p. 45.
13 *The Sword and the Stallion* (New York: Berkley, 1974).
14 Harry Harrison, 'Worlds Beside Worlds', *Science Fiction at Large*, ed., Peter Nicholls (London: Gollancz, 1976), pp. 107–8 (author's italics).
15 Cf. Jorge Luis Borges, 'The Garden of Forking Paths', tr. Donald A. Yates, in Borges, *Labyrinths: Selected Stories and Other Writings*, ed. Yates and James E. Irby (Harmondsworth, Middx: Penguin, 1970), pp. 44–54.
16 *An Alien Heat* (London: MacGibbon & Kee, 1972); *The Hollow Lands* (New York: Harper & Row, 1974); *Legends from the End of*

Time (New York: Harper & Row, 1976); *The End of All Songs* (New York: Harper & Row, 1976).

17 'Behold the Man', *NW*, no. 166 (September 1966), pp. 4–58.

18 *Behold the Man* (London: Allison & Busby, 1969), p. 117.

19 Ibid., p. 130.

20 Ibid., p. 135.

21 Ibid., p. 52.

22 Interview with Robert E. Toomey, Jr., *Science Fiction Review*, no. 34 (December 1969), pp. 7–15.

23 *Behold*, op. cit., p. 63.

24 *The Adventures of Una Persson and Catherine Cornelius in the Twentieth Century* (London: Quartet, 1976), p. 17.

25 Ballard, 'Which Way to Inner Space?', *NW*, no. 118 (May 1962), p. 118.

26 *Behold*, op. cit., p. 73.

27 Ibid., p. 7.

28 Undated transcript of an interview with Alan Burns; see *The Imagination Trial: British and American Writers Discuss their Working Methods*, eds Burns and Charles Sugnet (London: Allison & Busby, 1981), p. 113.

29 *Breakfast in the Ruins: A Novel of Inhumanity* (London: New English Library, 1972).

30 Ibid., p. 130.

31 Ibid., p. 123.

32 Ibid., pp. 90–2.

33 *An Alien Heat*, op. cit., p. 13.

34 *The English Assassin* Notebook, p. [47]; dated 10 June 1971.

35 Jenni Calder, *Heroes: From Byron to Guevara* (London: Hamilton, 1977), p. xi.

36 Ibid., p., 183.

37 Leslie Fiedler, quoted in Ann Banks, 'Symposium Sidelights', *Novel*, 3 (1970), 208–9.

38 'New Worlds – Jerry Cornelius', *Sojan*, op. cit., pp. 144–55. See also 'Lead In', NW, no. 191 (June 1969), pp. 2–3.

39 *The Final Programme* (London: Allison & Busby, 1969), p. 67. Extracts from the novel first appeared as 'Preliminary Data', *NW*, no. 153 (August 1965), 'Further Information', no. 157 (December 1965), and 'Phase Three', no. 160 (March 1966).

40 'The Swastika Set-Up', *The Lives and Times of Jerry Cornelius* (London: Allison & Busby, 1976), p. 56.

41 Neil Spencer, review of *The Condition of Muzak*, *New Musical Express*, 2 July 1977, p. 36.

42 *Programme*, op. cit., p. 138.

43 Ibid., pp. 37–8.
44 *A Cure for Cancer* (London: Allison & Busby, 1971), p. 61 (author's italics). Moorcock first published the novel as a serial of the same title in *NW*, nos 188–91 (March–June 1969).
45 From an unpublished dialogue in which Cornelius is interrogated about his part in the novel.
46 'Jerry Cornelius Novels' Notebook, p.[5], dated 12 December 1967.
47 *Cancer*, op. cit., p. 21.
48 'In Lighter Vein', *Sojan*, op. cit., pp. 156–7.
49 James Sallis, 'The Anxiety in the Eyes of the Cricket', *The New SF: An Original Anthology of Modern Speculative Fiction*, ed. Langdon Jones (London: Hutchinson, 1969), p. 39.
50 *The English Assassin: A Romance of Entropy* (London: Allison & Busby, 1972), pp. 13–14.
51 *The Condition of Muzak* Notebook, p. [71]; cf. *The Condition of Muzak* (London: Allison & Busby, 1977), p. 216.
52 At about this time Moorcock was also writing *The Warlord of the Air* (New York: Ace, 1971) and *The Land Leviathan* (London: Quartet, 1974), scientific romances about Oswald Bastable, a hapless Edwardian precipitated into alternative twentieth centuries similar to the ambience of *The English Assassin*.
53 *Assassin*, op. cit., p. 120.
54 Ibid., p. 65.
55 Ibid., p. 146.
56 Ibid., pp. 213–14 (authors' italics).
57 Ibid., p. 236.
58 Ibid., p. 236.
59 Moorcock uses the same analogy in his *Muzak* Notebook, p. [17], dated 3 February 1976.
60 *Muzak* Notebook, pp.[163–4], dated 18 April 1976 (author's italics).
61 *Muzak*, op. cit., p. 222.
62 Ibid., p. 241.
63 Théophile Gautier, quoted in Enid Welsford, *The Fool: His Social and Literary History* (London: Faber, 1935), p. 307. See *NW*, no. 213 (Summer 1978), pp. 16–19.
64 *Muzak* Notebook, p. [123].
65 An American edition of the tetralogy in one paperback volume: *The Cornelius Chronicles* (New York: Avon, 1977).
66 John Clute, 'The Repossession of Jerry Cornelius', *Chronicles*, op. cit., pp. ix–xv.
67 Jonathan Raban, *Soft City* (London: Hamilton, 1974), pp. 153–7 (author's italics). Robert E. Park was a pioneer of urban sociology writing in the 1920s who asserted that urban man has a fundamentally

rational attitude to his habitat, unlike tribal man.
68 *Muzak*, op. cit., pp. 211–12.
69 Ibid., p. 213.
70 Clute, op. cit., p. viii.
71 See Moorcock and Jones, eds, *The Nature of the Catastrophe* (London: Hutchinson, 1971).
72 Letter to Brian Tawn, 8 July 1976.
73 M. John Harrison, letter to Moorcock, January 1978.

9 Angst and angströms: stylistic practice

1 James Sallis, 'The Anxiety in the Eyes of the Cricket', *The New SF: An Original Anthology of Modern Speculative Fiction*, ed., Langdon Jones (London: Hutchinson, 1969), p. 37.
2 T.S. Eliot, 'East Coker', *Collected Poems 1909–1962* (London: Faber, 1963), p. 203.
3 D.H. Lawrence, quoted in Ihab Hassan, 'The Literature of Silence', in *Innovations: Essays on Art and Ideas*, ed., Bernard Bergonzi (London: Macmillan, 1968), p. 93.
4 Quoted by Bill Butler, 'William Burroughs', *NW*, no. 161 (April 1966), p. 152.
5 Burroughs, *The Ticket that Exploded* (London: Calder and Boyars, 1968), pp. 49–51 (author's italics).
6 Tony Tanner, *City of Words: American Fiction 1950–1970* (London: Cape, 1971), p. 114.
7 Alain Robbe-Grillet, *Snapshots* and *Towards a New Novel*, tr., Barbara Wright (London: Calder, 1965), p. 63.
8 B.S. Johnson, Introduction, *Aren't You Rather Young to be Writing Your Memoirs?*, (London: Hutchinson, 1973), p. 17.
9 David Lodge, *The Novelist at the Crossroads and Other Essays on Fiction and Criticism* (London: Routledge & Kegan Paul, 1971), pp. 17–18.
10 Wayne C. Booth, *The Rhetoric of Fiction* (Chicago University Press, 1961), pp. 34–6 (author's italics).
11 Benjamin Lee Whorf, 'Language, Mind, and Reality', in his *Language, Thought, and Reality: Selected Writings*, ed., John B. Carroll (Cambridge, MA: Technology Press of MIT, 1956), p. 246.
12 Steve Hall, 'Now is the Time', *NW*, no. 141 (March 1964), p. 48.
13 Michael Moorcock, 'Onward, Ever Onward', *NW*, no. 159 (February 1966), pp. 2–5.
14 Christopher Priest, 'New Wave', *Encyclopaedia of Science Fiction*,

ed., Robert Holdstock (London: Octopus, 1978), p. 170 (author's italics).

15 Judith Merril, *England Swings SF: Stories of Speculative Fiction* (Garden City, NY: Doubleday, 1968).

16 Priest, op. cit., p. 170 (author's italics).

17 *NW*, no. 197 (January 1970), for example.

18 Roger Zelazny, 'The Keys to December', *NW*, no. 165 (August 1966), pp. 115–41 (author's ellipses).

19 Sam Wolf, 'Eyeball', *NW*, no. 161 (April 1966), pp. 79–81.

20 See, for example, John Sladek, 'The Master Plan', *NW*, no. 187 (February 1969), pp. 34–40, and 'Alien Territory', *NW*, no. 195 (November 1969), pp. 24–5; Michael Butterworth, 'Circularisation', *NW*, no. 192 (July 1969), pp. 46–9; Thomas Disch, '334', *NWQ*, no. 4 (April 1972), pp. 58–155.

21 David Rome, 'There's a Starman in Ward 7', *NW*, no. 146 (January 1965), pp. 81–8.

22 Booth, op. cit., p. 152 (author's italics).

23 Ken Kesey, *One Flew Over the Cuckoo's Nest* (New York: Viking Press, 1962).

24 Don't tell your poppa or he'll get us locked up in fright.
There's a Starman waiting in the sky,
He'd like to come and meet us
But he thinks he'd blow our minds.
David Bowie, 'Starman', *The Rise and Fall of Ziggy Stardust and the Spiders from Mars*, RCA, SF8287, 1972.

25 M. John Harrison, 'Baa Baa Blocksheep', *NW*, no. 184 (November 1968), pp. 52–9 (author's italics).

26 See John Barth, 'The Literature of Exhaustion', *Atlantic Monthly*, 220 (August 1967), pp. 29–34; rpt. *The Novel Today: Contemporary Writers on Modern Fiction*, ed. Malcolm Bradbury (Manchester University Press, 1977), pp. 70–83.

27 Brian Vickers, 'Area Complex', *NW*, no. 184 (November 1968), pp. 5–20.

28 See Ballard, 'The Voices of Time', *The Four-Dimensional Nightmare* (London: Gollancz, 1963), pp. 9–41.

29 Vickers, 'The Coded Sun Game', *Quark*, ed. Samuel R. Delany and Marilyn Hacker, vol. 3 (New York: Paperback Library, 1971), pp. 169–235.

30 Ibid., pp. 171–2 (author's italics).

31 Ibid., pp. 195–6.

32 Ibid., p. 214.

33 Ibid., p. 191.

10   A higher albedo: stylistic theory

1   A. Alvarez, 'Beyond All This Fiddle', *Beyond All This Fiddle: Essays, 1955–1967* (New York: Random House, 1969), p. 5, quoted in James Sallis, 'Orthographies', *NW*, no. 187 (February 1969), pp. 2–5.
2   James Sallis, op. cit., p. 3.
3   S.R. Delany, 'About Five Thousand One Hundred and Seventy Five Words', *Extrapolation*, no. 10 (1969), pp. 52–66; rpt. in Delany, *The Jewel-Hinged Jaw: Notes on the Language of Science Fiction* (Elizabethtown, NY: Dragon Press, 1977), pp. 33–49.
4   The organ of the school is the journal *Science-Fiction Studies*, in which the principal documents of its foundation were published. See, for example Stanislaw Lem, 'On the Structural Analysis of Science Fiction', *SFS*, vol. 1 (1973–4), pp. 26–33; Joanna Russ, 'Towards an Aesthetic of Science Fiction', *SFS*, vol. 2 (1975), pp. 112–19; Marc Angenot, 'The Absent Paradigm: An Introduction to the Semiotics of Science Fiction', *SFS*, vol. 6 (1979), pp. 9–19. See also Darko Suvin, *Metamorphoses of Science Fiction: On the Poetics and History of a Literary Genre* (New Haven and London: Yale University Press, 1979). Suvin was an editor of *SFS* from 1973–81.
5   Sacchetti, the narrator of 'Camp Concentration', writes a poem containing the line: 'The jaw's jewelled hinge that we can barely glimpse': Disch, 'Camp Concentration', pt 2, *NW*, no. 174 (August 1967), p.8. Moorcock calls *The Jewel-Hinged Jaw* 'fundamentally illiterate', Delany a 'parochial pedant': *NW*, no. 214 (1978), p. [47].
6   Sallis, 'Orthographies', p. 5.
7   Sallis, 'Boris Vian and Friends', *NW*, no. 183 (October 1968), pp. 60–1 (author's italics).
8   Sallis, 'Orthographies', p. 5 (author's italics).
9   T.S. Eliot, 'Tradition and the Individual Talent', in his *Selected Prose*, ed. Frank Kermode (London: Faber, 1975), pp. 37–44.
10   Sallis, 'Orthographies', p. 2.
11   Ibid.
12   Ibid.
13   David Lodge, *The Novelist at the Crossroads and Other Essays on Fiction and Criticism* (London: Routledge & Kegan Paul, 1971), p. 18.
14   Langdon Jones, 'The Eye of the Lens', *NW*, no. 180 (March 1968), pp. 4–24; Introduction, pp. 2–3.
15   Anton Ehrenzweig, *The Hidden Order of Art: A Study in the Psychology of Artistic Imagination* (London: Weidenfeld & Nicolson, 1967). Ehrenzweig's book was the subject of an unsigned leading article in *NW*, no. 174 (August 1967), pp. 2–4.
16   Ehrenzweig, op. cit., p. 65.

17   Ibid., p. 121.
18   Ibid., p. 66.
19   Michael Moorcock, 'Onward, Ever Onward', *NW*, no. 159 (February 1966). p. 3.

11   No more with feeling: entropy and contemporary fiction

1   Jerry Casale, quoted in Paul Rambali, interview with Devo, *New Musical Express*, 18 March 1978, pp. 32–3.
2   Norbert Wiener, *The Human Use of Human Beings: Cybernetics and Society*, 2nd edn (London: Eyre & Spottiswoode, 1954), p. 40.
3   Rudolf Arnheim, *Entropy and Art: An Essay on Disorder and Order* (Berkeley, CA: University of California Press, 1971), p. 9.
4   J.J. Mundis, 'The Luger is a 9mm. Automatic Handgun with a Parabellum Action', *NW*, no. 188 (March 1969), p. 38.
5   Frank Kermode, *The Sense of an Ending: Studies in the Theory of Fiction* (New York: Oxford University Press, 1967), pp. 93–5.
6   'Modernisms', Kermode's reply to 'The New Mutants', may be found, together with Fiedler's essay, in *Innovations: Essays on Art and Ideas*, ed., Bernard Bergonzi (London: Macmillan, 1968), pp. 23–45 and 66–92.
7   John Barth, 'The Literature of Exhaustion', *Atlantic Monthly*, 220 (August 1967), pp. 29–34; rpt. *The Novel Today: Contemporary Writers on Modern Fiction*, ed. Malcolm Bradbury (Manchester University Press, 1977), pp. 70–83 (author's italics).
8   Ibid., p. 73 (author's italics).
9   Ibid., p. 76
10   Ibid., p. 74 (author's italics).
11   Thomas Disch, '334', *NWQ*, no. 4 (April 1972), p. 88 (author's italics).
12   Barth, op. cit., p. 70.
13   Letters to the author, 10 September 1977.
14   Arnheim, op. cit., p. 10.
15   Robert Scholes, *The Fabulators* (New York: Oxford University Press, 1967).
16   Tony Tanner, 'Everything Running Down', *City of Words: American Fiction 1950—1970* (London: Cape, 1971), pp. 141–52.
17   Tanner, op. cit., p. 141. In 1963 Saul Bellow mentioned 'the conception of entropy' as a strong influence on European writers: 'Some Notes on Recent American Fiction', *Encounter*, 21 (November 1963), pp. 22–9; rpt. Bradbury, *Novel Today*, op. cit., pp. 54–69.
18   William Burroughs, *The Naked Lunch* (rev. edn, London: Calder, 1964), p. 136 (author's italics).

19 Ibid., p. 222 (author's ellipses).
20 Thomas Pynchon, *V.* (London: Cape, 1963), p. 286.
21 Pynchon, *The Crying of Lot 49* (London: Cape, 1967).
22 Charles B. Harris, 'Death and Absurdity: Thomas Pynchon and the Entropic Vision', *Contemporary American Novelists of the Absurd* (New Haven, CT: College and University Press, 1971), p. 95.
23 Pynchon, 'Entropy', *Kenyon Review*, 22 (Winter 1960), pp. 277–92.
24 Tanner, op. cit., p. 141.
25 See, for example, Norman Spinrad, 'The Entropic Gang-Bang Caper', *NW*, no. 193 (August 1969), pp. 24–5; and George Alec Effinger, *What Entropy Means to Me* (Garden City, NY: Doubleday, 1972).
26 Robert Scholes and Eric S. Rabkin, *Science Fiction: History – Science – Vision* (New York: Oxford University Press, 1977), pp. 136–7. Barrington Bayley at least attempted a story about a closed system in *NW*: 'Exit from City 5', *NWQ*, no. 1 (June 1971), pp. 139–65.
27 P. Zoline, 'The Heat-Death of the Universe', *NW*, no. 173 (July 1967), pp. 32–9.
28 Wiener, op. cit., p. 12.
29 Ibid., p. 40.
30 Claude Lévi-Strauss, *Tristes Tropiques*, tr. John and Doreen Weightman (London: Cape, 1973), p. 413.
31 Ibid., pp. 413–14.
32 Wiener, op. cit., p. 12.
33 Arnheim, op. cit., p. 51.
34 Burroughs, *The Ticket that Exploded* (rev. edn, London: Calder & Boyars, 1968), pp. 54–5.
35 Harris, op. cit., pp. 77–8.
36 Ihab Hassan, 'The Literature of Silence', *Innovations*, op. cit., ed. Bergonzi, p. 107.
37 Ballard, 'Myth-Maker of the 20th Century', *NW*, no. 142 (May–June 1964), pp. 121–7. In return Burroughs contributed a preface to the American edition of Ballard's *The Atrocity Exhibition*, ironically re-titled *Love and Napalm: Export U.S.A.* (New York: Grove Press, 1972).
38 Philip José Farmer, 'The Jungle Rot Kid on the Nod', *NW*, no. 200 (April 1970), pp. 26–7; Barrington Bayley, 'The Four-Color Problem', *NWQ*, no. 2 (September 1971), pp. 83–120.
39 Pynchon, 'Entropy', *NW*, no. 187 (February 1969), pp. 50–6.
40 Wiener, op. cit., p. 181; Sigmund Freud, *Collected Papers*, ed. J. Riviere, tr. A. and J. Strachey, vol. V: *Miscellaneous Papers 1888–1938* (London: Hogarth and The Institute of Psycho-Analysis, 1950), p. 345.
41 Disch, op. cit., p. 152 (author's italics).

42 Moorcock, 'A New Worlds Index: Introduction', *NW*, no. 201 (March 1971), p. 12; 'New Worlds – Jerry Cornelius', *Sojan* (Manchester: Savoy, 1977), p. 149; 'New Worlds: A Personal History', *Foundation: The Review of Science Fiction*, no. 15 (January 1979), p. 18.

43 Moorcock, Introduction, *NWQ*, no. 2 (September 1971), pp. 9–11.

44 Charles Platt, 'Lead-In', *NW*, no. 193 (August 1969), p. 1.

45 Bernard Bergonzi, *The Situation of the Novel* (London: Macmillan, 1970), pp. 92–3, 75.

46 Moorcock, 'New Worlds – Jerry Cornelius', *Sojun*, op. cit., p. 150.

47 Undated transcript of an interview with Alan Burns; see *The Imagination on Trial: British and American Writers Discuss their Working Methods*, eds Burns and Charles Sugnet (London and New York: Allison & Busby, 1981), p. 106.

Bibliography

This bibliography is not definitive, but lists all principal sources referred to in the text, together with others consulted in the course of research. First editions only are cited unless specific reference has been made to a revised, foreign, or translated edition. In the case of works by Aldiss, Ballard and Moorcock which received their first publication in America, first British editions are also listed.

Primary texts

Moorcock, Michael *et al.*, eds, *New Worlds*, nos 142–201 (May 1964–March 1971).

Moorcock, Michael, *et al.*, eds, *New Worlds Quarterly*, nos 1–10 (Summer 1971–Autumn 1976).

Related texts: other magazines and anthologies of New Wave sf

Aldiss, Brian W. and Harry Harrison, eds, *Decade: The 1960's*, London, Macmillan, 1977.

Delany, Samuel R. and Marilyn Hacker, eds, *Quark*, vols 1–4, New York, Paperback Library, 1970–1.

Ellison, Harlan, ed., *Again, Dangerous Visions*, Garden City, NY, Doubleday, 1972.

Ellison, Harlan, ed., *Dangerous Visions*, Garden City, NY, Doubleday, 1967.

Jones, Langdon, ed., *The New SF: An Original Anthology of Modern Speculative Fiction*, London, Hutchinson, 1969.

Knight, Damon, ed., *Orbit*, vols 1–12, New York, Putnam, 1966–73.

Knight, Damon, ed., *Orbit*, vol. 13, New York, Berkley, 1974.
Knight, Damon, ed., *Orbit*, vols. 14–18, New York, Harper & Row, 1974–6.
Merril, Judith, ed., *England Swings SF: Stories of Speculative Fiction*, Garden City, NY, Doubleday, 1968.
Merril, Judith, ed., *SF12*, New York, Delacorte Press, 1968.
Moorcock, Michael *et al.*, eds, *New Worlds*, nos 212–16 (Spring 1978–September 1979).
Silverberg, Robert, ed., *New Dimensions*, vols 1–3, Garden City, NY, Doubleday, 1971–3.
Silverberg Robert, ed., *New Dimensions*, vol. 4, New York, Signet, 1974.
Silverberg, Robert, ed., *New Dimensions*, vols 5–6, New York, Harper & Row, 1975–6.
Spinrad, Norman, ed., *The New Tomorrows*, New York, Belmont, 1971.

Critical and other sources consulted
1 THE CYBERNETIC CUCKOOS

Clarke, Arthur C., *Childhood's End*, London, Sidgwick & Jackson, 1954.
Downing, David, *Future Rock*, London, Panther, 1976.
Farren, Mick, *Watch Out Kids*, London, Open Gate, 1972.
Fiedler, Leslie, 'Cross the Border – Close the Gap', in his *Collected Essays*, New York, Stein & Day, 1971, vol. II, pp. 461–85.
Fiedler Leslie, 'The New Mutants', ibid., pp. 379–400.
Hoffman, Abbie, *Woodstock Nation: A Talk-Rock Album*, New York, Random House, 1969.
Leary, Timothy, *The Politics of Ecstasy*, London, MacGibbon & Kee, 1970.
Neville, Richard, *Playpower*, London, Cape, 1970.
Nicholls, Peter, ed., *Science Fiction at Large*, London, Gollancz, 1976.
Roszak, Theodore, *The Making of a Counter Culture: Reflections on the Technocratic Society and its Youthful Opposition*, Garden City, NY, Doubleday, 1969.
Rubin, Jerry, *Do It!: Scenarios of the Revolution*, New York, Simon & Schuster, 1970.
Wyndham, John (pseud.), *The Midwich Cuckoos*, London, Joseph, 1957.

2 THE 'FIELD' AND THE 'WAVE'

Aldiss, Brian W., 'The Stars My Detestation', in his *Billion Year Spree: The History of Science Fiction*, London, Weidenfeld & Nicolson, 1973, pp. 285–317.

Anon, 'The Nova Venture: Thursday's Child', *Fantasy Review*, no. 13 (February–March 1949), pp. 4–6, 31.

Arnold, Francis, 'The Circle of the White Horse', *NW*, no. 14 (March 1952), pp. 61–5.

Ashley, Michael, 'The Way to Revolution', in his *The History of the Science Fiction Magazine*, pt IV: 1956–65, London, New English Library, 1978, pp. 65–70.

Atheling, William, Jr. (pseud.), 'Making Waves', in his *More Issues at Hand: Critical Studies in Contemporary Science Fiction*, Chicago, Advent, 1970, pp. 117–46.

Bailey, Hilary, 'Some Corner of a Funny Field', *Foundation: The Review of Science Fiction*, no. 13 (May 1978), pp. 78–83.

Gunn, James, 'Science Fiction and the Mainstream', *Science Fiction, Today and Tomorrow: A Discursive Symposium*, ed., Reginald Bretnor, New York, Harper & Row, 1974, pp. 183–214.

Merril, Judith, 'What Do You Mean: Science? Fiction?', *SF: The Other Side of Realism: Essays on Modern Fantasy and Science Fiction*, ed., Thomas D. Clareson, Bowling Green, OH, BG University Popular Press, 1971, pp. 53–95.

Moorcock, Michael, 'Play with Feeling', Guest Editorial, *NW*, no. 129 (April 1963), pp. 2–3, 123–7.

Moorcock, Michael, 'New Worlds: A Personal History', *Foundation: The Review of Science Fiction*, no. 15 (January 1979), pp. 5–18.

Moorcock, Michael, 'New Worlds – Jerry Cornelius', in his *Sojan*, Manchester, Savoy, 1977, pp. 144–55.

Nicholls, Peter, 'Jerry Cornelius at the Atrocity Exhibition: Anarchy and Entropy in "New Worlds" Science Fiction 1964–74', *Foundation: The Review of Science Fiction*, no. 9 (November 1975), pp. 22–44.

Nicholls, Peter, and John Clute, eds, *The Encyclopedia of Science Fiction: An Illustrated A to Z*, London, Granada, 1979.

Priest, Christopher, 'New Wave', *Encyclopedia of Science Fiction*, ed., Robert Holdstock, London, Octopus, 1978, pp. 163–73.

3 LOVE AMONG THE MANNEQUINS

Aldiss, Brian W., *The Shape of Further Things: Speculations on Change*, London, Faber, 1970.

Brown, Howard, ed., *Amazing Stories*, British edn, nos 4–22 (December 1950–December 1953).

Campbell, John W., Jr., ed., *Astounding Stories/Analog*, British edn, vol. 15, no. 1–vol. 17, no. 6 (January 1959–June 1961).

Crispin, Edmund, Introduction, *Best SF Three*, ed. Crispin, London, Faber, 1958, pp. 9–13.

Delany, Samuel R., 'To Read *The Dispossessed*', in his *The Jewel-Hinged Jaw: Notes on the Language of Science Fiction*, Elizabethtown, NY, Dragon Press, 1977, pp. 239–308.

Freas, Frank Kelly, *Frank Kelly Freas: The Art of Science Fiction*, Norfolk, VA, Donning, 1977.

Godwin, Tom, 'The Cold Equations', *Astounding Science Fiction*, British edn, vol. 11, no. 1 (January 1955), pp. 48–66.

Harrison, Harry, *Great Balls of Fire!*, London, Pierrot, 1977.

Harrison, Harry, 'We Are Sitting on Our. . . .', *SF Horizons*, no. 1 (Spring 1964), pp. 39–42.

Hill, Douglas, Introduction, *The Shape of Sex to Come*, ed., D. Hill, London, Pan, 1978, pp. 7–11.

Laing, Ronald D., 'The Ghost of the Weed Garden: A Study of a Chronic Schizophrenic', in his *The Divided Self: A Study of Sanity and Madness*, London, Tavistock, 1960, pp. 195–225.

Rorvik, David M., *As Man Becomes Machine: The Evolution of the Cyborg*, Garden City, NY, Doubleday, 1971.

Russ, Joanna, 'The Image of Women in Science Fiction', *Vertex*, vol. 1, no. 6 (February 1974), pp. 53–7.

Sargent, Pamela, 'Introduction: Women and Science Fiction', in *Women of Wonder: Science Fiction Stories by Women about Women*, ed. Sargent, New York, Vintage, 1975, pp. 11–51.

Thomas, D.M., *Penguin Modern Poets*, 11, Harmondsworth, Middx, Penguin, 1968.

4 PULLING OUT OF THE SPACE RACE

Aldiss, Brian W. and Harry Harrison, eds, *Farewell, Fantastic Venus!: A History of the Planet Venus in Fact and Fiction*, London, Macdonald, 1968.

Ballard, J.G., 'Which Way to Inner Space?', *NW*, no. 118 (May 1962), pp. 2–3, 116–18.

Bowie, David (pseud.), 'Space Oddity', Phillips, BF 1801, 1969; reissued on his *Space Oddity*, RCA, LSP 4813, 1972.

Le Guin, Ursula K., 'Science Fiction and Mrs. Brown', *Science Fiction at Large*, ed. Peter Nicholls, London, Gollancz, 1976, pp. 15–33.

Lewis, C.S. *et al.*, 'Unreal Estates', in Lewis, *Of Other Worlds: Essays and Stories*, ed. Walter Hooper, London, Bles, 1966, pp. 86–96.

Malzberg, Barry N., *Beyond Apollo*, New York, Random House, 1972.

Malzberg, Barry, N., *The Falling Astronauts*, New York, Ace, 1971.

Slayton, Donald K., Shepard, Alan B. and Gordon Cooper, L., 'Introduction to Space Flight', pt II, *Man in Inner and Outer Space:*

Selected Lectures on the U.S. Manned Moon Landing Programme, the Sun and Our Own Planet, ed. S.T. Butler and H. Messel, University of Sydney Press, 1969, pp. 393–472.

5   FOOTHOLDS IN THE HEAD

Aldiss, Brian W., Foreword to Pamela Zoline, 'The Heat-Death of the Universe', *The Mirror of Infinity: A Critics' Anthology of Science Fiction*, ed. Robert Silverberg, New York, Harper & Row, 1970, pp. 287–92.
Bachelard, Gaston, *The Poetics of Space*, tr. Maria Jolas, New York, Orion Press, 1964.
Dunlap, Jane (pseud.), *Exploring Inner Space: Personal Experiences Under LSD-25*, London, Scientific Book Club, 1961.
Fordham, Frieda, *An Introduction to Jung's Psychology*, revised edn, Harmondsworth, Middx, Penguin, 1966.
Harrison, M. John, *The Committed Men*, London, Hutchinson, 1971.
Laing, Ronald D., *The Politics of Experience* and *The Bird of Paradise*, Harmondsworth, Middx, Penguin, 1967.
Lessing, Doris, *Briefing for a Descent into Hell*, London, Cape, 1971.
O'Brien, Barbara (pseud.), *Operators and Things: The Inner Life of a Schizophrenic*, 2nd edn, New York, Ace, 1964.
Priestley, J.B., 'They Come from Inner Space', *New Statesman and Nation*, 16 (1953), pp. 712, 714; rpt. in his *Thoughts in the Wilderness*, London, Heinemann, 1957, pp. 20–6.
Simak, Clifford D., *Out of Their Minds*, New York, Putnam, 1970.

6   THE WORKS OF BRIAN W. ALDISS

Works by Brian W. Aldiss
Space, Time and Nathaniel, London, Faber, 1957.
Non-Stop, London, Faber, 1958.
Equator, London, Digit, 1958.
The Canopy of Time, London, Faber, 1959.
Bow Down to Nul, New York, Ace, 1960; retitled *The Interpreter*, London, Digit, 1961.
The Primal Urge, New York, Ballantine, 1961; London, Sphere, 1967.
The Long Afternoon of Earth, New York, New American Library, 1962; extended and retitled *Hothouse*, London, Faber, 1962.
The Airs of Earth, London, Faber, 1963.
The Dark Light Years, London, Faber, 1964.

234/Bibliography

Greybeard, New York, Harcourt, Brace and World, 1964; London, Faber, 1964.

Best Science Fiction Stories of Brian W. Aldiss, London, Faber, 1965; rev. edn. 1971.

Earthworks, London, Faber, 1965.

The Saliva Tree and Other Strange Growths, London, Faber, 1966.

An Age, London, Faber, 1967; retitled *Cryptozoic!*, Garden City, NY, Doubleday, 1968; London, Sphere, 1973.

Report on Probability A, London, Faber, 1968.

Barefoot in the Head: A European Fantasia, London, Faber, 1969.

Intangibles, Inc. and Other Stories, London, Faber, 1969.

The Moment of Eclipse, London, Faber, 1970.

The Shape of Further Things: Speculations on Change, London, Faber, 1970.

The Book of Brian Aldiss, New York, DAW, 1972; retitled *The Comic Inferno*, London, New English Library, 1973.

Billion Year Spree: The History of Science Fiction, London, Weidenfeld & Nicolson, 1973.

Frankenstein Unbound, London, Cape, 1973.

The Eighty-minute Hour: A Space Opera, Garden City, NY, Doubleday, 1974; London, Cape, 1974.

The Malacia Tapestry, London, Cape, 1976.

Secondary sources

Abrams, M.H., *The Mirror and the Lamp: Romantic Theory and the Critical Tradition*, New York, Oxford University Press, 1953.

Anderson, Poul, 'The Creation of Imaginary Worlds: The World Builder's Handbook and Pocket Companion', *Science Fiction, Today and Tomorrow: A Discursive Symposium*, ed. Reginald Bretnor, New York, Harper & Row, 1974, pp. 235–57.

Dick, Philip K., *Martian Time-Slip*, New York, Ballantine, 1964.

Greenland, Colin, 'The Times Themselves Talk Nonsense: Language in *Barefoot in the Head*', *Foundation: The Review of Science Fiction*, no. 17 (September 1979), pp. 32–41.

Heinlein, Robert A., *Orphans of the Sky*, London, Gollancz, 1963.

Hoyle, Fred, *October the First is Too Late*, London, Heinemann, 1966.

Mathews, Richard, *Aldiss Unbound: The Science Fiction of Brian W. Aldiss*, San Bernadino, CA, Borgo Press, 1977.

Pringle, David, 'Time Must Have a Stop', review of Aldiss, *The Malacia Tapestry*, *Foundation: The Review of Science Fiction*, no. 11 (March 1977), pp. 93–6.

7 THE WORKS OF J.G. BALLARD

Works by J.G. Ballard
The Wind from Nowhere, New York, Berkley, 1962; Harmondsworth, Middx, Penguin, 1967.
The Drowned World, New York, Berkley, 1962; London, Gollancz, 1963.
The Four-Dimensional Nightmare, London, Gollancz, 1963.
The Burning World, New York, Berkley, 1964; retitled *The Drought*, London, Cape, 1965.
The Terminal Beach, London, Gollancz, 1964.
The Crystal World, London, Cape, 1966.
The Day of Forever, London, Panther, 1967.
The Disaster Area, London, Cape, 1967.
The Overloaded Man, London, Panther, 1967.
The Atrocity Exhibition, London, Cape, 1970; retitled *Love and Napalm: Export U.S.A.*, New York, Grove Press, 1972.
Vermilion Sands, New York, Berkley, 1971; London, Cape, 1973.
Crash, London, Cape, 1973.
Concrete Island, London, Cape, 1974.
High-Rise, London, Cape, 1975.
Low-Flying Aircraft and Other Stories, London, Cape, 1976.

Secondary sources
Balakian, Anna, *Surrealism: The Road to the Absolute*, revised edn London, Allen & Unwin, 1972.
Ballard, J.G., 'Some Words About *Crash!*', *Foundation: The Review of Science Fiction*, no. 9 (November 1975), pp. 44–54.
Ballard, J.G., 'The New Science Fiction', transcript of a conversation with George MacBeth, *The New SF: An Original Anthology of Modern Speculative Fiction*, ed. Langdon Jones, London, Hutchinson, 1969, pp. 46–54.
Barthes, Roland, *Mythologies*, sel. and tr. Annette Lavers, London, Cape, 1972.
Berger, Harold L., *Science Fiction and the New Dark Age*, Bowling Green, OH, BG University Popular Press, 1976.
Goddard, James and David Pringle, eds, *J.G. Ballard: The First Twenty Years*, Hayes, Middx, Bran's Head, 1976.
Hayman, Martin, 'Future Perfect: The Crystalline World of J.G. Ballard', *Street Life*, 7 February 1976, pp. 16–17.
Linnett, Peter, Interview with J.G. Ballard, *Corridor*, no. 5 (1974), pp. 4–7.

Malzberg, Barry N., *The Destruction of the Temple*, New York, Pocket,
1974.
Pringle, David, *Earth is the Alien Planet: J.G. Ballard's Four-Dimensional
Nightmare*, San Bernadino, CA, Borgo Press, 1979.
Shea, Robert and Robert Anton Wilson, *Illuminatus!*, New York, Dell,
1975.

8   THE WORKS OF MICHAEL MOORCOCK

Works by Michael Moorcock
This is a simplified list of Moorcock's most important fiction; a complete
one would be too copious and complicated for this bibliography. In
accordance with the theme of this chapter I have arranged this list mainly
in series, which comprise the chronicles of the principal heroes.

Michael Moorcock's Elric *cycle*
Elric of Melniboné, London, Hutchinson, 1972.
The Sailor on the Seas of Fate, London, Quartet, 1976.
The Stealer of Souls, London, Spearman, 1963.
The Singing Citadel, London, Mayflower, 1970.
The Sleeping Sorceress, London, New English Library, 1971.
Stormbringer, London, Jenkins, 1965.

Michael Moorcock's Dorian Hawkmoon *cycle*
The Jewel in the Skull, New York, Lancer, 1967; London, Mayflower,
1969.
Sorcerer's Amulet, New York, Lancer, 1968; retitled *The Mad God's
Amulet*, London, Mayflower, 1969.
The Sword of the Dawn, New York, Lancer, 1968; London, Mayflower,
1969.
The Secret of the Runestaff, New York, Lancer, 1969; retitled *The
Runestaff*, London, Mayflower, 1969.
Count Brass, St. Alban's, Mayflower, 1973.
The Champion of Garathorm, St. Alban's, Mayflower, 1973.
The Quest for Tanelorn, Frogmore, Mayflower, 1975.

Michael Moorcock's Corum *cycle*
The Knight of the Swords, London, Mayflower, 1971.
The Queen of the Swords, New York, Berkley, 1971; London,
Mayflower, 1971.
The King of the Swords, New York, Berkley, 1971; London, Mayflower,
1972.

The Bull and the Spear, London, Allison and Busby, 1973.
The Oak and the Ram, London, Allison and Busby, 1973.
The Sword and the Stallion, New York, Berkley, 1974; London, Allison
   & Busby, 1974.

Michael Moorcock's Erekosë *cycle*
The Eternal Champion, New York, Dell, 1970; London, Mayflower,
   1970.
Phoenix in Obsidian, London, Mayflower, 1970.

Michael Moorcock's Oswald Bastable *cycle*
The Warlord of the Air: A Scientific Romance, New York, Dell, 1970;
   London, Mayflower, 1970.
The Land Leviathan: A New Scientific Romance, London, Quartet, 1974.

Michael Moorcock's Karl Glogauer *cycle*
Behold the Man, London, Allison and Busby, 1969.
Breakfast in the Ruins: A Novel of Inhumanity, London, New English
   Library, 1972.

Michael Moorcock's Jerry Cornelius *cycle*
The Final Programme, New York, Avon, 1968; London, Allison &
   Busby, 1969.
A Cure for Cancer, London, Allison & Busby, 1971.
The English Assassin: A Romance of Entropy, London, Allison & Busby,
   1972.
The Condition of Muzak: A Jerry Cornelius Novel, London, Allison &
   Busby, 1977.
The Cornelius Chronicles (all four Cornelius novels in one paperback
   volume), New York, Avon, 1977.
The Lives and Times of Jerry Cornelius, London, Allison & Busby, 1976.
*The Adventures of Una Persson and Catherine Cornelius in the Twentieth
   Century*, London, Quartet, 1976.

Michael Moorcock's Jherek Carnelian *cycle*
An Alien Heat, London, MacGibbon & Kee, 1972.
The Hollow Lands, New York, Harper & Row, 1974; London, Hart
   Davis MacGibbon, 1975.
The End of All Songs, London, Harper & Row, 1976.
Legends from the End of Time, New York, Harper & Row, 1976;
   London, W.H. Allen, 1977.

Michael Moorcock's other works including early writings and story collections
The Fireclown, London, Compact, 1965; retitled *The Winds of Limbo*, New York, Paperback Library, 1969; London, Sphere, 1970.
The Sundered Worlds, London, Compact, 1965; retitled *The Blood Red Game*, London, Sphere, 1970.
The Twilight Man, London, Compact, 1966; retitled *The Shores of Death*, London, Sphere, 1970.
The Wrecks of Time, New York, Ace, 1967; retitled *The Rituals of Infinity*, London, Arrow, 1971.
The Black Corridor, London, Mayflower, 1969.
The Ice Schooner, New York, Berkley, 1969; London, Sphere, 1969.
The Time Dweller, London, Hart-Davies, 1969.
Moorcock's Book of Martyrs, London, Quartet, 1976.
Sojan, Manchester, Savoy, 1977.

Secondary sources
Ashley, Michael, 'Behold the Man Called Moorcock', *Science Fiction Monthly*, 2, no. 2 (25 February 1975), pp. 8–11.
Bilyeu, Richard, *The Tanelorn Archives: A Primary and Secondary Bibliography of the Works of Michael Moorcock, 1949–1979*, Manitoba, Pandora's Books, 1981.
Blishen, Edward, 'Her(o)maphrodite', review of Moorcock, *The Lives and Times of Jerry Cornelius, New Society*, 8 April 1976, p. 92.
Calder, Jenni, *Heroes: From Byron to Guevara*, London, Hamilton, 1977.
Clute, John, 'The Repossession of Jerry Cornelius', in Moorcock, *The Cornelius Chronicles*, New York, Avon, 1977, pp. vii–xv.
Lehmann, A.G., 'Pierrot and Fin de Siècle', *Romantic Mythologies: Essays*, ed. Ian Fletcher, London, Routledge & Kegan Paul, 1967, pp. 209–23.
Moorcock, Michael and Langdon Jones, eds, *The Nature of the Catastrophe*, London, Hutchinson, 1971.
Pirie, David, 'The Chaos Machine of Michael Moorcock', *Time Out*, 17 September 1971, pp. 49–51.
Raban, Jonathan, *Soft City*, London, Hamilton, 1974.
Spencer, Neil, review of Moorcock, *The Condition of Muzak, New Musical Express*, 2 July 1977, p. 36.
Welsford, Enid, 'The Harlequinade: Punch, Pierrot, Clown and His Successors', in her *The Fool: His Social and Literary History*, London, Faber, 1935, pp. 300–13.
Willett, Ralph, 'Moorcock's Achievement and Promise in the Jerry Cornelius Books', *Science-Fiction Studies*, vol. 3 (1976), pp. 75–9.

9 ANGST AND ANGSTRÖMS: STYLISTIC PRACTICE

Booth, Wayne, C., *The Rhetoric of Fiction*, Chicago University Press, 1961.
Burroughs, William, *The Ticket that Exploded*, rev. ed., London, Calder & Boyars, 1968.
Hall, Steve, 'Now is the Time', *NW*, no. 141 (March 1964), pp. 40–50.
Johnson, B.S., Introduction to his *Aren't You Rather Young to be Writing Your Memoirs?*, London, Hutchinson, 1973, pp. 11–13.
Kesey, Ken, *One Flew Over the Cuckoo's Nest*, New York, Viking Press, 1962.
Lodge, David, *The Novelist at the Crossroads and Other Essays on Fiction and Criticism*, London, Routledge & Kegan Paul, 1971.
Robbe-Grillet, Alain, *Snapshots* and *Towards a New Novel*, tr. Barbara Wright, London, Calder & Boyars, 1965.
Whorf, Benjamin Lee, 'Language, Mind, and Reality', in his *Language, Thought, and Reality: Selected Writings*, ed., John B. Carroll, Cambridge, MA, Technology Press of MIT, 1956, pp. 246–70.

10 A HIGHER ALBEDO: STYLISTIC THEORY

Angenot, Marc, 'The Absent Paradigm: An Introduction to the Semiotics of Science Fiction', *Science-Fiction Studies*, vol. 6 (1979), pp. 9–19.
Delany, Samuel R., *The Jewel-Hinged Jaw: Notes on the Language of Science Fiction*, Elizabethtown, NY, Dragon Press, 1977.
Eliot, T.S., 'Tradition and the Individual Talent', in his *Selected Prose*, ed., Frank Kermode, London, Faber, 1975, pp. 37–44.
Ehrenzweig, Anton, *The Hidden Order of Art: A Study in the Psychology of Artistic Imagination*, London, Weidenfeld and Nicolson, 1967.
Lem, Stanislaw, 'On the Structural Analysis of Science Fiction', *Science-Fiction Studies*, vol. 1 (1973–74), pp. 26–33.
Russ, Joanna, 'Towards an Aesthetic of Science Fiction', *Science-Fiction Studies*, vol. 2 (1975), pp. 112–19.
Suvin, Darko, *Metamorphoses of Science Fiction: On the Poetics and History of a Literary Genre*, New Haven and London, Yale University, 1979.

11 NO MORE, WITH FEELING

Arnheim, Rudolf, *Entropy and Art: An Essay on Disorder and Order*, Berkeley, CA, University of California Press, 1971.

Bergonzi, Bernard, *The Situation of the Novel*, London, Macmillan, 1970.

Bergonzi, Bernard, ed., *Innovations: Essays on Art and Ideas*, London, Macmillan, 1968.

Bradbury, Malcolm, ed., *The Novel Today: Contemporary Writers on Modern Fiction*, Manchester, Manchester University Press, 1977.

Burroughs, William, *The Naked Lunch*, rev. ed., London, Calder, 1964.

Effinger, George Alec, *What Entropy Means to Me*, Garden City, New York, Doubleday, 1972.

Harris, Charles B., *Contemporary American Novelists of the Absurd*, New Haven, CT, College and University Press, 1971.

Hassan, Ihab, 'Fiction and Future: An Extravaganza for Voice and Tape', in *Liberations: New Essays on the Humanities in Revolution*, ed. Hassan, Middletown, CT, Wesleyan University Press, 1971, pp. 176–96.

Kermode, Frank, *The Sense of an Ending: Studies in the Theory of Fiction*, New York, Oxford University Press, 1967.

Ketterer, David, *New Worlds for Old: The Apocalyptic Imagination, Science Fiction and American Literature*, Bloomington and London, Indiana University Press, 1974.

Lévi-Strauss, Claude, *Tristes Tropiques*, tr. John and Doreen Weightman, London, Cape, 1973.

Olderman, Raymond M., *Beyond the Waste Land: A Study of the American Novel in the Nineteen-Sixties*, New Haven, CT, Yale University Press, 1972.

Pynchon, Thomas, *The Crying of Lot 49*, London, Cape, 1967.

Pynchon, Thomas, *V.*, London, Cape, 1963.

Rambali, Paul, Interview with Devo, *New Musical Express*, 18 March 1978, pp. 32–3.

Scholes, Robert, *The Fabulators*, New York, Oxford University Press, 1967.

Scholes, Robert, and Eric S. Rabkin, *Science Fiction: History – Science – Vision*, New York, Oxford University Press, 1977.

Tanner, Tony, *City of Words: American Fiction 1950–1970*, London, Cape, 1971.

Wiener, Norbert, *The Human Use of Human Beings: Cybernetics and Society*, 2nd ed., London, Eyre & Spottiswoode, 1954.

Index